THE NEW JERSEY SHORE

Maps by William N. Canfield

JOHN T. CUNNINGHAM

THE
NEW JERSEY
SHORE

Rutgers University Press

NEW BRUNSWICK   NEW JERSEY

TO THE SAYRES

TO ARLENE, WHO BY SHARING HER KNOWLEDGE AND ENTHUSIASM
HAS HELPED ME TO KNOW AND APPRECIATE NEW JERSEY

and

TO HOWARD, WHO BY SHARING HIS LOVE OF THE NEW JERSEY SHORE
HAS GIVEN US FOUR CUNNINGHAMS SO MANY PLEASANT HOURS

Contents

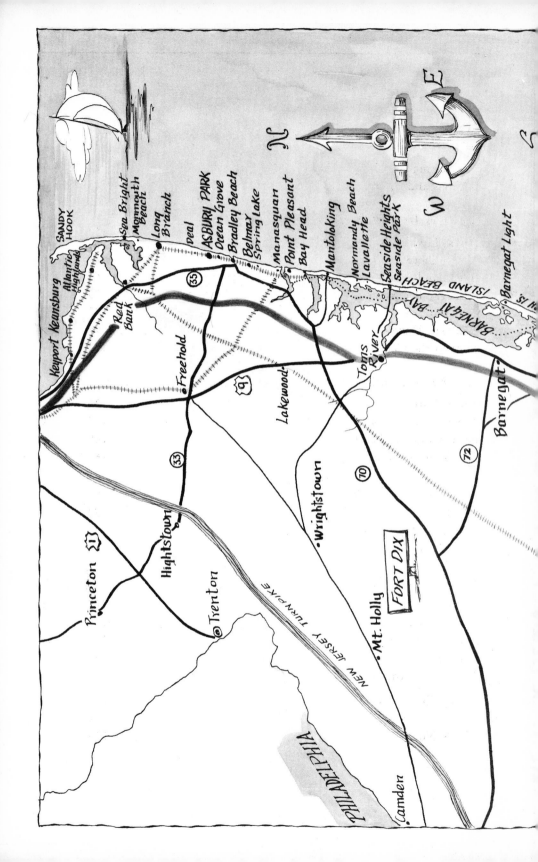

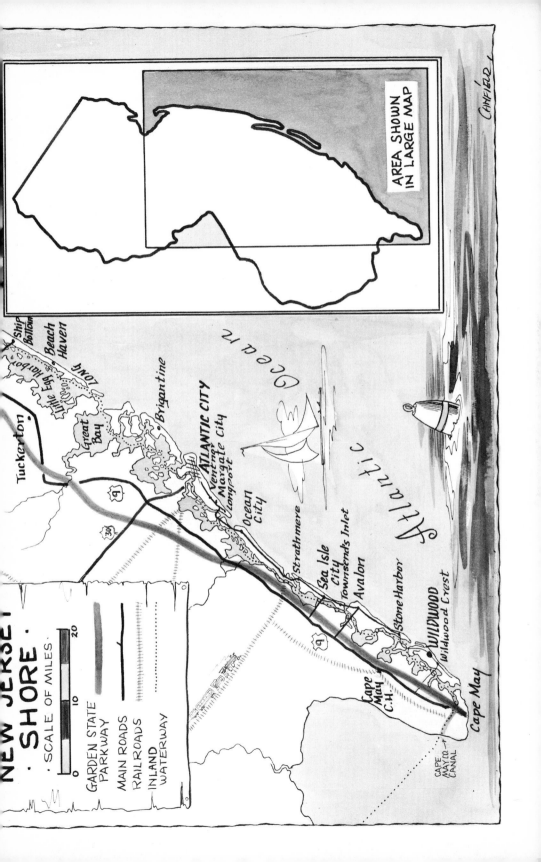

Preface

Perhaps no single area of the country, or possibly even the world, is so much frequented and so little understood as the New Jersey Shore. No one knows for sure how many people seek its charms each year: at least five million, conservatives say; something like 50,000,000 the promotion-minded insist—but publicists cheerfully admit they do on occasion count the same sunburned noses at least three or four times.

Still, for all the millions of admirers who return every year, how many people *really* know this remarkable 127-mile strip of sand between Sandy Hook and Cape May? How many know it at all times of the day—from the pre-dawn hours when fishermen rise in a score of towns to seek their livings, to the after-midnight hours when night clubs lure those who feel the need to "live"? How many know it at all seasons of the year—through fall hurricanes, in the dead of winter, in the midst of the spring awakening, at the height of summer glory?

Many months of my life have gone into these pages. The prelude consisted of precious vacations at Manasquan and Point Pleasant and Long Beach Island, of long-remembered trips to Asbury Park and Atlantic City. This made me part of the millions who seek only the pleasures of the Jersey Shore, with neither the need nor the desire to understand it. Then, for this book, I invested many off-season months trying to get a complete picture of the year-around aspects of this fabled land.

Thus, within this book are—in addition to the familiar pleasures known to all—the hurricanes and violent seas of fall and winter, the plain life of the commercial fisherman, the joy of a cruise on the Inland Waterway. There is the story of a vacation-land awakening in spring, the story of amusements, the story of noise and of quiet. There are occasional legends, true; but this is essentially a book of verifiable facts. It is my representation of my belief that the Jersey Shore is more—far more—than the much-sung summertime months of July and August.

Certainly, the hand of the promotion man is apt to touch any account of this land of amusement and pleasure. He, too, has a tale to tell, and if in telling it he usually reaches too deeply into his bag of adjectives,

11

that is the calling card of publicists everywhere. Nevertheless, the reader must know that at all times I have tried to stand outside the publicity man's reach. If I am sometimes amused by his passionate pamphlets, I also am aware that he *does* have his own story to present, a story of vital concern to many millions of individuals.

Let me admit that I like the Jersey Shore, particularly those areas still untouched by rampaging amusement. Let me declare, despite this preference for the less-populated beaches, that I never fail to feel a tingle of excitement in my spine as I drive across the marshlands to amusement-oriented Atlantic City. If I like Atlantic City better in *any* month but July or August, that is a minority opinion. Millions flock to the city's beaches in summertime to prove what *most* people seem to prefer.

My thanks go particularly to *The Newark News,* where most of these chapters originally appeared, and to Editor Lloyd M. Felmly, who granted permission to assemble these chapters into this book. I am grateful, too, for the help accorded me by many colleagues on *The News,* particularly by Joseph Taddeo, who edited the articles in their original form.

There are so many others to whom I am indebted. I would be less than fair if I failed to mention the help accorded me by Harold Wilson's three-volume work, *The Jersey Shore: A Social and Economic History.* His point of view is that of the scholarly historian, of course, and his volumes merit the careful attention of the person seeking a full history of the region.

I give thanks to many publicity men and single out for special thanks these, because their help was of a broad nature: George Zuckerman, Asbury Park; Richard Gibbons, Ocean Grove; Jack Lamping, Ocean County; Mall Dodson, Atlantic City; Norman Sargent, Ocean City, and John Kay, Wildwood. The William A. Hafferts—Sr. and Jr.—of Sea Isle City, while not publicity men *per se,* also helped me greatly in their unofficial public relations capacities for their area.

Many others helped: Lieutenant Commander Benjamin Kowalski and BMC Richard R. Terhune of Sandy Hook Coast Guard Station; Peter J. Gannon and James Rankin of the State Bureau of Navigation; A. Heaton Underhill of the State Division of Fish and Game; Wilson R. Meyers of Atlantic City Electric Company; and Frank W. McLaughlin and Robert C. Alexander, both of the New Jersey Audubon Society.

I am grateful, as always, to Arlene R. Sayre of the State Department

12

of Conservation and Economic Development for her encouragement, her knowledge, and her aid in contacting many people. My thanks go as well to Marion M. Manning, who did my stenographic work, and to Stanley W. Grupy, who prepared the index.

Most of the pictures in the book were taken by Irving Tuttle and Robert Anderson, both of *The Newark News*. I wish also to express my appreciation to Walter F. Pullinger, Jr., who gave permission for use of many pictures from his breathtakingly beautiful book, *The Island*, a pictorial study of Long Beach Island. Other pictures were supplied by public relations men, by the Coast Guard, and by several divisions of the State Department of Conservation and Economic Development.

The maps for this book have been drawn by William N. Canfield of *The Newark News*. Readers of one of my previous books, *This Is New Jersey*, for which Bill also prepared the maps, will be pleased again to see his crisp, clear style in these pages.

This book, as I have said, represents in large measure a personal point of view. It also represents a point of view I have shared with my family for five just-passed summers at Long Beach Island—and to my wife, Dot, and our Jay and Ruth, I extend this last word of appreciation for their helping me to achieve a philosophy about the Jersey Shore.

JOHN T. CUNNINGHAM

Florham Park, N. J.

THE NEW JERSEY SHORE

Beyond every dune lie adventure and mystery

1. The Setting

Most important is the sea in its ever-changing moods.

Man seeks the sea, some declare, because he came from the sea and yearns to return there. He seeks it because of the mystery, the constant air of potential excitement and the unceasing struggle of sea against land. *This* is the fundamental appeal of the shore, and until a visitor watches the sea in all its varying moods and seeks to understand these changes, he never gets full enjoyment from the Jersey Shore—or any other shore. He'll never really love the ocean-swept strand until he knows it as Rachel Carson captures it in her prose or as Walt Whitman sang about it in his poetry.

Even the boardwalk can't give anywhere near the pleasure to be derived from trying to know the complex sea—so predictable that the rising and the falling of its tides can be charted long in advance to the exact minute, so changeable that the ocean never on ebb tide leaves the shoreline exactly as it found it on flood tide.

Sometime or another practically everyone who ventures down by the sea falls under the mystic spell. The rising waves come on and on, rolling from far out, reaching a height, then curling under to collapse with a thunderous sound and a sudsing of the receptive sands. On and on they've rolled, day in and day out, back to the beginning, millions of years ago.

At present the New Jersey Shore stretches about 127 miles between Sandy Hook on the north and Cape May on the south, shaped like the arc of a curving, limp bow ranged from Sandy Hook southwestward. Most shoregoers, even the veterans, assume that when they gaze at the Atlantic Ocean they are looking east. They are not. Most of the beaches on the New Jersey Shore face southeast. Atlantic City's streets which parallel the ocean run almost east and west—rather than north and south as most believe.

17

Each day the Atlantic Ocean sweeps in her tides—twice high, twice low—against this curving land, to rearrange and to tidy up, like a fussy housekeeper never satisfied with her day's doings. The sea never gives up the fight to reclaim the New Jersey Shore as its rightful own. This is the nagging concern of every resort town: the awareness that time is on the side of the sea, the knowledge that erosion is a never-ending problem.

Swirling seas take away—at Long Branch, at Cape May, at Barnegat Light, at Longport. Land between Manasquan and Monmouth Beach has been cut back a thousand and more feet in recorded history, sometimes collapsing a full 30 feet back in one stormy night fight with the waves.

What the implacable sea takes away in one place it puts back somewhere else, often in the place frustrated man would least select. Sand silts across inlet mouths, fills in channels. Sandy Hook is visible evidence of where Long Branch's beach has fled. Even as waves lap hungrily at Barnegat Light, directly across the troubled inlet to the north new land builds up on the tip of Island Beach.

This matters only because humans in the past century and a half have decided that the sea and all the sands fronting thereon rightfully belong to them. Without giant hotels and boardwalks set rigidly in place, erosion wouldn't matter one bit. Untroubled by maps and charts and property rights, Indians who visited the shores each summer centuries ago didn't worry about the shifting sands. If an inlet changed location a half mile or so to the north or south—and inlets did—who cared?

This has been going on through all time. Geologists, who see today only as a passing interlude between millions of years past and millions of years hence, have some interesting facts to divulge about the New Jersey Shore of long ago.

For one thing, this present-day coastline, for all the year-in and year-out changes, is relatively stable—basically unchanged for many centuries. Once, however, the seas of the "Jersey Shore" washed most of the Coastal Plain on a line just to the south and east of the modern cities of Camden and New Brunswick. Out in the ocean were scattered islands—the occasional "high" spots such as the Highlands of Navesink or the hills in the Pine Barrens of the Coastal Plain of today. At that time, during an interglacial period, the sea level was 25 feet higher than at present because of melting glaciers pouring into the sea.

Most important is the sea in its ever-changing moods

Then, the geologists tell us, there followed a period of low seas, when another glacial age locked up land waters and the ocean dropped 300 feet. Consider the consequence: The "New Jersey" coast was 90 miles to the east—meaning that Atlantic City, if it had existed, would have been 90 miles inland, or about as far from the "Jersey Shore" as Reading, Pennsylvania, is today.

Fortunately, however, for Atlantic City and Asbury Park and all the other shore resorts which must shudder at the mere thought of no ocean within 90 miles, the Atlantic Ocean settled down thousands of years ago and began to operate about where it is today. Day after day, nevertheless, alterations went on.

The restless Atlantic began to build offshore islands, or barrier

19

beaches—the familiar sandy island strips running all the way south from Point Pleasant to just below the Wildwoods. The formation was gradual; great currents dragged along the bottom of the Continental Shelf, toppling hundreds or thousands of feet out from the mainland shoreline. The waves dropped loose bottom material oceanward of the mainland and gradually built up an underwater ridge. This in turn caught more material, and eventually the ridge peeped above the ocean level to become a string of narrow offshore islands of varying lengths and widths.

At the same time, northward-drifting seas gradually pushed sands out past the mouths of the Shrewsbury and Navesink Rivers and laid the foundation for Sandy Hook. The shoreward movements of waves and currents past the spit of Sandy Hook have continued to influence its growth as an ever more pronounced "hook." Cape May mistakenly might be thought to have grown the same way, but that formation apparently came about differently. Two things built up the Cape— interglacial deposits and outwash gravels carried down the Delaware River. Unlike Sandy Hook, Cape May has been eroding away rather than building outward since colonists first started to record such vital statistics about 200 years ago.

There are only two spots along the entire New Jersey coast where the mainland meets the ocean directly: Cape May and a region from Manasquan Inlet to just north of Long Branch. Elsewhere the entire stretch is a series of the above-described offshore islands, broken by intermittent inlets. Atlantic City, for example, is on an island well at sea; so are all of Cape May's resorts (except Cape May town).

The sea has never been satisfied with the job it did on the offshore islands. It keeps nibbling away here and building up there. Sometimes the ocean's decision to change an inlet is spectacular in its results, the prime example being the complete elimination in 1812 of Cranberry Inlet at what is now Seaside Park. No amount of man-inspired digging ever brought that inlet back. Sometimes the Atlantic can't make up its mind; several times in the eighteenth and nineteenth centuries the inlet at Shrewsbury River opened and closed—until man put an end to that nonsense (or thinks he did) with a strong stone sea wall.

Inlets owe their existence to tidal range. Where tidal ranges are small, inlets are far apart (Texas, with one- to two-foot ranges, has offshore bars as much as 100 miles long). New Jersey's tidal range is four to five feet, so inlets are found more frequently—every seven miles or so off the Cape May coast and about 18 miles apart on either end of Long Beach Island.

A summer northeaster snarls against a Monmouth seawall

Inside these inlets and offshore beaches are the hundreds of marshy islands or "sedges" filling the bays and sounds to the west of the barrier beaches. Seldom does a Shore visitor see these islands; they are the province of the hunters and bird watchers and the explorers of the Inland Waterway. Most plentiful in Cape May County, these "sedges" also abound west and northwest of Atlantic City and throughout Barnegat Bay. Someday some of these islands may become "civilized" (meaning a real estate developer will see the chance to build homes there at a profit), but for the moment they belong to the birds—and those who watch or hunt them.

The New Jersey resort promoters wish they could keep the customers coming around the calendar, but after Labor Day most go home—few of them to return before the next Memorial Day at the earliest and the next Fourth of July at the likeliest. The sea takes over, occasionally becoming furious in a fall nor'easter whipping across deserted boardwalk and through barren streets.

Nature expends most of her meanness in the off-season months. When spring softens the wintry pounding of the sea and smooths it to alluring gentleness, the strand is reborn. Swept away is the debris left by humans a vacation ago. The wind-ruffled sand is white and clean. At surf's edge are treasures from the sea—the shells, the wrack, the driftwood and, on rare occasions, an ancient coin.

Consider, too, the summer moods of the Jersey Shore.

There is the prevailing mood, when the breeze blows off the surf, cools the strand with a briny freshness, ruffles the curtains in bungalow and hotel alike and cools the occupants. This is the breeze to free the air of pollen and to make hay fever sufferers feel as if heaven has come

Wind and waves clean the beach, challenge man to spoil it

to earth. If this gives way to a mainland breeze from the west, laden with green flies and pollen, then it makes the wind swinging around east by southeast that much more welcome.

Sometimes—but rarely—the breeze stiffens into a howling gale, whipping rain into the deserted beaches, and the calamity-filled voices of every-hour-on-the-hour radio announcers frighten bungalow occupants with portents of impending doom: "Hurricane Diane is moving north. . . ." Despite the potential disaster, many people find in a summer nor'easter a welcome surcease from the dogged pursuit of pleasure.

A summer storm, if it stops short of the savagery of a hurricane, is something to remember with pleasure always. The winds pound vengeful waves against the boardwalks and stone jetties. Surf skims down the streets and piles sand over the sea walls, and the storm changes the shape of beaches for days, cutting steep ledges in one place and tearing away dunes elsewhere. The nor'easter may cover the sand with strange seaweed or bring to the strand seashells dredged up from the ocean bottoms.

These are the storms so feared through the ages before electronics and motors ruled the Atlantic. These winds and waves cast hundreds of ships on the New Jersey coast before 1900. This is the cold sea which swept the flaming *Morro Castle* to the very esplanade of the Asbury Park Convention Hall in 1934. This is the cruel sea which edged the strand in black oil during World War II, telling a mute story of the many tankers sunk within sight and sound of New Jersey coastal towns.

This is the sea which, in all its moods of cantankerousness and of loving gentleness, calls back millions of people every year. Sea and sand (and boardwalk)—that's enough for millions. Not many come really to understand the New Jersey Shore, to heed the lessons of time, to ponder the immutability of the sea; it's enough to be in her romantic spell for a few days.

There are people who never even look at the sea: those who come down to the strand, spread a blanket, read a book, turn over as if by clockwork to roast evenly, then pack up and go home without much caring about that moody, hungry, challenging sea. They are in the minority. See the child stop suddenly when he hears for the first time the pounding of the surf or the roaring of a strange ocean wind. See even the veteran beachcomber shudder at the mystery of the sea on a cold, black night when a hurricane roars.

See these—and recognize that to know the sea is to know the Shore.

23

Nature was almost enough at Cape May a century ago

2. Business and Pleasure

Many seaside entrepreneurs firmly declare that no one—well, no one with a modicum of sense and a spare dollar—would visit the New Jersey Shore if the boardwalks, the games of chance and the dimly lit nightclubs had not been perfected. Without these, nothing would be left but the mysterious ocean, the sparkling white sand, the azure-blue sky and the pleasant breezes. Surely no one would care for those.

Then, of course, there are people who wouldn't give two cents for the entire 127-mile strip of bleached white sand between Sandy Hook and Cape May—with or without boardwalks. That's all right with the keepers of the Jersey Shore cash registers; millions of people each year sample the briny charms of this New Jersey playground. How many millions is a matter of controversy. A publicity estimate says 30,000,000 to 50,000,000, but that undoubtedly permits counting the same visitors many times. Certainly, however, at least 5,000,000, perhaps 10,000,000, *different* persons make an annual stopover.

On a hot summer weekend Atlantic City entertains 500,000 persons and Asbury Park welcomes another 200,000. That same weekend, 50 other seaside resort towns find thousands upon thousands vying for a place in the sun.

Not all those hundreds of thousands come merely to get boardwalk relief from boredom. They also come to sail on the bays, to watch the herons at Stone Harbor, to find seashells at the edge of the strand, to soak up the sun, to be soothed by the surf, to head out through the inlets to fish in the deep sea.

There are publicists who feel that their colored prose made the New Jersey Shore desirable. As one put it for *Holiday* magazine a few years ago:

"Nature you can get on a park bench. You gotta sell entertainment, and for every ton of sand, ten tons of schmaltz."

25

Amusement *does* rule supreme at a score or more towns where boardwalks hem in the sand. A boardwalker at Atlantic City can buy anything from a hot dog to a mink stole. Rare is the boardwalk town where the visitor can't invest his dimes in "skill" games. He can be spun and twisted and tossed in rides. He can watch summer stock, hear band concerts, go to bathing beauty parades (official and unofficial), see the latest movies, hear the "name" singers of the age. He can be wined and dined and entertained like a king out of the Arabian Nights.

The main idea is that millions of people can be—and are—certain they never are more than a billfold away from dazzle and glitter and carefree hours in July and August.

Nonetheless, when Labor Day comes, the Jersey Shore wraps itself in the loneliness which envelops any area where vibrant activity suddenly gives way to quiet. Except for an occasional convention at Asbury Park, Ocean City or Wildwood, only Atlantic City stays alive after September.

Home go the stand proprietors, the pitch men, the food sellers, the yacht clubbers, the souvenir pushers, the sun worshippers and the skin burners. The natives in their villages breathe collective sighs of relief, enjoy themselves for a spell, then get ready for the long sleep until the boardwalks sprout a new growth of tourist dollars. By mid-October many a resort public relations man is lonely enough to take a vacation—somewhere else.

Uncommon is the seaside vacationland which wouldn't like to stretch "the season" at least from April to October. Talk of the advantages of vacationing the "year around" at the Shore continues every year, just as it has for at least 50 years. There are descriptions of the "warm" weather, the alleged absence of snow, the healthfulness of the winter spray. Few listen; most are home trying to make enough money to be able to come back when school closes and vacations begin again.

It's a shame that more people can't know the Jersey Shore in the months from September to June. A few surf fishermen know the joy of casting without fear of hooking into a well-packed bathing suit on the sand. Lucky October honeymooners know the romance of the harvest moon shimmering across the sea. Those who witness a February snow sifting silently down on the Atlantic City boardwalk find neon lights never were more fetching.

Mountains of dollars will be heaped up by that sea in any summer nudging over the horizon. Vacationists (according to one official survey) account for $1,683,540,000 changing hands in Monmouth, Ocean, Atlantic and Cape May resorts in 1955. A tidy sum—five times the total annual New Jersey state budget.

Viewed in terms of dollars, that sand isn't white, it's golden. That surf isn't salty, it's pure nectar.

Consider upward of a billion and a half dollars, then cast that sum against one point: this is income derived from land that, measured by any ordinary economic yardstick, should be wasteland. Little of agricultural value could be grown there; no industrialist in his right mind would build a factory on the shifting sands.

Early settlers recognized this fact. The first purchaser of what is now Atlantic City paid four cents an acre for the land in the 1690's—as against 24 cents an acre for mainland. Even in 1871, when James Bradley bought the 500 acres on which Asbury Park grew, he paid only about $2,000 an acre. These days a foot—*one* foot—of Atlantic City Boardwalk frontage could bring $4,000 or more.

The difference, of course, is accessibility married to desirability. Steamboats and wagon roads served Cape May and Long Branch as they rose to be the first prime resorts. A railroad from Camden to Atlantic City in 1854 made that resort accessible. Later, between 1870 and 1890, railroads coaxed into being an entire string of seaside towns from Atlantic Highlands to Wildwood. Since the 1920's, highways and automobiles have brought the New Jersey Shore closer to more millions.

Precisely defining the fundamental appeal of the New Jersey Shore is impossible. It might very well be the boardwalks and the games of chance and the other monuments to man's inability to suffer his own company. More than half the total annual shore income from vacationists is spent in Atlantic City—and the most fervent admirers of Atlantic City will agree that whatever else she is, the "Queen of Resorts" is neither natural nor inexpensive.

No part of the Jersey Shore is more vital, from an economic viewpoint, than Atlantic City. One out of every four persons who visit the New Jersey strand goes to Atlantic City. Conventioneers from all over the world have spread its fame. There is some reason to believe the apocryphal story that the words "Atlantic City" have been beaten on the drums in deepest jungles.

Atlantic City is geared to pleasure. Its hundreds of hotels outnumber those of any other resort city. Its boardwalk is unsurpassed in length and width. Its amusement piers have no equal. Often, on a steaming August day, as many as 225,000 people of all sizes and shapes and ages stake out their tiny patches of seaside sand in Atlantic City. They come back, year after year after year. Atlantic City is a flirtatious Queen who never grows old; who adapts herself to every generation.

To dwell on Atlantic City overlong is to slight the other 120 or so miles of Jersey's ocean front. After all, if it is pertinent that 25 per cent of all visitors head for that city annually, it is equally pertinent that the other 75 per cent go somewhere else between Sandy Hook and Cape May.

Millions of people gain millions of impressions of the Jersey Shore. Some think of the dunes at Avalon, the broad, level beaches of Wildwood, the stately charm of Cape May. Some remember forever the old lighthouses at Sandy Hook or Cape May or Barnegat or atop the Navesink Highlands. Some dwell on the seclusion in Deal or Spring Lake, the allure of Asbury Park, the uncompromising standards of Ocean Grove, or the thin strip of sand called Long Beach Island.

Others recognize the Jersey Shore only as the inlets through which party boats ride oceanward to track down stripers and porgies and weaks and blues. Thousands of others, particularly in recent years, regard the shore as Barnegat Bay, where they sail and fish or wander aimlessly using up gasoline in outboard motors.

The average shoregoer, in short, gets to love one tiny town or region and there he returns year in and year out. Those who seek the wild dunes of Avalon find lovers of Atlantic City baffling. Atlantic City pleasure seekers don't even return that sentiment; most of them never even heard of Avalon.

However, to view the Jersey Shore only in terms of favorite towns or areas is to fall into a thinking pattern which mesmerizes all but a few visitors to the shore. It is to overlook the colorful commercial fishing fleets which sail up to the back doors of Cape May, Wildwood, Sea Isle City, Point Pleasant—and, of all places, Atlantic City. It is never to catch crabs off the piers and bridges, never to watch the clammers feeling with their toes for shellfish in the bays. It is never to see the bird migrations at Cape May, never to pick up a Cape May diamond near the lighthouse, never to sail the lagoons of the Inland Waterway, never to know the joys of beachcombing before breakfast.

The point is that the Jersey Shore has as many personalities as there

Sea Isle City's fleet has charm, too

are millions of people to seek them out. Some insist in wistful, nostalgic letters-to-the-editor that "her charms long since have fled," meaning that she isn't what she was in 1900. She isn't, that's certain, but whether this year's high school senior class misses the old charms can be questioned. Charms have different meanings for different generations.

These disappearing 1950's are days of great transition for all the Shore, rivaled in importance only by the coming of the railroads in the 1850's and 1860's and the surge of hotel building in the 1920's. The Garden State Parkway and, to a lesser extent, the New Jersey Turnpike are arteries circulating new blood through the area. Long ago Walt Whitman said the railroads gave the Jersey Shore a spine; today roadways are giving it a whole new lease on life.

29

New roads increase the number of "day trippers," the modern versions of the almost-forgotten one-day dollar excursionists who jammed railroad trains to Asbury Park and Atlantic City and Wildwood three or four decades ago. Already the Garden State Parkway has generated so much new traffic that it is antiquated in parts, as thousands of people stalled in Sunday night jams can testify—then forget as they return the next Sunday.

Return they do, return they must. The pull of the Jersey Shore is and always has been intense.

Centuries before the white man saw America, Indians walked from inland slopes to the coast every summer, to fish, to hunt and to find seashells suitable for wampum. At last the waves brought them, in September, 1609, Henry Hudson's ship, skimming like a great, white bird. The braves watched silently from the Atlantic Highlands as the *Half Moon* anchored inside Sandy Hook, in their ignorance enjoying an Indian Summer that was soon to end for them.

The first colonial vacationists came to hunt and to fish, too, and by 1765 a boardinghouse had been opened on Tucker's Beach, south of Long Beach Island. Long Branch welcomed visitors to a boardinghouse in 1788, and in 1801 Ellis Hughes of Cape May advertised in the Philadelphia *Daily Aurora* that he had prepared himself "for entertaining company who use sea bathing."

Those who boil in unhappy impatience on days when traffic on the Parkway stalls to a mere 20 or 25 miles per hour should know what that company "who used sea bathing" endured. A wealthy few came by carriage or by steamboat; most crossed state from Philadelphia in "shore wagons," crude affairs which hauled fish or oysters to the Quaker City and hauled vacationists back. Travel, said one, "was more a penance than a joy."

One item should be strongly emphasized—Philadelphians first discovered the commercial potential of the Jersey Shore, and they continued to dominate the entire coast until after the Civil War. Even today the region south of Bay Head is predominantly a point of call for Philadelphia folk and everything from Ocean City south is overwhelmingly Philadelphian. Even "blocks" are called "squares" down that way.

The chief exception is Atlantic City, now definitely an outpost of New York City, but that started as a seaside terminal for a railroad from Philadelphia in 1854. Until Atlantic City became a name on a railroad map, Cape May and Long Branch—both magnets for Phila-

Boardwalks, such as Asbury Park's, coax bathers off the beach

delphia people—vied for superiority as the nation's prime vacationlands. Only Saratoga questioned their claims for resort supremacy; Long Branch and Cape May agreed on only one thing—both felt themselves better than Saratoga.

Railroads transformed the Jersey Shore, until by 1900 practically every town now in existence by the strand had been organized, had known commercial success and had sent out roots to feed on visiting pocketbooks. By 1900 Asbury Park and Atlantic City wrestled for the leadership once fought for exclusively by Cape May and Long Branch. Changes in the shore since 1900 have been in degree rather than in kind.

Founding fathers dipped deep into the bag of reasons for establishing each resort town between 1870 and 1900. Some wanted fashionable

31

exclusiveness, some wanted religious exclusiveness. Some wanted vacation spots for teetotalers, some didn't mind demon rum at all. Some wanted quiet, some wanted noise. Some wanted boardwalks, some would just as soon walk in the sand. Regardless of the reason for founding, most of the fathers were not averse to making fortunes.

Promotion, with those fortunes for a goal, ran the full gamut by 1900. The adjective wasn't invented by the Jersey Shore, but there it reached peak popularity. Today the four-color folder is as much a part of a resort town as the sand.

Promotion follows promotion, each dedicated to the proposition that a beauty queen looks like a million. The Miss America contest is surrounded by an aura of high respectability; the main difference between Miss America in 1957 and Miss America in 1921 is that Miss America in 1957 wears tighter bathing suits, is "talented" and is going to get a college education. Talent or no, she exists to promote Atlantic City, as did her older sister.

Still, the Jersey Shore has charms which usually don't get mentioned in the four-color folders or the 36-24-36 promotion.

What do you like?

Buried treasure? There almost certainly is buried treasure somewhere on the Jersey Shore—at Sandy Hook, maybe, or Long Beach Island or on one of the Jersey Keys between Ocean City and Cape May. Captain Kidd and other pirates put in to the Jersey Shore often. To get water, say the practical. Nay, to bury chests filled with fabled treasures, say the hopeful who poke their toes into the sand.

There is simpler treasure for the finding. There are the varied seashells, particularly out on the flat, marshy islands in Great Bay. The "diamonds" at Cape May Point are but glassy stones to the unimaginative, but they sparkle like gems for him who wills it so. The sea wrack to be gathered at tide line near Ocean City draws the knowledgeable.

Indeed, come to think of it, those promotion folders which publicity offices pile up like seashells at the edge of the strand aren't *completely* fanciful. The Jersey Shore *is* a "place of magic"; it *is* "fabulous"; it *is* "known throughout the world." Those millions by the sea *do* find (or think they find) "the elixir of youth, the wonder drug for good health." It *is* a place "where tired nerves relax."

See It as Its Different Regions . . .

One man's pleasure, along the Jersey Shore, is another man's boredom—and, fortunately, vice versa. The individual who is enthralled by Atlantic City might be yawning by 9 o'clock in Cape May. The Cape May enthusiast, on the other hand, could find Atlantic City unattractive.

Somehow, the right people find their way to the right areas, and once they find that *right* area, usually come back year after year. One way to an understanding of the Jersey Shore is to consider it as made up of various regions, each of them well-defined and each of them quite different from the others.

Look at these seven regions: Sandy Hook and vicinity; the North Shore between Ocean Grove and Sea Bright; the land of fisherman-attuned inlets between Ocean Grove and Point Pleasant; Barnegat Peninsula from Bay Head down to Barnegat Inlet; Long Beach Island; Atlantic City and its neighbors; and, finally, Cape May's long string of ocean-front keys.

See them change in character, from one to the other, in the advance southward along the coast. See how each contrasts with the others. See that what charms one man is drab or empty to another.

See the New Jersey Shore, in short, as a series of segments—and thus better understand the whole.

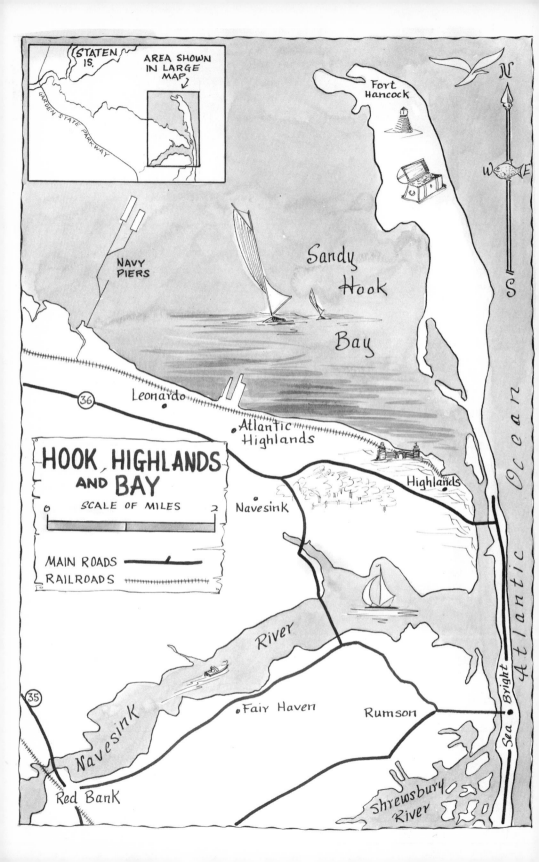

STATEN IS.

AREA SHOWN IN LARGE MAP

GARDEN STATE PARKWAY

Fort Hancock

N

W E

S

Sandy

Hook

Bay

NAVY PIERS

Atlantic Ocean

36

Leonardo

Atlantic Highlands

Highlands

HOOK, HIGHLANDS AND BAY

SCALE OF MILES

0   2

MAIN ROADS

RAILROADS

Navesink

River

35

Navesink

Fair Haven

Rumson

Sea Bright

Red Bank

Shrewsbury River

3. Hook, Highlands and Bay

The familiar and the mysterious exist side by side where the long, thin finger of Sandy Hook reaches out from the Highlands of Navesink to fend off 3,000 miles of rolling Atlantic Ocean.

There is familiarity: The Highlands of Navesink are the boldest coastal landmark from Maine to Key West; Sandy Hook, spread below the Highlands, is easier to see in full than any strip of Jersey Shore. Yet there is mystery, too—mystery as evanescent as Captain Kidd's treasure and James Fenimore Cooper's *Water Witch,* and mystery as real as the military censorship which blankets Sandy Hook like a morning fog.

Through the years the Hook, the Highlands and the Bay have played host to a fascinating parade of transients, from Henry Hudson to last summer's surf fishermen, from Captain Kidd to the motorists who sweat out a summer on Route 36. The tranquil waters inside the Hook have welcomed everything from pirates to bootleggers, from clammers to yachtsmen, from the sails of the old Gloucester fishing fleet to the motors of modern pleasure cruisers.

The theme of the entire region is the subtle interplay of war and peace. Revolutionary War heroics and treachery touched hill and peninsula alike. Since the building of a military fort in 1812, Sandy Hook has served as first line of defense for the vital harbor waters of New York. Guided missile Nike has replaced giant coastal guns, but the defensive purpose is not one whit different. Sandy Hook was—and is— a vital bastion of defense.

Whoever peers out over Sandy Hook from any of a dozen vantage points in the Highlands sees little to suggest the potential violence of mysterious defenses. The Nike base is well camouflaged, just as the tremendous 16-inch rifles of World War II folded back behind sand dunes and holly trees when their earth-shuddering practice sessions ended. The peace of pleasant bygone days seems supreme.

Sandy Hook lighthouse, built in 1764

Far out on Sandy Hook stands the old lighthouse, bleaching whiter with each passing sun. Built in 1764, the light stopped glowing only during the Revolution and World War II and it shines on now, the oldest lighthouse in the Western Hemisphere.

The Twin Lights of Navesink rise in stony prominence above the spot where the waters of the Navesink and Shrewsbury Rivers mingle before washing into the bay. Those lights, once the most powerful beacon in the United States, have been dark since 1949. They now serve only artistic or historic purposes. The Twin Lights welcome visitors as a museum; Sandy Hook light is viewed close up only by military men, who may even regard it as an outdated relic.

Is there more past than present in this hill-hook-bay land? If that is the impression, it is false. There is likely to be more in the future than in either past or present for the region if the military ever lets go of some of the Sandy Hook acreage it has possessed for more than 60 years.

Many times since 1930 the United States Government has appeared about to permit development of the lower half of Sandy Hook as a state park, in the best traditions of Jones Beach. Indeed, in June, 1950, the State moved rapidly toward creating its long-sought park land, only to be halted abruptly by war in Korea. Nonetheless Sandy Hook Park is certain to come some day.

Nature has worked overtime forming Sandy Hook, a classic example of unstable sand pulling itself together to defy the pounding force and fury of an ocean gathering power all the way from Spain. Geologists find Sandy Hook very simple to explain; observers without benefit of geology find it a marvel.

Long ago there was no Hook. The Navesink and Shrewsbury Rivers flowed directly into the sea east of the Highlands. Slowly, grain of sand by tiny grain of sand, prevailing longshore currents pushed a narrow spit of land to the north, uncertainly moving across the river estuaries—although not completely closing them. The spit lengthened and, out beyond the full influence of the rivers, it widened.

Then incredibly, the sands, incited by the mischievous ocean, stood up to the Navesink and Shrewsbury Rivers and closed their mouths—forcing them to flow northward inside the new hook. Periodically the ocean has recanted; several times in recorded history angry seas have smashed the river inlets through to the ocean again. Only the building of buttresses in the last 70 years has kept the capricious Atlantic in check.

37

Today Sandy Hook is a geological adolescent, still growing; its area has quadrupled since the Hook first was surveyed in 1685. The old lighthouse when erected in 1764 stood near the lapping waves on the spit's end. Now the end of the Hook is a mile and a quarter away from the light.

Tight military censorship has kept the secrets of Sandy Hook hidden for a half century from all but a relatively small number of soldiers, Coast Guardsmen and fishermen. Some two miles north from the gate near Highland Beach is a Nike base—everyone with the slightest curiosity knows that, even the Russians. Whoever desires a more intimate impression need only drive up Scenic Drive on the Highlands, unlimber a pair of high-powered binoculars and look. Seldom is a vital military base so temptingly spread out for spying eyes—and for spies who forget their glasses there are dime-in-slot magnifiers everywhere.

It would be a pity to be occupied with spying atop the Highlands. Too much else sweeps into binocular view to make Nike of more than passing concern to the average visitor.

Immediately below, the two-mile-long dock of Earle Naval Ammunition Depot protrudes far out into Sandy Hook Bay. This dock, said to be the longest of its type in the world, is capable of servicing Navy ships as large as cruisers. On the bay shore's fringe, marinas at Leonardo and Atlantic Highlands shelter enough boats to assure the bay's being aswarm with hulls on a warm Sunday.

Far off at the edge of the mist to the north are the towers of Manhattan, framed on the east by Coney Island and on the west by the Statue of Liberty. Between Manhattan and the tip of the Hook is Ambrose Channel, alive with ships outward bound to adventure and inward bound from exotic far-away.

Sandy Hook itself swims into the range of the moving binoculars, its curving area blanketed by the dark green of thousands of ancient, gnarled holly trees. On the bay side of the Hook is serenity. Inside the cove called The Horseshoe, Jersey Central steamships long ago made connections with trains bound for Long Branch. Peaceful, too, is Spermaceti Cove, the almost landlocked waters where in times past a giant whale washed ashore and bequeathed a name.

The Highlands fall away quickly, even precipitously in spots, to the bay on the north, the Atlantic Ocean on the east and the Navesink River on the south. The crouching hills of the Highlands are the best-known landfall on the Atlantic coast. Mount Mitchell in the

On the Highlands stand the Twin Lights, now a museum

Highlands, at 260 feet the highest point on the coast, has been the first glimpse of America for millions of immigrants—all the way back to the seventeenth-century Dutch.

The rugged and thickly wooded Highlands are only moderately changed in appearance since that day in September, 1609, when Henry Hudson dropped the *Half Moon*'s anchor and sent his men ashore to seek water. Roads entwine the heights and houses spread discreetly over the slopes, yet, to one looking at the Highlands from Raritan Bay, most of these twentieth-century encroachments are masked by the tall hardwood forests.

Deep in those trees is the very same flow of clear, cool spring water

39

from which Hudson's men refilled their casks. Even up to 1900, sailing ships stood in behind the Hook to get water from "The Spout." Thomas H. Leonard in his 1923 history recalled the 300 sails of the New England fishing fleet clustered on the bay—a "sight beyond description" as they awaited a favorable wind after getting Highlands water.

Of all the ships which found refuge in the bay, however, none loom larger in tradition than Captain William Kidd's buccaneer ship or the fanciful *Water Witch*, launched by a push of James Fenimore Cooper's pen in 1830.

Cap'n Kidd drank from "The Spout," he did. He buried treasure out on Sandy Hook by a lone pine tree, or he tossed it overboard in Sandy Hook Bay to escape a man-of-war, or he buried it in the sands on the bay shore. Anyone with an ounce of romance in his heart believes these things, aye, *knows* them. How else to account for those old coins dug from the sand near the Highlands in 1948? If some say Cap'n Kidd never really unfurled a sail off the Hook, it remains a fact that no one ever delves into the region's story without coming up with at least a bit of Kidd stuff.

As for the *Water Witch*, she was a seagoing lady of a different nature. James Fenimore Cooper drew that full-rigged "Skimmer of the Seas" out of thin air, writing hastily in a Paris hotel in 1830 before the elusive ship escaped him altogether. *The Water Witch* is one of America's finest sea legends and her sailing lanes unmistakably were the waters at the feet of the Highlands of Navesink.

Cooper remembered well the Highlands where he often had visited, and he transplanted his memories into his novel as a background for the bewitched ship. A half century ago the ruins of the book's villa, "Lust in Rust," could be shown visitors. Today nothing remains—except the sign "Water Witch" on a railroad station, a section of the Highlands named Water Witch and, of course, Cooper's book.

For all their foreboding topography, the Highlands had permanent settlers by 1664, and a year later 100 families lived on or near the heights. One of the early arrivals, Richard Hartshorne, by 1671 controlled nearly all of Sandy Hook and the Highlands—then called Portland Poynt, but a nice parcel of real estate by any name. Hartshorne bought the land from the Indians for the usual beads and guns and firewater, then, annoyingly enough, later had to buy from the Indians their rights to harvest beach plums on the Hook.

The Revolution provided an interlude, dominated by the activities

The Hook: where mystery and familiarity combine

of vengeful Tories who made Sandy Hook light a fort from which they struck at American rebels. The Tories achieved a measure of fame—or infamy—by hanging Joshua Huddy from a tall tree on the Highlands on April 12, 1782. Captain Huddy, they claimed, had cruelly put to death one Philip White. The story did not hold water; White had been shot while Huddy was a prisoner. The Tories exacted their vengeance anyway.

After the war clammers and fishermen found the peaceful bay to their liking. At what is now Keyport they took from the waters the celebrated Chingarora oysters—named by the Indians before white men arrived. At Parkertown, where the Navesink met Sandy Hook Bay, men lived of, by and for the clam. One writer said in 1890 that clams were to Parkertown "what the whale once was to Nantucket."

41

Some who gazed across the Highlands to New York in 1860 recognized the true destiny of the Highlands and the Hook—to warn the city of an approaching enemy, to fight that enemy if he arrived, and, in days of peace, to guide ships into the harbor. Sandy Hook, tied to New Jersey by a narrow isthmus, owed its vitality to New York harbor.

The city and those who came to it by sea had depended on Sandy Hook light since 1764, and later depended even more on the tall twin stone towers erected in 1862 on the Highlands of Navesink. Still, what could bring friends could bring foes equally well; in 1858 the United States Government began to replace 50-year-old wooden forts along the top rim of Sandy Hook with something more substantial.

Government builders labored mightily and spent greatly. They brought in huge blocks of New England granite and threw up a wall a mile in circumference. They put 75 enormous cannons in place in case any Confederate ships hove in sight. Perhaps even as they worked they suspected that the walls couldn't withstand a pounding by heavy artillery, and in the end they spent $10,000,000 without even finishing the job.

Someone suggested naming the fort for President Lincoln, although at least one man wrote, "No one who respects the memory of the martyred President calls the fort by that name."

As the years rolled on, the land-conscious government added to the original holdings it had bought from the Hartshornes in 1807. By 1892 the entire Hook rested in government hands. Far out on the sandy waste, amid the poison ivy and ancient holly, Fort Hancock grew in strength.

Meanwhile on the Highlands a few artists and actors had built homes after the Civil War, and *Harper's Magazine* sent a journalist down nearly every summer in the 1870's and 1880's to write about the pristine loveliness and the ever-present loneliness. There just wasn't much reason for summer folks to come down in numbers; so, said enterprising holders of land along the bay shore, let's build something for the folks.

The Reverend William W. Ramsey, out at Granville, and the Leonard family at Bay View got that same idea at about the same time. From their ideas grew Keansburg and Atlantic Highlands.

Mr. Ramsey saw possibilities over and above his thin church collections and he gave more and more attention to developing the resort. He helped change the name of Granville to Keansburg in honor of United States Senator John Kean of Elizabeth (senator from 1899 to

42

1911). Mr. Ramsey was Mayor Ramsey in 1881, the year he spent $70 for view postcards. The post office canceled $65 worth of cards the first year; Mayor Ramsey lost $5.

Well, he didn't *lose* $5, he invested $5. He induced boardinghouse people to make up postcards the next year and he made up another 20 different views of his own. Keansburg boomed. Thousands who received postcards telling of others "having a wonderful time" came to see for themselves. By 1913, as many as 40,000 people a year visited Mayor Ramsey's postcard-primed beach resort.

The Leonard family (for whom Leonardo is named) laid out Bay View in 1880—complete with restaurant, 100 bathing houses and a pier to receive steamships from the city. Bay View, which quickly was renamed Atlantic Highlands, was projected as a camp meeting town with heavy overtones of temperance.

Atlantic Highlands, said the founders, existed for lofty reasons, unlike those excursion resorts, "which were largely lager beer gardens, frequented by roughs and pickpockets." One of the Leonards said in 1881 that the Highlands camp meeting would be on such a scale as to "throw Ocean Grove out of business."

Ocean Grove didn't shut up shop, even after the building of the New York & Atlantic Highlands Railroad in 1883 gave the Highlands a link with Red Bank and the outside world. Soon few even discussed the Highlands camp meeting. For that matter, few discussed anything. Few came. Growth for Atlantic Highlands came unexpectedly in 1882 because when the government bought all of Sandy Hook that year the New Jersey Southern (Jersey Central) Railroad switched its terminal to the bay town.

Happy times settled over the Highlands, the Hook and the Bay in the first two decades of the twentieth century. The bay resorts, paced by Keansburg, found vacationists much better for the pocketbook than clams. Some built boardwalks, some enlarged their beaches, some inaugurated annual promotion feats.

Guns sounded from the ramparts of Fort Hancock during World War I, usually just to make sure they still worked, although on one occasion in 1918 they blasted away at a real, honest-to-goodness German U-boat. At least, the Army announced that when its guns spoke on August 13, 1918, they did so because a "Hun U-boat" had rifled 16 shells on the tip of the Hook during an afternoon fog. The Sandy Hook guns roared back with the rage of a sleeping giant stung by a hornet.

Except for that one incident, the 7,000 men and officers at Fort Hancock scarcely disturbed the local quietude during World War I, any more than the 9,000 Coast Artillery troops training out in the sand during World War II did much beyond rattling dishes on china closet shelves during practice sessions with the great guns.

War of a somewhat more intimate nature took over the placid bays and the quiet bay shore during Prohibition. Some local clammers-turned-businessmen disagreed with the law so violently that they decided to bring in illicit rum, in their fervent protest. Throughout the long reign of the Eighteenth Amendment the bay shore echoed and re-echoed with scandal, punctured occasionally by a shot aimed at or by a bootlegger or by a Coast Guard vessel at a rum runner. Venturing out at night sometimes became dangerous, and an Atlantic Highlands Association formed in 1923 begged an end to "bootleggers, gangsters and gunmen."

Prohibition and the strange bedfellows it created did no permanent damage to the region. The building of good concrete highways in the 1920's brought thousands of new visitors to Laurence Harbor and Union Beach, to Keyport and Keansburg and Atlantic Highlands. The concrete ribbons doomed the railroads and the Sandy Hook Bay boats. Prosperity, tempered of course by the depression, rode the highways to the bay.

That's the way today was born. The Garden State Parkway brings in new business, but who knows how much it also tempts drivers to look a few more miles down the beach? The bay villages are never likely to rival Atlantic City in size, but who is to shrug off as unimportant the weekend crowds of 75,000 at Keansburg, where major overhauling of the beach in 1954 was aimed to keep Keansburg abreast of public demand?

Economics is the thing that all seaside or bay resort owners fret about all the time. Many worry privately that a public park at Sandy Hook will ruin business in established resorts. One Shore mayor at a public session in the early 1950's said the proposed park will bring in "riffraff"— roughly defined by him to mean people who come only for a day with a lunch packed in a box and don't even spend a nickel on a pinball machine, much less rent a bungalow.

A casual visitor is relieved of such incidental worries. He can see the handsome old Twin Lights up close, can gaze long-distance at the remarkably long-lived lighthouse out on Sandy Hook. He can visit "The Spout" where Cap'n Kidd and Henry Hudson and the Gloucester fish-

44

They say Hudson's crew found good water at this Spout

ermen filled their casks. He can locate a marker to Captain Huddy, can find enough mementoes to make Cooper's legend clear. He can guide his car along the tortuous roads winding through the Highlands and be rewarded with ever-changing—and often most unsealike—landscapes.

This is only icing on the cake. The enduring thing is the essential romance of the place, a place touched by the sea, yet apart from it. Nothing—wind, storm, hurricane, even people—changes the High-lands much.

Philip Freneau, celebrated New Jersey "Poet of the Revolution" who lived at nearby Matawan, well summed up the Highlands in the Eighteenth century:

> These hills, the pride of all the coast,
> To mighty distance seen,
> With aspect bold and rugged brow
> That shade the neighboring main;
> These heights for solitude designed,
> This rude resounding shore,
> These vales impervious to the wind,
> Tall oaks that to the tempest bend,
> Half Druid I adore.

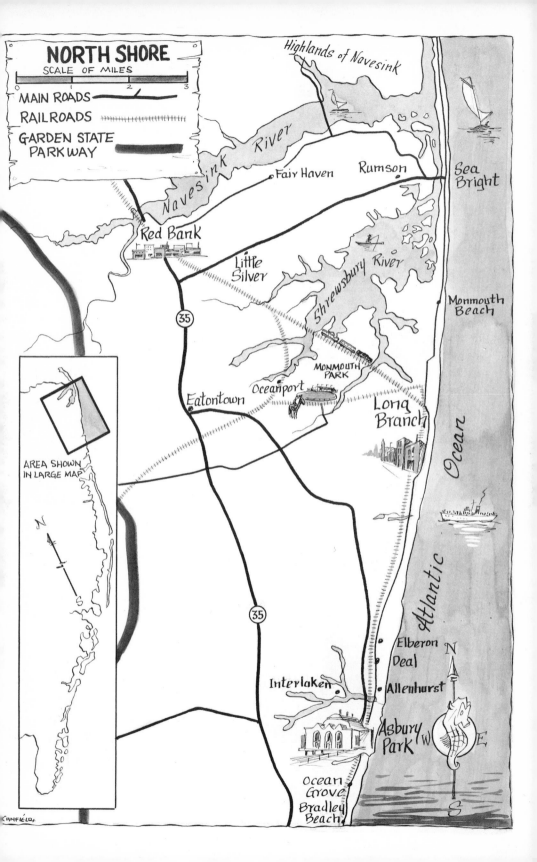

Asbury Park is the acknowledged Duchess of the North Shore

4. North Shore

Down in a little triangle in Monmouth County the green New Jersey mainland meets the blue Atlantic Ocean on uniquely solid terms, and there the Jersey Shore is at its stable best—its gold-making waves and its greenback-sprouting boardwalks supplemented by vital, if unspectacular, everyday living.

That triangle—the North Shore—is loosely bounded on the east by the ocean, on the west by the Garden State Parkway and on the north by the Navesink River. It stands, more or less, on its point at Ocean Grove. Here, in an area of perhaps 125 square miles, the Parkway is booming year-around living. Here, too, industry for two decades has been putting some economic starch in a region long washed only in salt water.

That is not to deny the value of the North Shore's narrow strip of sea-caressed sand. The ocean-front towns between Sea Bright and Ocean Grove rise on a flood of vacation cash in June, ebb in September as dollars fall away with the homegoing tide. Good July sunshine and sea air restore brightness to the eyes and quickness to the step of the North Shore entrepreneurs just as they do to resort businessmen everywhere.

Nevertheless, towns like Asbury Park and Long Branch have a year-around vigor over and above summer trade. Their boardwalks in off-season, except for an occasional Asbury Park convention, are as dead as last summer's seaside romances. Inland a few blocks, though, both have all the bustle and hustle of mainland towns of 25,000 to 30,000 people—which is exactly what each happens to be.

The key word here is "mainland." Much of this North Shore is good, solid earth coming right down to meet the ocean, unusual for the New Jersey Shore, where 90 per cent of the beachland is a string of sandy bar islands at varying distances off the mainland.

North Shore mainland characteristics are readily apparent: the prominent ridge bisecting the Rumson peninsula between the Navesink

49

and Shrewsbury Rivers, the good stands of hardwood trees still seen in many places, the abundance of fresh-water streams and lakes—rare so close to the briny sea. This is, by and large, green land, and that helps coax people to the triangle for all-year living.

The most obvious meeting of mainland and ocean is where the bluffs of Long Branch drop 25 to 30 feet to ocean level. Even in the short space of two centuries of recorded time the Atlantic has eaten the bluffs back more than 1,000 feet.

As the bluff has fallen before relentless waters, Long Branch sands have shifted northward with the longshore currents. Today the sandy North Shore area north from Monmouth Beach to Highland Beach is held in place by a solid sea wall, a granite tribute to the never-ending desire of the sea to move that sand again. Often the Atlantic has threatened Sea Bright and even the high wall can't keep away entirely the power of a hurricane.

Few resorts on the Jersey Shore suffer as badly from the battle with the ocean as Long Branch. Seventy-five years ago Long Branch had no peer among American resorts; these days even its most fervent admirers admit it is no Gold Coast—although that may in the final analysis be a tribute. People who are serious about Long Branch's present and future can become ill at thoughts of what the Gold Coast days did to a fine resort.

Long Branch attracted its first summer vacationists in 1788 and grew steadily in stature until by 1850 only Cape May could claim to be on a par with it. Happy and uncomplicated traditions pleased Long Branch visitors; docilely they followed the swimming flags—red meant gentlemen only on the beach, white meant ladies only. For years the gentle folk laughed about the day a joker hoisted both red and white flags at once ("which created some awful squinting and no little confusion").

Two great waves swept over the nation when the Civil War ended— a gilt-edged wave of materialism verging on debauchery and a guilt-edged wave of religious fervor. The two met head-on along the North Shore, rising respectively at Long Branch and Ocean Grove and eventually colliding with an impact which has echoed down through the years.

The rise of Long Branch gathered momentum when Ulysses Simpson Grant, war hero and president, arrived in 1868 for a summer visit. Grant liked the bluffs and agreeably accepted a home given him by influential men who summered in Long Branch.

James A. Bradley's statue at Asbury Park

The rich came—the old rich and those with new fortunes. The prominent came—those prominent in business and in the theater. The bored and the high-spirited came. Once the bluffs and the exciting possibility of mixed-up flags had been enough, but most of these new people needed constant amusement and they could pay for it.

As naturally as darkness follows the sunshine, the dice rollers and the roulette spinners and the famed ladies of ill repute arrived at Long Branch. One town official proudly proclaimed Long Branch to be "The Monte Carlo of America." Monmouth Park Jockey Club started its track in 1870 to give the wealthy a chance to become poor. Those who hated fresh air could lose their money in smoke-filled, gold-domed gambling houses, particularly those made famous by Phil and John Daly.

The pace quickened. The gamblers indentified themselves with Long Branch in such homey little ways as giving money to fire departments (there is still a Phil Daly Hose Company in town). America's burgeoning industrial might created fortunes overnight and many a million went to build fabulous homes on the bluff. Diamond Jim Brady and Jim Fisk and their camp followers and hangers-on frequented the Branch. By 1885 no resort matched Long Branch in glitter—a glitter disguising dangerous hollowness.

A few miles down the strand at Ocean Grove, a counterwave swelled. Ocean Grove typified the many camp meetings of the day, when huge crowds gathered under tents to hear powerful voices warn them of the consequences of sin. Several camp meetings started along the Jersey Shore—at Ocean Grove, at Sea Grove (Cape May Point), at Ocean City, at Island Heights, at Seaside Park and at Atlantic Highlands. Only Ocean Grove survived in the full extent envisioned by the founders.

The barrenness of the North Shore attracted the Ocean Grove Camp Meeting Association in 1869. Except for Long Branch, not more than 100 persons lived on the beaches between Shark River and Atlantic Highlands. One family lived in what is now all of Ocean Grove and Asbury Park. The entire area from Long Branch to north of Sea Bright was owned by the Widow Wardell in 1865, her claim being based mainly on the fact that her boys always "whipped" any other boys they caught gathering driftwood on the beach.

Ocean Grove grew rapidly. By 1891 as many as 6,000 people attended a single camp meeting service. Two years later the Reverend Elwood Stokes, first president, broke ground for the remarkable Auditorium (engineers still marvel at it). Its seven main trusses, sound after all these years, stretch over 151 feet and cover an area capable of seating well over 9,000 people.

The Grove never clashed openly with the Branch. That remained for one of its sons, James A. Bradley, the self-made New York brush manufacturer, who in 1870 came for a rest at Ocean Grove and wound up buying 500 acres of briars on the north side of Wesley Lake. Bradley named his wretched and uninhabited wilderness Asbury Park, in honor of Bishop Francis Asbury, first Methodist bishop in the United States.

Bradley, known as "a benevolent czar with a twirling foot rule," wielded the most influence exhibited by any single individual anywhere along the New Jersey Shore. He laid out streets and made them wide and straight; he built cottages and hotels, selling only to those who would abide by his temperance beliefs. Asbury Park was no camp meeting, but Bradley fought liquor traffic and gambling and sin—measuring sin, like most reformers, by his own foot rule.

Inevitably, James A. Bradley, reformer, took up battle with Long Branch, his personal dragon. Monmouth County sent Bradley to the State Senate in 1893 and a year later he cast the deciding vote on a bill outlawing bets on horse races in New Jersey. The bill crippled and then closed Monmouth Park Jockey Club. Long Branch's scantily supported golden dome swayed, then fell crushingly when a 1907 anti-gambling bill closed the gambling houses. People who wanted "a Monte Carlo" went elsewhere.

Many persons of wealth and discrimination long since had fled from the Golden City. The exodus could be dated as early as 1880, when the wealthy moved outward to Elberon, to West End or even farther, to Sea Bright and Monmouth Beach and Allenhurst and Deal on the south.

Elberon, named for the L. B. Brown who subdivided its 100 acres in the 1870's, was the nation's pulse for 13 days in 1881 when President James A. Garfield came there hoping to recover from the assassin's bullet which felled him in Washington on July 2. Some 2,000 volunteers built a $5/8$-mile spur from the New York and Long Branch Railroad to the Francklyn cottage on Ocean Avenue. The stricken president arrived on September 6, seemed to revive for a time, then died on September 19.

Sea Bright gained fame in a different way; an 1889 guidebook called it "one of the gayest resorts on the coast." Its Lawn Tennis and Cricket Club, sporting the colors of the Zingaree Cricket Club of England, started its Invitational tennis tournaments in 1884—and continued them until 1949 except for two wars. The world's greatest court players

53

competed on the springy turf imported (from England, naturally) in 1886.

Monmouth Beach rose swiftly after developers cut up the old Widow Wardell holdings in 1871. The town soon became a center for the wealthy and musical. Moneyed New Yorkers often entertained 50 or more guests on a weekend—and never really forgave the Nauvoo fishermen for discovering the beach first. As late as 1928 a court action to halt fishing failed, despite fervent presentations to the court that noisy commercial fishermen got up too early and that their fish smelled. The fishermen still fish on.

Minor annoyances failed to stop the flow of brilliant musicians to Monmouth Beach. Such musical personalities as Walter Damrosch and Albert Spaulding found the Beach helpful to their art. Often Spaulding played to the accompaniment of Clara Clemens, daughter of Mark Twain.

The greatest visible display of wealth, however, stretched from the lower end of Long Branch down through Loch Arbour. Much of the moneyed area centered around St. James Chapel on Ocean Avenue, across the street from where Garfield died. St. James in 1886 claimed a congregation whose pew holders enjoyed an aggregate wealth of $120,000,000. Over the years seven presidents worshiped there—Grant, Hayes, Garfield, Arthur, Harrison, McKinley and Wilson. Today this "Church of the Presidents" is a historical museum, preserved only by a dedicated struggle on the part of a few/persons, despite the wealth of its past pew holders.

Millions poured into huge homes between 1890 and 1910. Up went mansions like Solomon P. Guggenheim's 100-room "Aladdin's Palace," James A. Hearn's $1,000,000 scale reproduction of Shakespeare's home at Stratford-on-Avon, Nellie Fern Jones's Deal showplace which later became Frank Hague's home, and Arthur Horgan's Deal Conservatoire. There were more, many more—and sometimes town folk couldn't be blamed if they wondered what the beachfront displays did for their towns.

In the early 1920's, for example, when Long Branch sought to bestir itself from a long and unprofitable sleep, town officials bitterly reflected that the days of golden glory had left the city nothing. Deep ruts filled Ocean Avenue. Dilapidated mansions and the decaying gold-domed gambling houses stood along the avenue like haunted houses. Not one cent of the billions flipped at roulette wheels and galloping ponies had gone to save the ever-collapsing bluff.

Stone walls keep Sea Bright's narrow strip in place

One leader summed it up in 1923: "Long Branch was gold-domed to death."

Still, Long Branch fought back during the 1920's, when a surge of prosperity rolled up and down the entire Jersey Shore. The city made graveled Ocean Avenue a wide, paved parkway, rebuilt the boardwalk, pushed a hotel boom, built its beachfront stadium for automobile races (and later used the track for dog races). Some of the estates—such as George M. Pullman's acreage—were cut up for development.

By 1928, indeed, Long Branch's 6½-mile beachfront had vigor, even if the blood which pumped through its veins was no longer all blue. Depression closed down by 1932, the very year that the wild Atlantic sullenly warned that Long Branch's woes weren't all economic by carving away 30 feet of bluff in a single storm.

Ocean Grove and Asbury Park those same years experienced few of the financial and erosion complications besetting Long Branch and its near neighbors. Ocean Grove had its unrelenting religious strength; Asbury Park had its James A. Bradley.

If ever a resort community could be called uncomplicated, the community is Ocean Grove. The Grove has never deviated from its original aim to provide a quiet community where those who seek Methodist inspiration can find it. Its annual August camp meeting is as great a Methodist magnet as was the first camp meeting in 1870.

Hundreds of noted personages have spoken in the huge Auditorium— presidents, congressmen, state officials, Methodist leaders, vibrant evangelists from Billy Sunday to Billy Graham. President Grant, who spoke in Ocean Grove on a Sunday long ago, posed a problem. Should he be permitted to drive a carriage into town despite the law forbidding such traffic? Grant, as much at home in Ocean Grove as in Long Branch, settled the matter:

"Who should regard and uphold the law, if not the chief magistrate of the nation?"

That Sunday shutdown still pertains. Everything comes to a standstill on Sunday—automobiles cease to run; as many as 2,500 cars leave Ocean Grove before Saturday midnight in summer. The beach is empty. Few promenade the boardwalk. This is not calculated to please all who disagree on how Sunday should be kept; one writer in an article in 1953 apologized with probably unconscious naïveté: "Ocean Grove is not as bad as some say."

Asbury Park stayed for the most part under the personal control of James Bradley until he died in 1921. Many felt the founder's stubborn refusal to see his town change set the Park back a couple of decades. Bradley, on the other hand, thought his town so altered that in his declining years he said:

"I would have been much happier in my old age if I had never heard of the place."

Ocean Grove's unique camp meetings center on its Auditorium

Bradley, as noted, fought vice on his own terms. He also fought to keep Asbury Park exactly as he planned. He tried to keep the beach-front under his control, but when the city threatened condemnation in 1903, he sold his holdings east of Ocean Avenue for $100,000. Bradley's interest in Asbury Park began to decline, although he hung onto his huge holdings in the city.

The city administration pushed on rapidly to develop its beachfront. It improved the boardwalk, built wood piling jetties and in 1905 built a handsome boardwalk arcade. Arthur Pryor of West Long Branch, an unknown, came in 1904 to give the first of the public band concerts which are still a summer feature. Pryor, who later wrote "The Whistler and His Dog," one of 250 original compositions, was a fixture for 16 years. He captured world attention, but between 1926 and his death in 1942 he returned often to Asbury Park for concerts.

Asbury Park got around to dedicating a statue to James A. Bradley in June, 1921, the very month the bearded old patriarch died. One year after Bradley's death his large real estate parcels hit the market and Asbury Park soared into its biggest decade of growth. In 1922, building shot up to treble that of 1921. The boom culminated in construction of Convention Hall and the Casino in 1928 and 1929 and widening of the boardwalk to 60 feet in 1936.

The years, in general, have been reasonably kind to the North Shore, now virtually one town from Sea Bright to Ocean Grove. Streets run together from municipality to municipality, the whole area being tied together by Ocean Avenue. Time hasn't changed everything, by any stretch of the imagination. The area from Loch Arbour up through Elberon is still notable for fine mansions, many of them holdovers from the Gold Coast days and most of them still well kept—although scarcely a year goes by without a big auction.

Certainly Ocean Grove hasn't changed. Its Ocean Pathway, once called by *National Geographic Magazine* "the most beautiful short street in the United States," is still handsome in a vintage way. The town's old street names perpetuate memories of past Methodist Church leaders and events. Ocean Grove is the one total survivor of the immense post-Civil-War Methodist camp meeting movement. Symbolizing the meetings are the little two-part dwellings surrounding the Auditorium. The rear part is permanent wood; the front part is a tent erected in the summer.

Asbury Park, while much changed from 1920, is the acknowledged Duchess of the North Shore. Her wide streets, thanks to James Bradley, are as useful in the automobile age as they were decorative in the four-in-hand era. Her boardwalk, while not comparable in size or lavishness to Atlantic City's, is not so confusing or garish either.

Most seasonal visitors to Asbury Park's boardwalk and beaches would be surprised at the size and vitality of the year-around city separated from the resort area by six or seven blocks jammed with boardinghouses and medium-size hotels. The greatest contrast between Atlantic City and Asbury Park is the fact that Atlantic City's business is all within about three blocks of the Boardwalk—and dependent on the 'walk—while Asbury Park's business leads an inland life of its own.

The third of the North Shore's big three—Long Branch—continues to suffer from the ravages of the sea. It takes no erosion expert to see the immensity of the problem, which the city hopes a new sea wall will alleviate. Ocean Avenue, three times shifted since 1875, is in (in 1957) the process of being moved again.

Part of the northbound lane of Ocean Avenue has been converted into a boardwalk adjunct, with tables and chairs set on the asphalt street. Hurricanes in the past 15 years have ripped away huge chunks of the boardwalk; it is unlikely the boardwalk will ever again stretch over miles as it once did.

Erosion is a continuing problem for all the North Shore. The sea wall at Long Branch is hidden by the bluff, but the sea wall from Monmouth Beach north to Sandy Hook is a grim, ever-present reminder that the Atlantic Ocean doesn't really take people seriously.

The North Shore should get ever more popular because of the Garden State Parkway. Officials who grumble that motorists spend precious little in town could be too pessimistic. Many of these down-for-the-day visitors will be returning—for two days, for a week, for a month, to buy a home in one of the inland towns. Meanwhile, 300,000 to 350,000 people flock to the North Shore every blistering weekend, sometimes coming in such numbers that a hotel room is as hard to find as a knee-length bathing suit.

The North Shore's prosperity is based on more than its ocean-front income. Several industries and government installations in the area offer employment; many new home developments are springing up. The Parkway brings industrial areas surrounding New Brunswick, Elizabeth and Newark within a reasonable morning and evening drive.

Possibly the future of this northernmost of the Jersey Shore areas may be as much a matter of its industrial-residential character as of the shifting sands. The real potential of the "day trippers" may not be in what they spend this day on hot dogs—but that they may return tomorrow to invest in the North Shore as home owners.

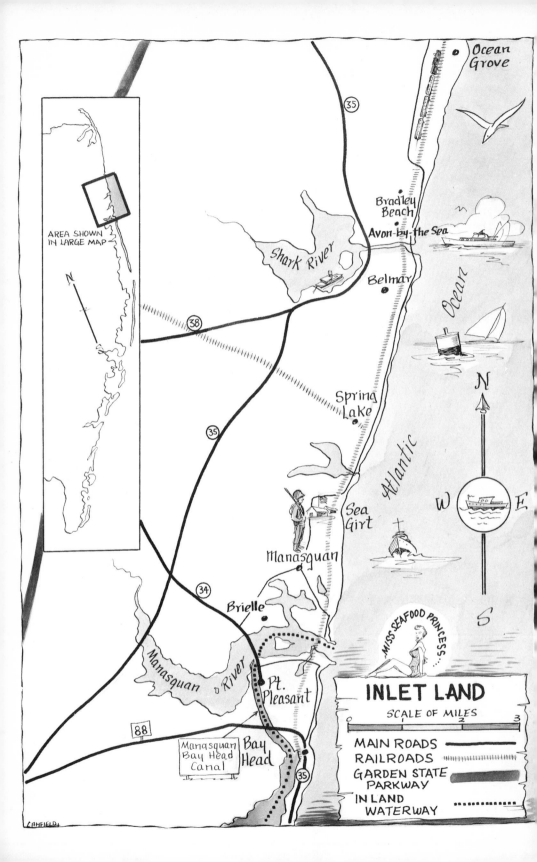

5. Inlet Land

Many a modern wife waiting for the party fishing boats to come home must be excused for agreeing the Indians turned a neat phrase when they called a meandering Monmouth County stream "Manatah-squawhan."

A very simple name, that: "Man-a-tah" for island; "squaw" for wife, "han" for stream. All together now—"Stream of the Island for Squaws," the place to park wives while the wampum winners hunted and fished. Breathes there a fisherman's wife who doesn't feel a kinship with the squaws when the boats swarm outward to the fishing banks?

The "Manatahasquawhan" today is Manasquan River, and that sluggish stream and its up-coast neighbor, Shark River, combine to give ten miles of seacoast between Bradley Beach and Point Pleasant a distinctive quality found nowhere else along the New Jersey Shore. This is Inlet Land.

Outward through the inlets on fair summer weekends pour thousands of deep-sea anglers bound for the Mud Hole, Shrewsbury Rocks, Squan Ridge, the Klondike and other favorite banks. Yachtsmen from Maine to Florida know Manasquan Inlet as the invitation to a long, protected run, down through the Inland Waterway to Cape May and beyond.

The uniqueness of this Inlet Land stems from the unusual number of lakes and ponds so close to the Atlantic Ocean that a good outfielder easily could toss a clam shell from beach to lake shore. The lakes are in several instances frustrated inlets, held in place now by dikes.

The region is given character by the lakes and inlets. At the same time, they rather well define town limits:

Sylvan Lake is the mutual boundary for Bradley Beach and Avon-by-the-Sea. Shark River Inlet divides Avon and Belmar. Lake Como is between Belmar and Spring Lake. Wreck Pond differentiates between

Shark River's inlet leads fishing boats to the sea

Spring Lake and Sea Girt. Sea Girt and Manasquan are kept apart by Stockton Lake. Glimmerglass Lake separates Manasquan and Brielle. Manasquan is only an inlet away from Point Pleasant.

The present rock-bound stability of both Manasquan and Shark River Inlets is a thing of the twentieth century. In recorded time they have tended to shift regularly, often as much as a half mile away from the present openings.

Millions of dollars have poured into Shark River and Manasquan Inlets during the past four decades. Keeping these exits to (and entrances from) the Atlantic open is a more or less full-time concern for the area; the inlets mean big business as well as big sport.

The entire Bradley Beach-Point Pleasant ocean frontage came to maturity between 1875 and 1890, given sustenance by the Jersey Central (New York and Long Branch) Railroad, whistling down from the north. Not all credit for discovering Inlet Land belongs to railroad engineers and real estate developers. The Indians knew its charms long before the surveyor's transit and a quitclaim deed became handy devices for measuring progress.

Each year during August Point Pleasant pauses to pay pleasant and profitable homage to those braves and their ladies who long ago gathered for their annual outing and/or squaw parking near the Manatahsquaw-han.

Point Pleasant calls this annual rite Big Sea Day, and let it be emphasized that squaw parking is no longer the rule. Indeed, the female of the species is venerated to such an extent that the fairest of them all becomes Miss Seafood Princess as the highlight of the day. The Indians never chose a Miss Seafood Princess, but then the backward Lenni Lenape had a distressingly poor promotion department.

Big Sea Day deserves celebration, and all credit to Point Pleasant for reviving the fete. After the Indians found they no longer could get at a white man's shore, farmers took up the red man's custom, gathering near Wreck Pond in Sea Girt on the second Saturday every August. The farmers, simple fellows, called their outing "Wash Day."

Farm wagons covered the beach for nearly a mile on Wash Day. An 1894 account in *Harper's Magazine* told of 10,000 rustics on the strand, with "hucksters, sharpers and gamblers" willing and able to help farmers dispose of harvest profits. Farmers and their families either swam in the clothes they wore down or changed into costumes which the *Harper's* correspondent said "were not for the better." If there was a Miss Sea-

63

food Princess in the lot, her charms remained well hidden in homespun.

Wash Day, Big Sea Day—call it what you will—was dying in 1894. The man from *Harper's* wrote that 20 years before crowds had been three times as large, "but the more recent settlement of the coast" cut the crowds drastically. Sea Girt had come a long way. The farmer eventually had to stay home; he was as unwelcome as the Indian.

Commodore Robert Stockton, Princeton 1813 and United States Navy hero, gave Inlet Land its first social significance in 1852, the year he bought a huge ocean-front farm and named it Sea Girt. The commodore built his ocean-front mansion as much like a ship as possible, to give the illusion of striding a deck at sea.

Tradition says Mrs. Stockton became *too* impressed with the ship-at-sea illusion. She insisted that the commodore build another home—"The Cottage"—somewhat back from the waves. There Mrs. Stockton and other landlubbers could enjoy a night's sleep, unperturbed by nightmares featuring a shiplike mansion carried out by the waves.

Annual arrivals of the Stocktons from Princeton assumed some of the atmosphere of a circus coming to town. The commodore liked his family about him for the six weeks he spent at Sea Girt; trailing behind his carriage came a parade of vehicles laden with children, grandchildren, friends, servants and friend's servants. Somewhere in line trotted the blooded horses which would exercise all summer on the ¾-mile track at the Stockton grounds.

Commodore Stockton and some summer visitors at Manasquan had the entire beachfront from Long Branch to Long Beach Island almost all to themselves by Civil War time. Squan Village (Manasquan) had attracted boatbuilder William Brown in 1808, and by 1834 *Gordon's Gazetteer* could report Squan's boardinghouses to be "much frequented for sea bathing."

Change came inevitably. The commodore sold his beloved Sea Girt to developers before his death in 1866. A group of Ocean Grove summer residents founded Ocean Beach (Belmar) in 1873 and two years later workers laid the tracks of the Jersey Central (New York and Long Branch) Railroad all the way to Manasquan.

Inlet Land expanded. James A. Bradley, founder of Asbury Park, established Bradley Beach in the 1870's, although he gave it only moderate personal attention until 1897. Philadelphia tobacco maker Edward Batchelor established Key East on the north bank of Shark River Inlet in 1878. Batchelor's town attracted tobacco-hating Baptists, who in 1883 started a camp meeting patterned after Ocean Grove. Nevertheless, by the time that Key East took the name Avon-by-the-Sea in 1900, it lacked both tobacco maker and camp meeting.

Credit in large measure one Colonel L. U. Maltby, owner of the Beach House at Sea Girt and two-thirds owner of the Monmouth House at Spring Lake, with keeping Sea Girt and Spring Lake just as Commodore Stockton would have liked them. In the 1880's the colonel approached the railroad with a proposition: If the railroad could run a train to make the 56 miles from Jersey City to Sea Girt in 90 minutes, the colonel would guarantee 150 Wall Street brokers to ride it.

The railroad agreed, but lengthened the time to two hours on the chance that there might be some brokers who would like to get off at Long Branch or Asbury Park or such way spots. Most brokers put up with the extra half hour to enjoy the cherished pine, oak and holly forests surrounding their Spring Lake and Sea Girt homes, or the ultra-fashionable Monmouth, Essex and Sussex hotels near the clear waters of Spring Lake.

Spring Lake vacationists chuckled in the late 1880's over the story of a young swain who sought to impress an heiress by taking her for a daily row on the lake. He tossed gold coins into the clear waters and the lovers watched them settle all the way to the bottom. Alas for young love, a rival swam to the bottom to recover some of the coins—and revealed them to be but gilded poker chips. The rival won the heiress; the pretender didn't even get his chips back.

Shark River's far-famed soft-shell crabs and oysters made it imperative through the nineteenth century to keep the inlet open, since the shellfish needed salt water. The worst fears of commercial shellfishermen were realized in the summer of 1877—shoaling sands completely closed the inlet. Shark River built up to a level three feet higher than normal behind the barrier. Shellfish began to disappear.

Volunteers worked desperately in August, finally succeeded in getting river water to trickle through the sand barrier at low tide. Quickly the pent-up river burst through the shoal, sweeping thousands of tons of sand along on what the *State Gazette* in August, 1877, called "a swift and turbulent current far out to sea." Unfortunately, sand returned to block the inlet on and off—even as recently as 1950.

Shoaling of Manasquan River Inlet had more serious implications, because considerable ocean-going commerce came and went in the Manasquan as the tides changed. The United States Government felt the situation serious enough in 1879 to invest $39,000 in jetties on the north side of the inlet—and a condition had to be serious indeed for the United States Government to invest $39,000 in anything in 1879.

The investment might as well have been spent for sand as jetties, in large measure because a Spanish brig laden with iron ore ran aground in the channel in the late 1880's. She became "solid as a rock," a picturesque and sentimental sight for all but commercial shippers, fishermen and government jetty enthusiasts.

Sentiment had its moments, of course. Ailing author Robert Louis Stevenson visited Manasquan for six weeks in 1888 and while there wrote part of *The Master of Ballantrae* in the Union House (later burned). In his memory a patch of sand in the Manasquan is still called Treasure Island. Across the inlet at Point Pleasant Beach, thousands came by 1900 to enjoy the "wild shore and ocean scenery," and cottagers strolled the uncommercial strand. A 1902 historian said artists "yet come in the hope that the coast storms of the previous winter have produced something new."

Happy days, those days of the 1890's when the artistic and the wealthy shared Inlet Land with the ever-dwindling ranks of Wash Day farmers and the ever-growing ranks of society seeking invitations to the Governor's Ball at the New Jersey National Guard encampment at Sea Girt.

The National Guard, finding its old rifle range at Elizabethport cramped, in 1885 rented land from the Sea Girt Land and Improvement Company for $3,000 annually. The State bought the grounds in 1891 and in 1907 enlarged its holdings to 165 acres—with 3,000 feet of ocean front, "affording the soldiery ample opportunity for healthful recreation in the water."

Soldiers on parade and at the firing range intrigued the citizenry, but the big thrill each year occurred on Governor's Day, when New Jersey's chief executive came to inspect the troops. As Governor's Day turned into magic evening, the Governor's Ball in the "Little White House" attracted socialites from all over the state and from New York and Philadelphia. The Little White House until 1906 was Commodore Stockton's old farmhouse, fronting on the roadway to the ocean.

In 1906 the State bought the New Jersey building at the Louisiana Purchase Exposition in St. Louis and moved it to Sea Girt as a replacement for the farmhouse. Governors usually summered at the Little White House until World War II. There Governor Woodrow Wilson

The "Little White House" at Sea Girt no longer draws society

received word of his 1912 nomination as Democratic presidential candidate.

Governors of both parties and their faithful followers used the Little White House extensively—and the public often wondered if "used" was not a two-edged word. Governor Charles Edison pretty well shuttered the Little White House in 1942 by questioning publicly a series of large Sea Girt bills.

The Little White House hasn't been the summer capitol since. Actually the Little White House began to assume Little White Elephant proportions by 1932, when first proposals were advanced to make the grounds a public park. Recently Governor Robert Meyner revived the state park notion. Sea Girt residents show no marked enthusiasm for the park either in 1932 or 1955.

Regardless of the quiet times at Sea Girt and Spring Lake and increasingly busy times on the boardwalks at Bradley Beach and Belmar, it became clear by 1906 that no matter what else happened to Inlet Land, something had to be done about the inlets—particularly Manasquan Inlet.

Shark River had local import, true, for fishermen and boaters, but Manasquan Inlet posed a twofold challenge—to keep it open for the commercial and party boat fishermen and to develop it as the northern entrance to a long, protected waterway down through inland bays and thoroughfares to Cape May.

In 1907, making sure it wouldn't break the taxpayers, the State Legislature allocated the modest sum of $200 for a survey to plan ways and means to keep the inlet open and to estimate costs. Professor Lewis M. Haupt carried out the survey with volunteers and came up with as good a $200 bargain as the State ever has got, summing up all that had gone before—and clearly proving the advantages of keeping both inlets open.

The following year work began on the Inland Waterway from Bay Head to Cape May and in 1925, after eight years of intermittent digging, a canal finally linked Manasquan River and Barnegat Bay. Thus yachtsmen could move into Manasquan Inlet from the open sea and proceed safely inside for 115 miles to Delaware Bay—always providing, of course, that the inlet stayed open.

Keeping the inlet open was not easily done. Soon after the canal opened the inlet closed, and many said bitterly that the canal caused the closing by siphoning off water from Manasquan River. In August, 1926, firemen and New Jersey National Guardsmen etched open a channel by shooting streams of water under pressure against the blocking sand.

The inlet was choked completely in 1928 and 1929, but in 1930 work began on a joint federal-state-county-municipal project to dig a 400-foot-wide opening through solid sand dunes ten feet high. Manasquan's familiar massive jetties date from that beginning, although they have been lengthened through the years. Ocean and river waters mingled through those jetties on February 10, 1931, embracing in the height of the full-moon tide.

Shoaling continues intermittently in the inlet, but constant vigilance (and money) keeps the channel open. The word with yachtsmen and fishermen today is that Manasquan Inlet is first class.

Not only is the inlet relatively easy for skilled pilots to navigate, it also offers several places inside where boats may tie up either temporarily or permanently. Many yachts berth in the large, square basin just inside on the south side of the inlet. Brielle boat basin, a mile inside on the north shore, is recognized as one of the nation's best.

The Manasquan River and Inlet fishing center is said to be the largest in the world; Coast Guardsmen have counted more than 1,600 boats of all sizes leaving and entering Manasquan Inlet on a Saturday or Sunday. Return of the party fishing boats in late afternoon brings regular crowds down to the rocky jetties to watch the parade in from the sea.

Fishing is the key word at Brielle, an attractive little haven founded in 1919 and named for Brielle, Holland. Heavily shaded avenues crisscross in front of quiet homes with their green lawns, but what fisherman notices trees or lawns when he is outward bound for the deep sea?

Fishermen on party boats gather in the early morning hours at the boat basins in Brielle and Point Pleasant and Belmar, ready to sail as soon after daybreak as possible. They go out in all seasons—for cod and pollack in the winter, mackerel in the fall and spring, porgies, sea bass, fluke, bonita and other fish in the summer. Often the boats cross shipping lanes eight and twelve miles at sea in search of the elusive fish. Party boat fishing is a humming year-around Inlet Land industry; deep-sea fishermen know neither time nor season.

Inlet Land is as varied as the founding fathers could have hoped. Spring Lake, Sea Girt and Avon-by-the-Sea founders long ago declared themselves firmly against "fanfare amusements." They have none. Point Pleasant Beach, Manasquan, Bradley Beach and Belmar, on the other hand, see nothing wrong with amusements along the boardwalk—and many a young Sea Girter or Spring Laker or Avon-by-the-Seaer comes to town in season to agree.

Once this area largely looked to Philadelphia for its well-being. Indeed, an 1889 commentator declared that a shaking of the genealogical tree of the average Sea Girt or Silver Lake resident "would likely reveal a Binney or a Biddle"—good Main Line names. The automobile age has made such tree shaking meaningless; northern New Jersey has been as close as Philadelphia for three decades.

Certainly the variety of Inlet Land is easy to perceive:

It's the cottages surrounding the Point Pleasant boardwalk pavilions, the huge Brielle boat basin as viewed from the Route 34 bridge rising over the Manasquan River (and over Brielle). It's the Manasquan cot-

Handsome swans find a peaceful setting on Spring Lake

tages set directly on the sand, their styling verging on the vintage. It's the National Guard encampment, the natural Sea Girt woods, the Silver Lake charm.

North of the pillars at Spring Lake's northern entrance, the character changes again. Often in Belmar and Bradley Beach the eye catches clusters of little cottages—very tiny cottages, mementoes of days when real estate men looked upon every acre as something to be sliced into the absolute minimum portions buyers would take.

The diminutive cottages may show the influence of Ocean Grove's camp meeting establishment, where the lots needed to be only wide

70

enough to accommodate a tent. Regardless of the reason, they are an interesting sight as they remain stubbornly in place, often in the shadows of very large hotels, large cottages or substantial business and amusement buildings.

Possibly Inlet Land is not due for a speedy growth on the beachfront. Most of its towns which have the room are by tradition not interested in growth. Expansion is more likely to move out along the Manasquan and Shark Rivers. There has already been such growth; the emergence of Point Pleasant as a major shopping area attests to that.

Inlet Land thus is many things to many people—to yachtsmen coming off the Atlantic, a haven; to fishermen, a place to begin; for home owners, a place to relax in reasonable quiet; for boardwalk stand proprietors, a place to relax in reasonable din. Those squaw-parking Indians knew a good thing when they saw it.

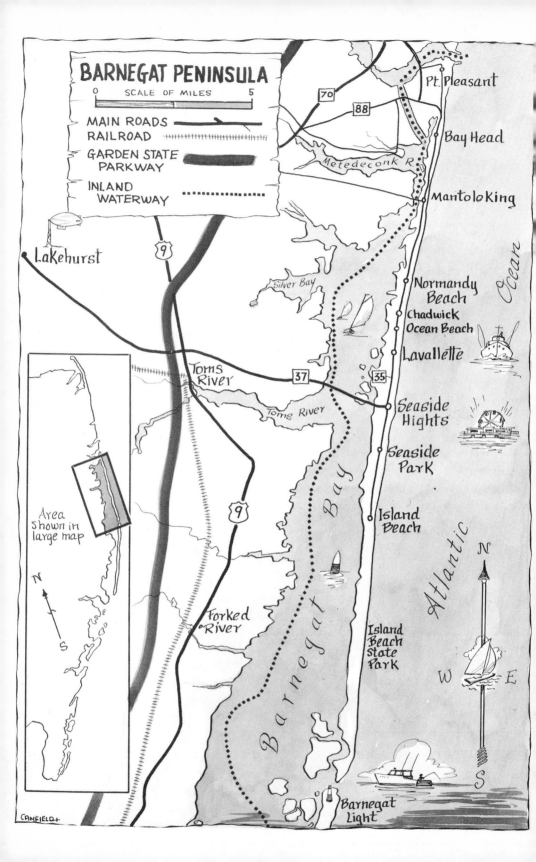

BARNEGAT PENINSULA

SCALE OF MILES
0 — 5

MAIN ROADS
RAILROAD
GARDEN STATE PARKWAY
INLAND WATERWAY

Pt. Pleasant

70

88

Bay Head

Metedeconk R.

Mantoloking

Lakehurst

9

Silver Bay

Normandy Beach

Chadwick
Ocean Beach

Lavallette

Toms River

37

35

Seaside Hights

Toms River

Seaside Park

Area shown in large map

N

S

9

Island Beach

Ocean

Atlantic

Forked River

Barnegat Bay

Island Beach State Park

N

W   E

S

Barnegat Light

CANFIELD

6. Barnegat Peninsula

Wild currents rolling in from the Atlantic Ocean slammed a wall of sand into Cranberry Inlet in 1812, closing off the finest Barnegat Bay passageway to the sea. That storm-tossed night Barnegat Peninsula was born and, strangely enough, in all the passing years neither man nor ocean has split asunder what God had brought together.

This is strange, because the Atlantic is known to slice its way through sandy barrier beaches whenever and wherever it pleases. The ocean seldom leaves any offshore sand bar alone for decades on end. This long, slender shoestring of a peninsula is 22 miles long and but a half mile or so wide; the ocean could breach that thin strand overnight if the stormy mood struck it.

Planners failed to bring back the inlet in 1821 and 1847, and the Atlantic hasn't cooperated once in 145 years. Nevertheless, Cranberry Inlet's old influence lingers on—even with no natural separation, Barnegat Peninsula is really two parts: deserted Island Beach to the south, and the string of resorts from Seaside Park north to Bay Head.

Island Beach, someday to be New Jersey's long-awaited seashore park, is no more island than Asbury Park, although a bay-to-ocean snow fence keeps out curious taxpayers. No one save Coast Guardsmen and squatters (some far from penniless, by the way) has ever lived on the "island." Island Beach, despite that isolation, gets far more newspaper attention than Squan Beach, where summer crowds flock.

Squan Beach? That goes back to before resorts came to the peninsula in the 1870's, back, indeed, to about 1750, when the surging sea cut Cranberry Inlet through from the ocean to Flat Bay Sound (as upper Barnegat Bay was called). Natives simply and directly called the region north of the inlet "Squan Beach" and south of it "Island Beach." Across the bay, a new world of opportunity opened for Toms River sea captains via that new doorway to ocean lanes.

Wind-whipped dunes face the sea on Island Beach

Heavily laden square-riggers sailed through Cranberry Inlet, named for the wild fruit sailors plucked from the inlet's banks to ward off scurvy in long weeks at sea. Whaleboaters and privateers skimmed in and out through the channel to ravage British shipping during the Revolution. Many a captured English merchantman was steered home to Toms River by triumphant privateers, some of whom sailed a very thin line between piracy and patriotism.

Sea captains needed Cranberry Inlet, in war and in peace. Consider, then, the consternation in 1812 when out of the skies came a storm to complete the job of filling the inlet. Consider how today's truckers would feel if George Washington Bridge should disappear in the night; Toms River sea captains felt much the same. Most ex-Cranberry Inlet users did nothing more than bewail their fate—and then sail 12 miles south to Barnegat Inlet.

Michael Ortley, who settled on the peninsula in 1818, proved the exception. Rallying fishermen and farmers, Ortley worked on and off for three years to create a new channel. Success of a pathetically limited nature came in 1821, when in the evening twilight Ortley and company watched the mingling of bay and ocean waters through their hard-dug inlet.

"Mr. Ortley and his friends had quite a merry time celebrating their work," says a contemporary account. They went to bed to dream of square-riggers once more maneuvering through Cranberry Inlet. They awoke to find the same old hang-over: The running tide, instead of sweeping open the channel, raised a bulkhead of sand to close it. That kept the diggers still until 1847, when a new generation drank to a new channel, completed on July 4. Came the night, came the tides— went the inlet.

There is a peculiar footnote to this history. On November 17, 1935, a northeast storm scoured a beautiful new inlet across Island Beach, between the vanished Cranberry Inlet and the existing Barnegat Inlet. This time, as a changing era would have it, human ingenuity worked not to keep open the 600-foot-wide channel, but to close it. Baymen and boatsmen hoped the channel would deepen. Owners of Island Beach wanted it to close.

Guards stood by to thwart channel users, said to be "rum-runners." Once in the darkness the guards came upon several boats backed up to the mud flats, their propellers swiftly turning in an attempt to churn out shoals and thus hasten the tidal flow. It made no difference; the following spring the waves closed the inlet.

Enough of lost inlets. Barnegat Peninsula now is a single entity, despite the fact that regulations and red tape (and lack of money to develop a state park) serve to keep Island Beach almost as isolated as Cranberry Inlet once did.

Island Beach possibly is as well known—in print—as virtually any Jersey Shore region except Atlantic City or Asbury Park. Its virtues as a botanical preserve and as a potential Jones Beach have been carefully exploited—in print, only. Somewhat overlooked is the fact that Island Beach is also a living history book; conditions on the State-owned stretch are much what they were along all the coast two centuries ago.

In addition, Island Beach is what all of Barnegat Peninsula was when vacationists discovered it after the Civil War.

An 1870 cartographer experienced but minor difficulty inking the 22-mile peninsula onto his map. He drew the thin bar, labeled the upper half "Squan Beach" and the lower half "Island Beach." If he wished to be precise, he printed in the name "Chadwicks" for the fishing village about halfway down Squan Beach. That took care of towns—and there was no need to worry about railroads. None existed.

Solitude and natural beauty mingled on the peninsula. A few fishermen lived at Chadwicks and a few lonely men manned the lifesaving stations. It took the soul of a poet to enjoy the surroundings: the high dunes with the curving swales between, the beach plums, the gnarled old holly, the bayberry and sedge, the cattails waving in the bay-side marshes.

Take such unmarred natural wonders, then see them as pioneers saw the peninsula from Bay Head south to Barnegat Inlet in 1875. See low, sandy hills capped with black moss, with bridges linking the hills to permit walkers to get about in times of high seas. See old wagons with wide-rimmed wheels laboring over the sand to bring in provisions. See as the chief contact with the world the little sailboats flitting across to Toms River.

Such quaintness attracted a limited number of vacationists, of course. When H. C. Woolman and T. F. Rose published their *Atlas of the New Jersey Coast* in 1878 (just about the handsomest thing ever done on the New Jersey Shore), they mentioned Lavallette-by-the-Sea, Chadwicks and Seaside Park. That was all. A decade of town-founding lay just ahead.

Albert Lavallette started in the middle 1870's the seaside resort he named for his father, Admiral Elie A. F. Lavallette of Baltimore, said

Once a sandy waste, Ocean Beach now is jammed with cottages

to be the first commissioned admiral in the U.S. Navy. The admiral's
son and his associates laid out squares of streets on the round dunes and
waited for customers.

Down beach a spell, members of the Baptist Church found the place
where they prayed they could emulate Ocean Grove's Methodist camp
meeting ground. In 1876 the Baptists founded Seaside Park, a 300-acre
camp ground, as "a place for rest and ease at moderate expense and free
from the blighting influences of immorality, drunkenness and Sabbath
desecration." In those days thousands of sheep wandered the peninsula,
and the Baptists heard tales of sheep so weighted down with wind-whipped sand that they couldn't return home. Not as many sheep of the

Biblical sort—lost or found—reached Seaside Park as the Baptists had hoped, and the camp meeting expired. The foundations of a quiet residential community stood firm, nevertheless; even today Seaside Park remains relatively sedate.

Up where the long peninsula took its slim hold on the mainland, Bay Head and Mantoloking came into being as the 1870's faded. Mantoloking was first, begun in 1878 by Captain John Arnold and his Sea-Shore Land and Improvement Company. Captain Arnold knew whom he wanted to attract: He laid over the entire tract with imported inland soil to grow grass. That cost money; it also attracted money. The exclusive seed of Mantoloking was sown in the first load of topsoil dumped on the sand.

Princetonians established Bay Head in 1879, on land purchased from Captain Elijah Chadwick, the only resident at Head of the Bay. Quickly the new little resort became a summer vacation place for many of Princeton University's faculty—a happenstance memorialized in some of Bay Head's streets since named for former university presidents and professors.

Bay Head's original stability rested on more than classical knowledge. From the time Benjamin Hance opened his small boatyard in 1878 until the present day, Bay Head has enjoyed a reputation for good boatbuilding. The best-known name—Johnson—first appeared in 1891, when Morton Johnson opened his yard. Hubert, Morton's son, started making boats in 1912; his cabin cruisers since have been sold around the world.

Boats loomed large in the insular life of the peninsula dwellers: Only by boat could they get their food, their clothes, their mail, even some of the materials for their shelter, from Toms River. Take, for instance, the building of Seaside Park's Hiawatha Hotel. The promoters built the hotel in Philadelphia, took it apart and shipped it to Seaside Park— making the last few miles across shallow Barnegat Bay on broad barges.

So they needed a railroad—badly.

That required some doing. In 1880 the New York and Long Branch Railroad had not even the inclination to build across Manasquan River to Point Pleasant, much less down to a hurricane-swept sand bar. In addition, the area seemed to hold more appeal for Philadelphians than upstaters or New Yorkers. A glance at the map tells why: The north and south latitudes of Philadelphia's city limits today almost exactly coincide with the latitudes of Barnegat Peninsula's two ends.

It took extraordinary vision for the Pennsylvania Railroad to bring rails to the barrier beach. First the Pennsylvania acquired an existing line from Camden to Pemberton, then extended its tracks to Barnegat Bay on the south side of Toms River. Ahead lay the toughest job of all—a trestle across the bay, a mile and a quarter of open water. To this could be added another half mile of sedgy marsh on the land side; this, too, had to be bridged.

Thus, nearly two miles of open water and shifty marshes had to be conquered. A savage winter in 1880 made the work doubly hard—the bay froze over so thickly that workmen had to chop through the ice before pilings could be driven into the bay bottom. Fortitude conquered all, and the first train rumbled over the frail trestle and up to Seaside Park in 1881. Soon after, rails reached all the way north to join the New York and Long Branch.

Here is something to ponder: Island Beach probably is isolated today chiefly because the railroad turned north only in 1881. True, that's where Seaside Park and Lavalette-by-the-Sea lay, and it was logical that that region beckoned the first trains. However, railroad pioneers who dared to bridge a mile and a quarter of bay and a half mile of uncertain sedgeland might have been expected to penetrate the southward dunes. The railroad never did go south, and as Squan Beach expanded, Island Beach began its deep sleep.

Not that the railroad immediately transformed Squan Beach into a heavily populated suburb of Philadelphia. The moneyed influences at Bay Head and Mantoloking discouraged that on the north, and the sedateness of Seaside Park on the south convinced fun-bent excursionists that Atlantic City offered greater opportunity for gaiety.

The peninsula's yachtsmen learned the virtues of Barnegat Bay. Henry J. West of Gloucester, New Jersey, a bay-front cottager in Seaside Park, in the 1880's started a series of races for the locally famed sneak box sailboats. The men who manned the Life Saving Stations entered eagerly, doubtless drawn as much by large cash prizes as by interest in racing.

Those sneak box races spawned the Seaside Park Yacht Club in 1899, and rivalry among sailboaters became intense on Barnegat Bay, with clubs from Bay Head, Island Heights, Toms River, Mantoloking and Lavallette vying with Seaside Park for bay supremacy. In 1926 an International Series for Class E sloops started, with the best of Barnegat Bay's skippers matching sails against the Royal St. Lawrence Yacht Club of Montreal. That rivalry continued until 1933, alternating be-

79

tween the Seaside Park course and the Maple Leaf course in Montreal.

Yacht racing was just about the height of Barnegat Peninsula excitement at the turn of the century. Coast chronicler William Nelson in 1902 allocated one sketchy paragraph in two fat volumes to the peninsula, "upon which have been built numerous pleasant little villages." Bay Head? "Splendid piscatorial sport is afforded," said Mr. Nelson. Seaside Park? "The nearest seaside resort to Philadelphia from which it derives a large and constant throng of visitors in season," summed up Mr. Nelson. The others? Mr. Nelson mentioned them not at all.

Certainly Bay Head and Mantoloking attracted new people, or at least second generations of old families, who came between 1890 and 1915 to build the comfortable two- and three-story villas fronting on the ocean. Those old houses still stand, conservatively similar in appearance, with their old shingles either darkened or silvered by ever-moving decades.

There is nothing quite like the Bay Head-Mantoloking atmosphere anywhere else on the Jersey Shore. Houses at Deal and Elberon or Margate may be bigger and brighter and more costly, but the Bay Head-Mantoloking homes, set comfortably in reasonably well-preserved dunes, are like the seaside "cottages" in old *Harper's Magazine* etchings. There is unshowy evidence of wealth, of conservativism—the expensive "natural" look, the "Ivy League" look, so to speak.

The automobile democratized Barnegat Peninsula. In 1909 the first road started southward from Point Pleasant; by 1911 the thin highway reached Seaside Park. Two years later a long wooden bridge carried automobile traffic across Barnegat Bay from Toms River to the uncertain sandy roads on the mainland. A new day dawned for the dunes.

Five brothers from Philadelphia—the Cummings boys—arose to greet that dawn, choosing to develop the exact spot where Cranberry Inlet had ceased to flow a century before. Along with the Manhasset Realty Company, the Cummings developed Seaside Heights, converting acres of moss-covered dunes into building lots just in time to take advantage of the new roads and the bridge.

Seaside Heights eventually outstripped all its peninsular neighbors in size, in large measure because the automobile bridge conveniently landed Quaker City motorists in town before they had a chance to look elsewhere. Seaside Heights also proved the value of a commercial boardwalk, frowned on in most other Bay Head-to-Seaside Park Towns.

The greatest Barnegat Peninsula development of all never got off

"Lagoon-dwellers" at Normandy Beach off Barnegat Bay

the drawing board, however. An announcement in 1926 said that buyers for Henry Phipps, partner of Andrew Carnegie in Pittsburgh steel ventures, had purchased everything from Seaside Park to Barnegat Inlet. The plan: to construct "a high-class private development on Island Beach."

Newspapers claimed the purchase to be the largest in many years along the Atlantic coast. The huge tract in colonial days had belonged to Lord Stirling, but as time passed some of the land titles had become clouded. One of the owners of property on Island Beach, for example, was Columbia University. No one even bothered to chase the squatters

81

who threw up shacks after 1900, partly because no one knew exactly who owned what. Phipps's lawyers finally gained the last parcel in 1926, although the squatters paid the new owners no more mind (or rent) than they had paid the old.

Speculation ran rife. Island Beach would be the "largest development ever undertaken on the Atlantic coast." A new highway would run southward to Barnegat Light. The Pennsylvania Railroad planned to nose its tracks southward after all these years. Rolls of blueprints showed fine homes, yacht clubs, tennis courts and a golf club, exactly right to appeal to the new millionaires and semi-millionaires aborning on Wall Street.

The 1929 business crash erased the projected Island Beach development, the fine homes, the yacht clubs and, of course, most of the millionaires who would have settled there. Then in 1930 the 90-year-old Mr. Phipps died, and as depression years rolled on the few squatters (ranging along an economic scale from rich to poor) called Island Beach theirs, more or less exclusively.

On and off for 30 or so years the State talked of buying Island Beach, without doing anything concrete until 1952—when $2,750,000 snatched Island Beach intact out of the grasp of a real estate company planning something in the line of what had been dreamed of in 1926. One of these decades Island Beach will be a big, fully utilized state park; the plans can be shown to anyone—but there's a big distinction between plans and the allocation of State money.

If a strip of land can be evaluated in terms of people who enjoy it, then the time from World War II—indeed, from 1950—to the present must be considered the most important in all the long existence of Barnegat Peninsula.

A 1939 impression of the peninsula showed little development outside of Bay Head, Mantoloking, Lavallette, Seaside Heights and Seaside Park. Bay Head and Mantoloking, of course, hadn't changed much since 1910 (and aren't likely to change much in the foreseeable future, as far as that goes). Lavallette, Seaside Heights and Seaside Park enjoyed only modest popularity in the days just before Pearl Harbor.

Informality ruled the peninsula until World War II. Trailers, tents and shacks in varying degrees of repair (or disrepair) could be found in many areas. Broad stretches of open seaside land rolled up one dune and down another. Perhaps the area seemed too far out of the way for North Jersey, perhaps the rickety old wooden bridge discouraged Pennsyl-

The busy boardwalk has meant prosperity for Seaside Heights

vanians. At any rate, the peninsula couldn't have been called a beehive
of activity.

The happenings since 1950 stand out in sharp contrast. The Thomas
A. Mathis Bridge, completed after the war to replace the old bridge to
Seaside Heights, coincided with the incredible demand for small shore
homes that began to swell about 1950.

Everywhere from Mantoloking south to Seaside Park new cottages
have replaced the dunes and the bayberry—and even Bay Head and
Mantoloking have, in a controlled way, each year gained some few new
residents.

83

When it comes to change, Exhibit A on Barnegat Peninsula is Ocean Beach. The only thing comparable is the sudden rise of small homes on lagoons on the land side of Barnegat Bay. Ocean Beach almost beggars description. Less than a decade ago there was nothing where the sprawling seaside resort now lies. Today, on lots just big enough to hold a small house, hundreds of vacation retreats dot the sand. Ocean Beach is even of sufficient economic vitality to merit a branch bank.

Ocean Beach's streets could be the closest together anywhere in the state—or just anywhere. Streets stretch seaward and bayward from Route 37, so many of them that the developers would seem likely to run out of street names. Street follows street—Penguin, Amberjack, Albacore, Marlin, Pelican, Kingfisher, Surf, Spray, Channel, Beach, Bay, Barnegat, and so on and on. Each, of course, is an "east" street and a "west" street, going on the one hand to the ocean and on the other to the bay.

Out on the bay side of Barnegat Peninsula, man-made lagoons are everywhere, proof of the fact that boating is just as popular today as it was when the yacht clubs began to enjoy the bay. Elsewhere, the old, established resorts are gaining new homes on the fringes of their built-up blocks.

Seaside Heights, which entered a period of second growth in 1939 and a third period of expansion after the war, is a busy boardwalk town. As many as 40,000 or more people pour over the Mathis Bridge on a summer weekend to visit the Heights and its amusements. In 1955 a $1,000,000 fire wiped out four blocks of boardwalk, but the borough and private operators calmly replaced it. Seaside Heights has prospered; boardwalks aren't rebuilt in bad times.

Barnegat Peninsula is in its rapid growth an astonishing manifestation of a nation on wheels with money in its pockets. In this respect it also demonstrates the sharp differentiation between the days when only the rich went to the shore, via the railroads, and these days, when anyone with an automobile and the courage to sign a mortgage can be a shore home owner.

Cranberry Inlet? Who needs an inlet?

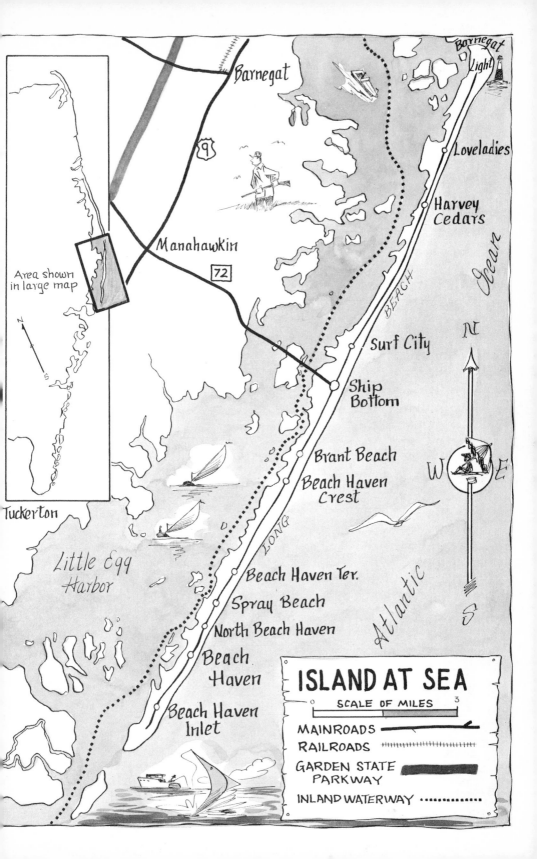

Uncomplicated is the word for Long Beach Island

7. Island at Sea

A lover of Long Beach Island is somewhat like the teenage boy who has a new and beautiful girl friend: He is just bursting to introduce her to the world, but he has the vague, uneasy feeling that to do so is the surest way to lose her.

Long Beach Island is not exactly unknown, nor is it nearly as naturally beautiful as it was a mere decade ago. Still, the narrow, 19-mile-long island maintains a reasonable enough facsimile of native charm to cause mixed feelings among its admirers about the new $12,000,000 causeway across Barnegat Bay linking island with mainland.

On the positive side, the span will eliminate the summer weekend traffic crushes on the low causeway which has more or less served Long Beach Island for some 40 years. It will also bring swarms of new customers to gladden the hearts of the shopkeepers and real estate men and to sadden the hearts of those regular visitors who are devoted to the skinny strip of sand.

Ah, well, no use crying over built bridges. Perhaps, in all truth, Long Beach Island too long has been too good a thing to reserve for so relatively few.

Long Beach Island begins an inlet away from the southern tip of Island Beach and runs southwest until it slopes off into Beach Haven Inlet. Vacationists readily accept the word of promoters that Long Beach is "Six Miles at Sea" (although it's really only four miles at the widest mainland-to-island separation).

Four miles is wide, at that, wide enough to stir idle curiosity about why someone decided six miles sounded better. Four miles is also wide enough to make Long Beach Island quite free of pollen, something which a hay fever sufferer can dream worth noting.

The past and the future clasp hands across the island, since century-old Barnegat Light is the number one attraction of the place, and the light's essential appeal is its romantic past. Still, as veneration of "Old Barney" increases, the new causeway forces attention on a changing future.

Between past and future stands the island of today. As of now, there isn't a foot of boardwalk on the ocean front, not one brash amusement center overlooking the waves. Two or three blocks from the ocean, youth can have a bit of a fling on some scattered miniature golf courses or in occasional buildings housing a few "amusement" machines and juke boxes. There are three or four movie houses and a summer theater with talent "direct from Broadway," but sometimes the pace slows to the point that even teenagers play shuffleboard.

Actually, except for visiting "Old Barney," the chief amusement is exploring the hold of the schooner *Lucy Evelyn*, a 140-foot sailing ship now beached on the bay side at Beach Haven. The *Lucy Evelyn* has been, since 1948, a unique gift store and memento of old windjamming days. Rare is the visitor who doesn't drop by there often.

Why under the sun would anyone ever cross a causeway, new or old, to go to Long Beach Island, when Atlantic City is at most only an extra half hour away?

The answer probably is that the island never has become complicated in a social or amusement sense. Its tone hasn't altered materially, despite the thousands of look-alike Cape Cod cottages built since World War II. Sure, Long Beach Island has some expensive homes, most of them nestling in the sand dunes north of Ship Bottom. By and large, though, the average Long Beacher is an ordinary, unexciting, moderate-income person, down with his family for a week or two or three in a rented cottage.

Barnegat Light is Long Beach Island's—and the New Jersey Shore's—most compelling symbol. The Sandy Hook Light is older by 94 years, but military rule keeps that beacon from being much more for most people than a white speck glimpsed off the Highlands at Navesink. Old Barney suffers no such handicap; its red and white tower can be painted, photographed, touched, entered—and, at one's own risk, climbed to the very top.

The lighthouse lives on borrowed time, rescued from oblivion by sentiment (and several millions of dollars). Its light glowed for the last time in 1927, when Barnegat Lightship was placed eight miles at sea. These days the tower serves to remind new generations that once men who went down to the sea in ships depended desperately on men who stayed behind to keep the lighthouses and to launch the lifesaving boats.

88

Around Old Barney's base swirl the currents of rushing Barnegat Inlet, named in 1614 by Captain Cornelius Jacobsen Mey, the ubiquitous Dutch sea captain, who usually named everything in sight for himself. This time he chose *Barende-gat*, meaning "Breakers Inlet"—a name descriptive enough to last three and a half centuries with only slight Anglicizing.

New England whalers maneuvered their ships through the inlet around 1690, setting up lookouts at "Great Swamp" (near what is now Surf City). Later, other whale hunters erected two more lookouts on the island, one about three miles north of Great Swamp and the other about three miles south.

Whalers lingered on Long Beach Island long after they left the rest of the New Jersey coast. John F. Watson visited the island in 1833, and in his classic *Annals* wrote:

"I was surprised to learn from old Stephen Inman, one of the 12 islanders of Long Beach . . . that he and his family have never ceased to be whale catchers along this coast. They devote themselves to it in February and March. Generally [they] catch two or three a season. . . ."

Even by Watson's day the litter of countless shipwrecks lay on the island's strand, mute evidence of the evil Barnegat shoals just offshore. Throughout the eighteenth and nineteenth centuries scores and scores of ships of all sizes and all types ended their days on those shoals.

Who knows for sure how many victims the shoals claimed—in ships and the men who sailed them? Charles Edgar Nash, in *The Lure of Long Beach*, estimates the number at between 400 and 500 wrecks. An official report to Congress in 1848 told of 158 vessels wrecked on the New Jersey coast in the ten years between 1839 and 1848, most of those lost at Long Beach Island or Squan Beach, directly to the north.

Occasionally ugly rumors drifted to the mainland of "Barnegat pirates" who lured ships ashore by false lights attached to mules wandering on the shore. No one ever proved the charges; most recognized that the wild island got far more than its share of tragedy without need of trickery.

Those who whispered of "Barnegat pirates" did particularly grave injustice to the small band of islanders who worked as volunteer life-savers for little or no reward. Others sought to warn ships off the shoals. Congress appropriated $6,000 in 1834 for a 50-foot whitewashed brick lighthouse overlooking Barnegat Inlet. The surly ocean picked away at the beach below the lighthouse and in 1856 toppled the tower into the waves.

"Old Barney"—the Jersey Shore's most compelling symbol

The government wasted little time replacing the light. Workmen under the direction of Lieutenant George Meade (later a hero as General Meade at Gettysburg) began construction in 1857 of a sturdy brick tower. The walls at the base were ten feet thick, tapering to 18 inches thick at the top, 168 feet above sea level.

This is today's "Old Barney," the "Grand Old Champion of the Tides," one of the tallest and best-known lighthouses on the Atlantic coast. Through all storms the tower has stood, swaying in hurricane gales but always casting its light 20 to 30 miles across the ocean until it was replaced by the lightship. Attracted by the light, birds would crash against its glass and fall dead to the ground, enough of them at times to cover the sand below the tower.

An occasional vacationist made his way to Long Beach Island before 1800, but the pace picked up measurably in 1822. That year, for the first time, anyone who made the jolting trip across-state from Philadelphia and then found someone to sail him across Barnegat Bay could be choosey—not one, but two establishments noised it about in 1822 that they would be willing to entertain boarders.

The choice was this: Joe Horner's old house, converted into a "first-class seaside hotel" by The Philadelphia Company, or the Mansion of Health, a "large house 120 feet long . . . well kept, and supported by a goodly number of inmates" (paying guests, by any name).

Others established boarding houses here and there—John Brown and his four sons, hosts after 1855 at the Ashley House near Barnegat Light; James James ("Double Jimmy"), proprietor of the Club House near Harvey Cedars; Captain Sammy Perrine, builder of the Harvey Cedars Hotel in the 1840's; and Captain Thomas Bond, owner and proprietor of The Long Beach House on the south end of the island.

No hotel keeper outdid Captain Bond—"Old Man" Bond—in hospitality. The bearded old captain recognized that people willingly paid to be housed and fed with rugged simplicity. Captain Bond was in every sense a Long Beach pioneer; his activities included not only hotel keeping, but also a brilliant career in the lifesaving service.

The captain put on no airs and permitted none. His guests hunted, fished, swam, enjoyed the billiard room and bowling alley or watched the owner's imprisoned golden eagle in the yard. "B'iled" shirts brought stares; the uniform at Bond's was an old straw hat, a red flannel shirt and overalls for males and a sunbonnet and calico gown for the ladies.

Much of the island's popularity came to depend on one thing—the

91

fact that the distance from the mainland made its breezes relatively free of pollen. Many came in the 1850's and 1860's seeking relief from August hay fever, and one of them stayed to found Beach Haven in 1872.

Archelaus R. Pharo, of Tuckerton, whose wife found surcease from sneezing in pollen time on Long Beach Island, decided in 1871 the time had come for a new resort town on the island. Pharo's decision rested on more than hay fever. That same year a railroad was completed between Philadelphia and Tuckerton, and in 1872 Pharo induced the railroad to build a spur to the bay.

Pharo bought a steamer and plied it between the railroad spur and the lots he owned on the island. The name for the development came from Pharo's daughter, who suggested Beach Haven. The resort was so christened with a minor and flattering dissent from one Dr. A. A. Willett, who said: "An 'e' should be inserted in Haven; this is Beach Heaven!"

Haven or Heaven, the resort caught the fancy of Philadelphians. Three Beach Haven hotels welcomed guests before 1876—the Parry House, the Hotel Baldwin and the Engleside. The latter two, modified through the years, still stand. The Parry House burned spectacularly in the summer of 1881, but none of its 200 guests perished.

The activity at Beach Haven naturally affected other parts of the island. Resorts started—Surf City in 1873, Barnegat City (in the shade of Old Barney) in 1881, Peahala in 1882, North Beach Haven in 1887, Spray Beach in 1890 and Ship Bottom in 1898.

Spare a moment for Ship Bottom, now the entranceway to all of Long Beach Island, and a town which won its name from a shipwreck. Back about 1817, the folklorists say, a ship floated ashore at the spot, bottom side up. Rescuers cut through the hull's planking and out stepped a young woman. She spoke a foreign tongue and apparently dazzled the rescuers so that they couldn't afterward remember either the name of the ship or that of the beauty herself, who soon departed from the island.

In the later days of the nineteenth century, visitors leisurely watched fishermen dry their nets on the beaches, sometimes went to the fishermen's dances, watched the artists trying to transfer sand dunes to canvas, observed the sailing ships pass by on the horizon—and listened openmouthed to tales of treasure and sagas of the sea.

They knew at first hand one treasure yarn, the most famed on the

92

The *Lucy Evelyn* is a Beach Haven landmark

island. Late on the afternoon of September 11, 1886, a sloop anchored in the ocean two miles below Beach Haven, and in the gathering dusk two men sailed a yawl ashore. They refused lodging at the Life Saving Station, and by dawn's early light the station lookout saw them digging rapidly in a hole they apparently had been working on all night. As the lookout watched, the pair hoisted an ironbound chest out of the hole.

The lookout summoned help, but by the time he and others reached the spot the pair had fled. They left behind the rifled chest, an old cutlass, a gold hilt, some time-stained Spanish coins—and a map, yellowed with age. It really happened; for years the cutlass hung in the office of the Superintendent of Life Saving Stations at Asbury Park.

Ships sailed past the island in a long, white-winged parade in the 1880's and 1890's, with as many as 200 recorded in the course of a day. Often, as noted, they came ashore with harrowing results, but not every shipwreck meant only suffering.

In 1868 the *Imperatrice Elizabetta* broke up on the beach and her cargo floated in. Natives opened box after box—all contained prunes. Tradition says that prunes appeared on every menu for years, served in every conceivable way. Nor could the wreck of the *Francis* in 1897 be called wholly tragic. The hold was filled with fine wines and liquors. If ever there was a Tight Little Island, Long Beach was it for many many days.

To know Long Beach Island was to love her. The Manahawkin and Long Beach Transportation Company built a railroad line across the bay to Ship Bottom and by the middle 1880's served the island north to Barnegat Light and south to Beach Haven. People came by train, but not until 1914 was beautiful Long Beach fully launched in resort society. That year the newly completed automobile bridge coaxed tourists across the bay. Just a wee bit of the fresh young bloom began to disappear.

The island experienced a modest growth, neat but not gaudy, you might say. Actually most motorists of the 1920's passed right on by the Manahawkin turnoff; practically everyone who got his puncture-riddled tires down Route 4 as far as Manahawkin generally figured he might as well try to make it to Atlantic City. A decent road westward to Philadelphia wasn't completed until 1936.

Old Barney fell upon trying days in the onrush of civilization. Talk spread at the end of World War I that Barnegat Light would be abandoned to the fates, a worn-out derelict on the scrap heap of time.

94

Old Harvey Cedars Hotel sits quietly on the "bay side"

Everyone knew a lightship anchored out in the sea lanes was coming, although it didn't arrive until 1927.

The United States Government said in 1920: "Let it fall over" (in bureaucratic innuendo, of course, but the natives got the point). The local people, mostly Scandinavian fishermen and their families, did an amazing thing—they raised their own taxes and they donated their own labor to construct a makeshift jetty to save their lighthouse in 1920.

Eventually, after State and Washington politicians finished kicking the matter back and forth to try to get some other government agency to pay for the project, the federal government deeded the lighthouse to

New Jersey in 1926. Eight years later local citizens again rallied to Old Barney's help, calling state-wide for abandoned automobiles to dump into the inlet to keep the waves away. Now, of course, Barnegat Light is a state park, still in constant need of protection, but definitely not abandoned.

The 1914 highway bridge brought some changes to the island, but despite its ardent supporters, not many people in comparison with other resorts came to Long Beach before World War II. That posed the paradox: enthusiasts wanted people to know of Long Beach's merits, but they really didn't want too many to come to enjoy them.

Long Beach Island's boom really started in 1950. By then so many devotees of the strip had extolled its merits so widely they suddenly woke up to realize that thousands of others were arriving to share the land "Six (well, four) Miles at Sea." Row after row of cottages, most of them seemingly built from the same Cape Cod blueprint, filled in scores of blocks of once vacant sand between Beach Haven and Ship Bottom.

North of Ship Bottom the growth has been more controlled. Houses are widely spaced and somewhat more estate-like than they are on the southern half of the island. Over on the bay side land is being developed, some of it fronting on man-made lagoons. Long Beach Island is growing; those devoted to widespread expansion wholeheartedly believe the greatest days in Long Beach's economy are immediately ahead.

Strangely enough, in the face of unquestioned growth, Long Beach Island maintains an atmosphere of charm, of mystery, and of suspense linked to the sea. It's easy to believe that the next step on the beach may reveal treasure in the sand, or that the next nor'easter may uncover the ribs of a long-forgotten wreck.

That new causeway, combined with the Garden State Parkway, may bring in enough newcomers to make Long Beach Island just another strip of sand jammed from bay to surf with houses and people. It may bring enough people to necessitate boardwalks and honky-tonks and night clubs and even a bridge across Barnegat Inlet to Island Beach to give the curious and the restless a chance to get away in a hurry to go someplace else.

Right now, though, if your craving is for excitement and glamour and the chance to spend your money so fast it won't pile up income taxes, don't go to Long Beach Island. You wouldn't like it.

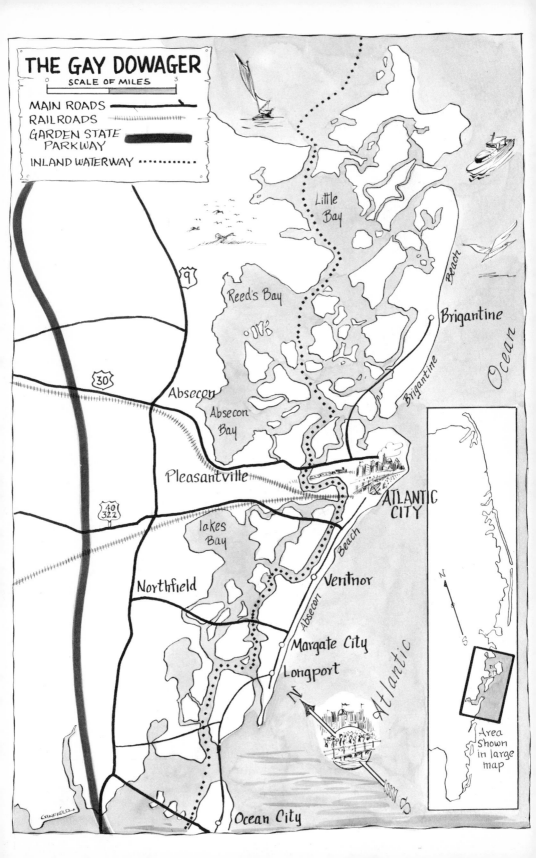

THE GAY DOWAGER

SCALE OF MILES

0   3

MAIN ROADS

RAILROADS

GARDEN STATE PARKWAY

INLAND WATERWAY

Little Bay

9

Reed's Bay

Brigantine Beach

Brigantine

Ocean

30

Absecon

Absecon Bay

Pleasantville

ATLANTIC CITY

40 322

lakes Bay

Northfield

Brigantine Beach

Ventnor

Absecon Beach

Margate City

Longport

Atlantic

N

S

Ocean City

N

S

Area shown in large map

CANFIELD

The Gay Dowager has amusement to meet any demand

8. The Gay Dowager

"Call it a sand patch, a desolation, a mosquito territory, but do not talk to me about a city. You could not build a city there in the first place. And, if you could, you could not get anyone to go there."

Logic touched those words spoken in 1854 by a good, hardheaded Philadelphia businessman approached by promoters who schemed to build "a city by the sea." They proposed to call it "Atlantic City" or some such name—and they sought to induce the Philadelphian to invest $17.50 per acre of sand on a barren island.

Laugh not in hindsight at that careful gentleman from Philadelphia— he merely tried to be logical about Atlantic City. The surest way to be confounded by Atlantic City always has been to try to view it as something logical, something to fit the ordinary pattern of things.

Imagine a city on a sand bar four miles at sea, where nothing can be grown and no fresh water is naturally available. Imagine skyscraper hotels built on sand, amusement piers jutting into the ocean nearly a half mile, boards spread over a million square feet to keep restless feet out of the sand—and all of these where there is no steel, no lumber, no clay. Imagine a city with 60,000 year-around residents in the most unlikely spot possible for a city.

That's Atlantic City.

Take this unlikely city and make it so elastic that it must absorb as many as a half million people every weekend in July or August—people who come or go unpredictably, and usually without advance notice, lured by hot sun or repelled by cool rain. The city must be prepared to feed, house, amuse, doctor and pamper these people on cue. Visitors expect sanitary and healthful beaches, so the waste of a half million humans must be disposed of.

Enough of logic or illogic. Atlantic City for 75 years has been America's best-known resort. Today its millions of annual visitors come from far and wide; it is safe to say that practically everyone in the country has been in Atlantic City or knows personally someone who has been there.

Atlantic City's shimmering glory reaches its peak in July and August, as is the case with all resort towns, but its strength has been the ability to keep people coming around the calendar. This is much more remarkable than attracting millions of people when cool breezes and sparkling ocean offer relief from the oppressiveness of hot inland city pavements.

A recent study by the Federal Reserve Bank of Philadelphia disclosed a startling fact: 75 per cent of Atlantic City's estimated annual $700,000,000 to $800,000,000 business is transacted in the "off" months, from September to June. That's contrary to all resort rules.

Atlantic City's off-season success lies largely in its ability to cater to the American propensity for birds of like feather to convention together. Sooner or later every organization chooses Atlantic City for its convention—one out of every five conventions held in America gathers on *the* Boardwalk.

Week in and week out they convene—doctors, lawyers, bankers, teachers, plumbers, industrialists, labor leaders, morticians, and a thousand and one other varieties of men and women who meet to exchange ideas and to hear of new developments. They come because the city's 300 to 400 hotels (some with as many as 1,000 rooms, some merely overgrown tourist homes) can house them, because the city's 500 restaurants can feed them, and because the gigantic Convention Hall can accommodate more people than live permanently in Asbury Park and Long Branch put together.

Rumor persists that some conventioneers, particularly males, need more than dull old meetings and dull new ideas to entice them back year after year. Atlantic City makes no bones about supplying amusement to meet virtually any tourist or convention demand, tailored to fit virtually any wallet. A writer for the *American Guide Series* summed it up about as well as can be done:

"Atlantic City is an amusement factory, operated on the straight-line, mass production pattern. The belt is the Boardwalk along which each specialist adds his bit to assemble the finished product—the departing visitor—sated, tanned and bedecked with souvenirs."

Two things—transportation and promotion—transformed Atlantic City from a barren island wasteland to what she is today.

100

First and foremost came transportation. Cape May and Long Branch had been beloved resorts for Philadelphia a full half century before a small band of enthusiasts, led by Dr. Jonathan Pitney, decided in about 1850 that Absegami Island could find favor in the Quaker City. In 1853 they took the wraps off a fanciful paper town, called in big, gold letters: "ATLANTIC CITY."

Dr. Pitney and his friends applied to the New Jersey Legislature for a charter to build a railroad, an undertaking deemed so ludicrous that the Camden & Amboy Railroad's powerful lobby let the legislature grant the request. Who wanted a railroad: the fishermen, the glass-blowers in the pines, the bay boatmen? Let Pitney and friends build; let them perish by the sea.

They built, over the rivers and through the woods and across the bay, and on July 1, 1854, a Camden & Atlantic Railroad train rolled across the South Jersey flatland from Camden to Atlantic City in two and a half hours. Aboard rode 600 dignitaries, and, of course, the Press. Never has the Press been very far from Atlantic City's heart or mind.

Other capitalists, reassured by the success of the "impossible" city, built the Narrow Gauge Railroad (so called because of its narrow width) from Camden to Atlantic City in 1877. They were astoundingly eager for the business—they laid 54 miles of track in the phenomenal time of 98 days. Then they cut fares and warred with the Camden & Atlantic for business. Atlantic City boomed.

Atlantic City couldn't be disputed in its 1900 claim that no seashore resort in all the world matched its glories. In less than 50 years the population of the island wasteland had soared from about 100 hardy beach squatters to about 28,000 full-time residents. Its real estate value—it was close to worthless in 1854—zoomed to more than $50,000,000 in 1900.

Seven hundred thousand visitors reveled in the joys of Atlantic City in 1900, and seemingly they couldn't wait to get there. In 1898 the Atlantic City Flyer thundered across the pine barrens between Camden and Atlantic City in 44 minutes for the 55½ miles—74.4 miles per hour. Regularly, a patron could make the trip in 50 minutes.

The passion for speed reached its peak in 1920, just as the automobile crippled railroad travel. That year a survey showed that of the 16 fastest trains in the world, 13 were in the Atlantic City service.

Fast trains to Atlantic City, along with a one-dollar round-trip fare, created the "day tripper," and the "Dollar Excursion" unquestionably

101

gave the city its wide popularity. Throughout the 1890's and up until World War I working men had freedom to play only on Sundays. That day, week in and week out, found swaying Atlantic City-bound coaches teeming with Philadelphia families, laden with their "shoe box lunches."

Naturally not all of Atlantic City viewed the "Shoe Box Lunch Set" with favor. Keepers of the swank hotels figured anyone who couldn't come for at least a week should stay home and get rested for his job. Hotel residents and the cottagers probably viewed the masses with alarm, too; in those days Atlantic City's "regulars" considered themselves genteely upper class.

The railroads didn't care: an excursionist's dollar looked the same as a millionaire's dollar. Keepers of the Boardwalk (the capital "B" has been correct since 1896) didn't care either. As a matter of fact, they loved the excursionists. The love was mutual.

Railroads brought millions to Atlantic City faster than many of them could get to their jobs during the week. The city, led by its hotel keepers, firmly decided that prosperity lay in spreading the magic name throughout the land—throughout the world, in case any Hindus or Egyptians or Mongols might be planning a world tour.

Promotion reached high peaks in Atlantic City long before the grandfathers of today's Madison Avenue hucksters even discovered the word colossal. Dr. Pitney and associates boasted about the attractions of their shore (candidly hopeful that their $17.50 land might one day be worth $500 per acre). Hotel keepers in 1900 raised $16,000 for advertisements in 60 newspapers in 20 cities and that year opened a year-around information bureau in New York City—with part-time offices in Chicago, St. Louis, Toronto and Montreal.

One bit of promotion caught hold and became a major tradition. Word of the Centennial Exposition in Philadelphia in 1876 caused some hustlers in Atlantic City to suggest an Easter Parade in the resort town on Easter Sunday. "Maybe," they reasoned, "some of the swells down to Philadelphia for the Exposition will come over."

Not many arrived on the 1876 Easter Special trains, but in 1896 nearly 40,000 folks strolled the Boardwalk to show their finery on a cool Easter Sunday. By leaving off their coats, though, "bright and chipper Easter girls and many fashionably attired young men . . . made themselves believe it was a balmy day." That could have been written about this year, or any of the years since 1896. The Easter Parade, widely imitated, has never ceased to be an Atlantic City institution.

Hotels and beach are laced together by *the* Boardwalk

Atlantic City made the beautiful girl its symbol, and with its mimeograph machines created the legend that every American female is shaped in a mold marked 36-24-36, give or take a bit. Promoters have put as many young women as possible into bathing suits and paraded them before judges to prove the figures.

Miss America rules supreme as the queen of American beauty, just as she has ever since the first of her royal family was discovered in Atlantic City in 1921. She also rules supreme as the top American promotional device; she has been imitated everywhere. Today, of course, Miss A. is chosen merely to prove that talent is not dead. The fact that the hotels and the Boardwalk get an extra week's business is merely a pleasant coincidence.

Atlantic City has been called many things (with views of visiting journalists sometimes disagreeing with typewriters in the city's publicity office). However, ever since the old resort paused in 1954 to celebrate its hundredth anniversary, the term "Gay Dowager" creeps into an occasional official press release.

"Gay Dowager"—that's good. That's a way to say that practically nothing under the Atlantic City sun is new—but that an annual spring repolishing hides the wrinkles and the gray hair and makes the old girl practically as chipper as a youngster.

What really is *new* at Atlantic City?

The Boardwalk? Not a bit of it—the present Boardwalk dates from 1896, allowing for a widening to 60 feet in 1902 and for the annual $100,000 refurbishing. The present Boardwalk is old, but at that is only the fifth in a line dating from 1870.

Atlantic City takes credit for inventing the Boardwalk, citing Alex Boardman, railroad conductor, and Jacob Keim, hotel keeper, as the discoverers. It seems that Boardman didn't care for sand in his cars any more than Keim liked sand on his hotel carpets—so the pair persuaded the city to lay a plank walk on the sand in 1870.

Atlantic City's rise dates from the first boardwalk, and to this day Atlantic City's charm centers around that wooden pathway. There is nothing like it on the face of the earth, and—even though shops may be featuring the latest fads and 'walk theaters may be showing the latest Hollywood smashes—the Boardwalk's appeals are old, old stuff.

Take the amusement piers which have stretched out over the Atlantic Ocean since 1882; the newest of the lot came into being in 1913. None is as much a magnet as the great Steel Pier, with its incredible variety of amusement, but that dates all the way back to 1898. Possibly no single amusement enterprise in any corner of the globe has been as widely advertised as the Steel Pier; probably no other single spot has featured as many different stars of show business.

Boardwalk amusements and Boardwalk shops, webbed together by year-around hotels—that's the modern Atlantic City. This year-around matter, too, is a story out of the past. Why the Brighton Hotel, first to try it, stayed open for 12 months as early as 1876!

The city claims 300 to 400 hotels, as we have noted, and at times has waxed quite indignant when writers for national magazines questioned whether some of the vintage wooden buildings a block or so back from the Boardwalk are really hotels. Everything's up-to-date in Atlantic

Lucy, the wooden elephant, dominates Margate City

City, the city thinks, and it publicly classes all hotels with the fabulous structures close by the ocean waves. Privately, progressive city boosters recognize many of the old relics must go—to make room for motels.

Even the magnificent 'walk hotels—and magnificent is a fair word—aren't new, unless 30 years old can be considered juvenile. All the Boardwalk hotels date from a splurge of frenzied building between 1900 and 1929, and many of them have old names going back to the turn of the century, the brick skyscrapers retaining the titles of old wooden hotels they replaced.

For all the hotels and amusements and promotion, Atlantic City's real attraction is its beach, which in its organization and its safety is one of the wonders of the modern resort world.

105

Each year as many as 10,000,000 people go down to the sea at Atlantic City. Often 200,000 people—half the population of Newark—swim on a Saturday or a Sunday. Just the immensity of these masses would make it seem inevitable that a few would be lost, stomped down to the ocean's bottom to perish. That makes the record of the Atlantic City Beach Patrol far more than laudable; it's fantastic.

The city hired its first paid life guards in 1892. Before that volunteer guards patrolled the beach, passing the hat after a rescue—and sometimes doing right well. One of them, Henry Rutter, Jr., dove into the surf one day and hauled out Jacob Whiting of Philadelphia. That was a big one for Henry; Mr. Whiting was wealthy and he reckoned his life to be worth $500. Henry took the money and established a bath house business which by 1907 brought an offer of $100,000.

Records carefully kept by the Beach Patrol starting in 1913 show some astounding facts. Since 1913 the patrol has rescued nearly 65,000 persons, with an average of well under a single drowning per year—less than *one* drowning a year, out of 10,000,000 people who enter the ocean.

No one knows for sure how many people have ridden out to Absecon Island by train or by wagon or by automobile since 1854. Surely the number from the time Absecon Boulevard was finished in 1919 approaches the half billion mark. Probably a billion people is not too high a guess at the total of visitors over a full century of time.

Not all of those billion or so humans have been Boardwalkers. Some, believe it or not, actually move right through Atlantic City, turning north to Brigantine or south to Ventnor, Margate and Longport. The last three share Absecon (Absegami) Island with Atlantic City; Brigantine has an island of its own, but for all purposes is a suburb of Atlantic City.

Brigantine is a puzzle. The island is desirable, the location is good, the proximity to the "Queen of Resorts" would seem to make it a natural spot for resort development. Yet, until the past decade, Brigantine knew only failure—cursed, legend says, by the brigantine cast on its beach in the early eighteenth century. The sea-tossed ship gave the island a name but, as the legend says, it was an omen of trying times.

Many have tried to cope with Brigantine. In the 1880's Philadelphia's Republican overlords, Matt Quay and Boies Penrose, gathered their GOP cronies at Brigantine to determine what Pennsylvanians (and Americans in general) should have in the way of government. Quay encouraged developers to build a railroad trestle across the bay in 1890, to construct hotels and to lay a trolley line over the sand.

A storm tore down the railroad bridge in 1903, the trolley gave up the ghost soon after, and the hotels stood vacant. By 1914 only 15 people voted in Brigantine. Periodically waves of real estate speculation dashed over the island—in 1914 and again in the 1920's, when a huge development program featuring a $1,250,000 hotel was lost in the 1929 Wall Street disaster. The hotel, still standing, has had difficult years. A $5,000,000 housing program started in 1947 has brought Brigantine along, but the town is unlikely to grab the headlines from its flamboyant big sister across the inlet.

The first railroad entered Atlantic City at what is now the northern part of the city—North Carolina Avenue. It turned south and moved all the way down the island to Longport in the early 1880's. Attracted by its steel right-of-way, Ventnor, Margate and Longport sprang into being. The names suggest their origins as real estate promotions—Ventnor and Margate, nice, fancy names borrowed from England; Longport named for the original owner, James Long.

Longport and Margate started at about the same time in 1882. The Longport promoters ran a special excursion train from Philadelphia that year and hauled prospective customers down to their sand dunes in fine carriages. Lots sold, particularly to Philadelphians interested in nature—who joined the Agassiz Association for "the pleasure and benefits derived from the study of the animal and vegetable life of the sea and the wild flowers of the shore."

Up island a stretch, James V. Lafferty entertained the notion that novelty rather than nature would entice prospective lot purchasers. In 1882 he built Lucy, the wooden elephant who still towers over Margate's boardwalk. Lucy cost $38,000 for the lumber for her wooden innards and the sheet metal for her hide. Her measurements are 45-38-80—45 feet high, 38 feet long and 80 feet around the waist. She's no beauty queen, but she's one of the most surprising Jersey Shore sights.

Ventnor, nearest neighbor of Atlantic City, very likely would be part of that city except that in the early days a narrow inlet stretched across Absecon Island. It eventually became "Dry Inlet" and is today Jackson Avenue. The wife of the secretary-treasurer of the land development company chose the name Ventnor, after a seaside resort she knew on the Isle of Wight.

All of Atlantic City's southern neighbors have boardwalks and hotels

107

A.C. Beach Patrol has 65,000 rescues to its credit since 1913

and modified amusements, but they have developed as suburban resort areas rather than in the manner of their much more noted neighbor. Many year-around homes house people who earn their livings in Atlantic City. Some of their homes are large and spacious, reminiscent of Deal and Elberon.

Back in 1929 Atlantic City politicians politely—if over-ardently—suggested that Ventnor and Margate come into the family as legal portions of the city. Both refused, with vehement impoliteness, aware that their charms for Atlantic City consisted mainly of multi-millions of dollars in ratables.

Atlantic City's financial collapse after the crash of 1929 points up the paradox of many a resort—a gold-planked boardwalk doesn't necessarily mean prosperity for the city which plays host. Atlantic City suffered badly; former banks became marble night clubs after the 1929 collapse. There was ample justification for believing that the politicians had used Atlantic City for their own purposes and left the Queen gasping for breath in the depression.

The city came back. During World War II Atlantic City performed nobly as a center for training troops and for receiving the wounded and weary military men from the world's battle fronts. Giant hotels became luxurious barracks and fine hospitals. World War II may well have been Atlantic City's shining hour.

These days Atlantic City is handsome (near the Boardwalk) and affable and charming—the year around. In November 20,000 to 30,000 New Jersey teachers crowd its hotels for their convention. In December the city and its neighbors sparkle with a splendorous Christmas glow. The New Year holiday attracts 50,000 or more people—a good mid-July crowd for most resorts. Huge crowds jam the Boardwalk when Washington's Birthday falls on a weekend. Easter Sunday finds the planks echoing to the tap of new high heels.

All year long the show goes on—for conventions, for reunions, for holidays. Atlantic City stays alive. Regardless of varying opinions about the Queen, she is remarkable. She loves people, she lives to welcome them, to entertain them, to send them home eager to return. She can take state and national off-season investigations of alleged gambling and vice with a yawn, secure that scarcely a devoted lover will think one bit less of her, come warm weather.

Atlantic City is exciting and warm-hearted. She makes a man spend a bankroll without a murmur, regardless of what regrets he might have when he gets home. She is nice to children, hints at excitement for their parents. She sparkles, she fascinates, she warms. You've got to like the "Gay Dowager"; she gives you a run for your money.

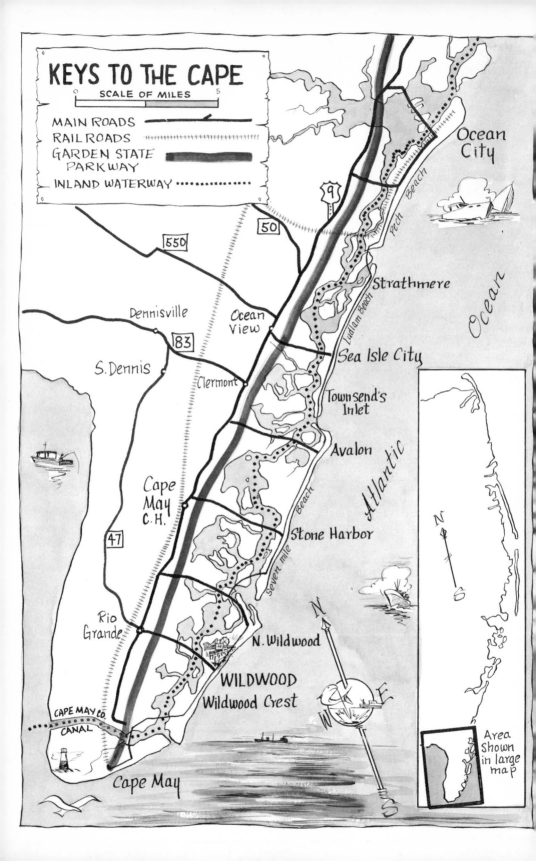

9. Keys to the Cape

Cape May County got into the resort business two centuries ago just by sticking its peninsular nose into the shipping trade sailing on Delaware Bay to and from Philadelphia. An occasional passing sea captain stopped off, liked what he saw, and eventually found the chance to pick up an extra shilling or two by bringing vacationists to the watering place. It was that natural.

Nothing much spectacular has happened since those easy beginnings, except maybe at Wildwood, where weekend crowds of 150,000 are no surprise. All other resorts on the Jersey Cape more or less pride themselves on being intimate, quiet, "family-type" towns. Growth they might accept—providing, of course, they could stay small at the same time.

The essential charm of Cape May resortland is its ability to stay simple, to be natural in a world that savors flash and show. Still, because of the Garden State Parkway, spectacular days could be on the horizon, days which will see great crowds of people overrun the lonely sand dunes and chase the migrating birds off to the Salem County marshes.

If wind-tossed dunes and quaint towns and uncrowded beaches and bird sanctuaries are of as much value as Cape May's devotees think, then the arrival of the Garden State Parkway may be a blessing only to real estate holders and concessionaires. Cape May right now is relatively unspoiled—the consequence of being off the beaten path.

Cape May's resorts all are on islands, if it is permissible to stretch a point and say that Cape May Canal—though man-dug—places Cape May town and Cape May Point on an island of their own. This isn't too farfetched, at that; until a century ago Cape May town actually was an island and bore the name "Cape Island."

Elsewhere, the islands exist beyond dispute. Islands abound off Cape

May peninsula, where marshy sedgelands taper out into the Atlantic Ocean. Even a casual glance at a road map discloses the islands; a close study of a detailed map shows nearly 150 sizable islands set among the sounds and thoroughfares—islands normally known only to birds and bird hunters or bird watchers.

Only four of these 150 islands have importance in a resort sense, and those are the four islands fronting directly on the sea. These four line up like giant footsteps—each footstep almost exactly the same length: seven miles, give or take a few rods. The sandy prints are as if they had been made by seven-mile boots, striding southward to the bay.

These insular quadruplets really could be called "The Jersey Keys," meeting as they do the dictionary definition of a key as "a low island . . . off the coast." More, they are as closely related to one another as the Florida Keys (not that anyone pretends the Jersey Keys are as unique or as renowned as those coral beads strung off Florida's cape).

Excitement smolders among those who wish for a tidal wave of dollars to flood down the Parkway from northern New Jersey and metropolitan New York. When Newarkers and New Yorkers become accustomed to the Parkway's lower reaches—the hopeful reason—they won't stop their automobiles short of Cape May County.

That's possible, but right now Cape May peninsula belongs heart and soul to Philadelphia, Baltimore and points south and west—and always has. This is mainly a matter of elementary geography: Newark is more than twice as far from Cape May than Philadelphia is, and Baltimore is 20 miles closer than Newark to Cape May. The cape's point, almost 55 miles below the imaginary Mason-Dixon Line, is on the same latitude as Washington, D. C.

Tradition plays a part in this Philadelphia and Southern orientation, too. Philadelphians first discovered Cape May's resort potential. They first exploited the Cape May sands, they provided the early transportation, they coaxed north the leading families of Maryland and Virginia. They set the pattern of dignity and quiet. They did practically everything but induce the birds to make Cape May the foremost northern stopover spot in their annual migrations. The birds took care of that themselves.

Cape May's resort hopes began to be based on Philadelphians many, many years ago—two centuries or so.

Two centuries? Resort hopes? Why, didn't folks have enough to do, in those days, what with battling the frontier and grumbling at Britain's

112

taxation, without needing vacations? They probably should have, but in 1766 a gentleman named Robert Parsons advertised in the *Pennsylvania Gazette* his willingness to sell his 254-acre Cape May plantation. Unless Parsons engaged in the exaggeration traditional in advertising resort property, vacationers already knew Cape May's attractions; he extolled the location thus:

". . . within One Mile and a Half of the Sea Shore, where a number resort for health and bathing in the Water. . . ."

The cape had this in its favor: Its bulbous nose was prominent. It was easy to find. Captain Cornelius Jacobsen Mey saw the cape in 1620 and modestly named it Cape Mey for himself. Whalers arrived through the seventeenth century to hunt whales where the broad Delaware merged with the limitless Atlantic. They came by boat and they lived by boat and they left by boat; there wasn't a landlubber in the lot of 'em.

First vacationers visited to improve their constitutions (no eighteenth-century Philadelphian could admit to anything so worldly as sitting in the sand for sheer enjoyment). The City of Brotherly Love by 1801 suffered sufficiently from the ills of civilization to make it feasible for Ellis Hughes to insert his memorable notice in the Philadelphia *Daily Aurora:*

"The Public are respectfully informed that the Subscriber has prepared himself for entertaining company who use sea bathing, and he is accommodated with extensive house room, with Fish, Oysters, Crabs, and good liquors. Care will be taken of gentlemen's Horses. . . ."

Customers of 1801 needed the ability to be easily pleased: the "extensive" Hughes house looked positively barnlike—and sleeping accommodations didn't include private rooms with bath. Brother Hughes drew a curtain across the middle of the cavernous guest room at night. Men slept on one side, women on the other. With such mass chaperonage, the hotel had no need for a house detective.

Transportation difficulties held down the crowds at first, but by 1815 the fast sailing sloop *Morning Star* made regular weekly trips to the cape, and the following year a steamboat and packet line advertised a schedule for the "bathing season." Steamboat service gained full stature within the next decade, and at the same time the roads to Philadelphia improved; by 1825 instead of being completely wretched, the roads were merely poor.

Sophisticated newcomers demanded something superior to Ellis

113

Hughes's curtained dormitory. Thomas Hughes built his three-story Congress Hall in 1816, partitioned off into rooms to accommodate 100 boarders. Congress Hall had no paint on the outside, no plaster or paint inside, but people shook their heads anyway at "Tommy's Folly" (too big, too grand for Cape May, they warned). Tommy laughed last; vacationers filled "the folly" the first year.

Cape May quickly became America's premier resort. By Civil War time no resort in the nation matched the Jersey Cape—provided fashion and dignity and the fame of its guests were the criteria. Saratoga boasted of pre-eminence (and Long Branch made some counterclaims), but by the 1850's Cape May probably ranked first among all vacationlands.

Southern planters and the elite of the North brought along their gleaming carriages, drawn by horses whose gold-ornamented harness glittered in the bright Cape sun. Nationally famous bands played in the fine hotels. Planters and statesmen whiled away fretful hours in such respected gambling establishments as Henry Cleveland's Blue Pig.

Two roaring fires between the seasons of 1856 and 1857 swept away hotels with rooms for 2,400 visitors, and the Civil War ended the visits of those from Virginia and the Old South. Cape May never fully regained its past glories (although it never fully lost them either, as did Long Branch in later years).

The chief blame for Cape May's subsidence, if blame there was, rode on the railroad tracks which in 1854 linked Camden and the seashore at Atlantic City. Philadelphians took to the rails, Atlantic City blossomed, and Cape May began to find comfort in traditions. Don't get the idea that Cape May city became a ghost town; in 1866 more than 50,000 visitors arrived during the summer. One acidulous New York writer of the day found the society less than dashing. Said he:

"No changeful and effervescent visitors are they; yearly come the spinster and dowager habitués . . . fond are they of whist and moderate are the stakes thereat. . . ."

Cape May whist players got their railroad in 1863, and it caused a spurt—but nothing sensational. Nothing moves fast in Cape May County. No one even thought to establish resorts on the four seven-mile islands out on the fringe of the sedgelands until 1879, when the Lake brothers of Pleasantville established Ocean City.

The Lakes—S. Wesley, Ezra B. and James E.—all were Methodist ministers, and they sailed out to Peck's Beach looking not for enjoyment, but rather for a place to establish a camp meeting. The brothers

114

Wildwood's amusement-packed 'walk is a powerful magnet

stood beneath the tangled branches of a cedar tree in late 1879 and dedicated the lonely island to clean living.

Ingeniously, by a system of cross-deeding, the Lakes (and their Ocean City Association) secured control of every square foot of the island. The Association wrote restrictions (including prohibition of intoxicants) into every deed. To the present day transfers of title are always made subject to those restrictions, "to insure the original purpose of the

115

party of the first part [the Association] in securing the whole island as a Christian Seaside Resort."

While the Lakes held their first camp meeting in 1880 and built their Tabernacle in 1881, men whose philosophies didn't rule out either demon rum or the possibility of making money looked with interest at the other islands.

It took an experienced eye to visualize the possibilities of those barren wastelands, and just such an experienced eye belonged to Charles K. Landis, who started to develop Sea Isle City in 1881. Landis 20 years before conceived the city of Vineland in the midst of the pine barrens; it didn't take nearly as much vision to see the resort possibilities of Sea Isle City on Ludlam Beach.

A railroad spur reached Sea Isle City in 1884 and the resort expanded mightily. Brilliant electric lights gained a measure of fame for Landis's town in 1893, and by the turn of the century the island spot had 30 hotels and a dedicated crowd of Philadelphia admirers, many of them both wealthy and noted.

Trains rolled all the way down to Townsends Inlet on the south end of Landis's island, and for two years in the late 1880's the railroad (and real estate promoters) wished mightily that rails could bridge the inlet and serve Avalon across the water. Avalon, founded by the Seven Mile Beach Company of Philadelphia in 1887, finally welcomed its first train in 1889 after the railroad received the right to cross the inlet on two drawbridges.

The fourth of the islands—Five Mile Beach—first received developers in 1880, the year Frank Swope and some friends used a day of fishing to plan Anglesea (now North Wildwood). They soon after built 50-room Hotel Anglesea, on a spot now long since eroded away by the ocean.

Wildwood waited for another Vinelander to arrive in 1890, however, before it achieved prominence. That year Philip Pontious Baker, state senator from Cumberland County, bought 100 acres—half of it in "grand timber," with many trees 100 feet tall. Gigantic grapevines reached through the treetops and festoons of beautiful green moss hung from the cedars and oaks. Underneath, huckleberry bushes grew as tall as 20 feet. The natural beauty of the spot attracted many naturalists to see the trees and plants; some claimed that every wild flower known to exist between Maine and Florida had been found in aptly named Wildwood before 1910.

116

Cape May Light, where Delaware Bay mingles with the ocean

Cape May city, happily serene with its memories of the days when Presidents Pierce, Buchanan, Grant and Arthur came for long splashes in the sea, received another joyous thrill in 1889 after President Benjamin Harrison found the cape exactly suited to a president and his family.

The Harrisons stayed slightly out of town, over at Sea Grove (now Cape May Point), founded in 1875 by Presbyterians who hoped their town would be "a moral and religious seaside home for the glory of God and the welfare of man." John Wanamaker, the Philadelphia store magnate, invited the Harrisons for a stay in 1889 and the following year friends of the president built him a handsome $10,000 cottage at the Point.

The cape stayed quiet, true, but it didn't stand completely still.

Pittsburgh financiers sparked a 1902 development in Cape May city, filling in hundreds of acres of marshland north of Madison Avenue and creating virtually a new city. This is the part of Cape May city surrounding the Hotel Admiral, a South Jersey landmark towering nine stories above the beach. Built in 1908 by the East Cape May Company, developers of the marshland, the Admiral still is the largest hotel south of Atlantic City.

Wildwood ranked only fourth among the Cape May resort towns in 1902, but many things happened in 1912 to propel Five Mile Beach into unquestioned Cape May resort leadership. That year Wildwood and Holly Beach merged, a new boardwalk was ready for the 1912 season, and simultaneously a new automobile bridge reached out over the marshlands to the mainland.

All these things in one year, and the Dollar Excursion, too! During the height of the season for the first 30 years of the twentieth century the railroads each weekend ran long excursion trains from Philadelphia to Wildwood. A noted "Fisherman's Special," bristling with angler's poles, also made the one-day, one-dollar run on weekends. Excursions built Wildwood into the big amusement-centered resort of the modern day.

Then came the boom—and the bust.

Maybe it started because Florida's wild land deals made the headlines. Maybe the building of the new Philadelphia-Camden bridge in the early 1920's misled speculators as to potential land values. Maybe too many people had too much money. At any rate, the Jersey Shore had an unparalleled land boom and bust in the 1920's. Nowhere was

118

the impact felt more cruelly than in the Jersey Keys.

Everyone experienced the tremendous urge to speculate in land. Even the bootleggers moaned that they made more money in real estate than in rum-running—and real estate was legal. The whole precarious land business evaporated in 1926; the South Jersey shore didn't need a Wall Street upheaval to indicate times could be tough. Memories of wild prices linger from Ocean City to Cape May; one authenticated tale tells of a $75,000 lot (boom price) being bought for $750 a year after the 1926 collapse.

Throughout all the twentieth-century story of Cape May has run the desperate hope that just around the corner would be a ferry across the bay to Delaware. This—even more than the Garden State Parkway— would bring rapid changes to the Jersey Cape and the Jersey Keys.

Ferries have crossed the bay several times. As early as 1900 an old side-wheeler made unsatisfactory runs and in 1903 the 200-foot *Caroline* tried without success to establish service. The most elaborate scheme, pushed in 1926 by "Colonel" Jesse Rosenfeld of Baltimore, tried to use outmoded World War I concrete ships as ferry slips. That failed also; one of the abandoned ships still rests in the water off Cape May Point.

The Cape May Ferry is much in the air—and much at sea. Delaware and most of the South are cut off from New Jersey by the broad bay. From Cape Henlopen, Delaware, to Cape May Point is 170 miles by highway—and 12 miles by water. Ferry proponents are numerous and enthusiastic; they claim one out of every five cars in the United States is within easy reach of the Capeline ferry.

The ferry, when completed (or if completed), is likely to make all Cape May's resorts look more than ever to the South. The area within an arc swung from Washington to Richmond to Norfolk will be within easy driving range of Cape May. The "grand old days" of the Southern aristocracy sojourning at the cape may come back—within limits; Southern aristocracy isn't what it used to be.

There's many a slip between ferry planning and ferry running. Meanwhile, one thing is certain: Cape May County's resorts have infinite appeal.

Say, for example, that the desire is for wide, safe beaches. The Keys have those—beaches as much as 1,000 feet wide from boardwalk to high-water mark. Wildwood, in fact, claims it has "the world's finest beach." The world is a big place, but unquestionably Wildwood has the finest natural beach in New Jersey and probably the finest among all Northern resorts. Wildwood is an increasingly forceful South Jersey magnet. Its amusement-filled boardwalk adds proof that most Jersey Shore visitors like mechanical rides and "skill" games and "name" bands and "name" singers as much as they like sand and surf and sea breezes. Wildwood is gay and amusing and—like most boardwalk towns —extracts from visitors much more in the way of cash than its neighbors.

Ocean City, old and secure and undeviatingly "dry," calls itself "America's Greatest Family Resort." Again that covers a big chunk of geography, but this can be said—whole generations of Pennsylvania and Delaware families have been coming to Ocean City through the decades since the Lakes began their resort.

Ocean City visitors love the long boardwalk, with just enough amusement to be appealing, and they love the famous Music Pier, where all season long free orchestral concerts are given. They appreciate the $7\frac{1}{2}$-acre municipal recreation center, where among other games, shuffleboard is a way of life. Ocean City has the largest shuffleboard courts north of St. Petersburg and the Ocean City Shuffleboard Club has a membership of more than 1,000 members. Religion also is significant; Ocean City thinks it may be the only major resort in the world where boardwalk theaters are given over to church services on Sunday evenings.

Between Ocean City and Cape May city are a half dozen or so seaside towns, each of them distinctive. All of them, incidentally, have been linked since the 1940's by the Ocean Drive—amply marked all the way from Atlantic City south by "The Sign of the Gull."

Sea Isle City, Avalon and Stone Harbor earnestly maintain their island personalities, set more than seven decades ago. Avalon's boast that it is the "Gem of the Jersey Coast" is best understood by walking through the magnificent dunes on the lower side of the town. Sea Isle City prides itself on its canals and its colorful fishing fleet and its quiet ways. Finally, there is Stone Harbor, established in about 1910 and now a town proud of its neatly landscaped streets and its seven back-door harbors and canals.

Cape May city stands alone, unique among all resorts. Here and there a modern motel proves progress, but essentially the city is proud of its past, of its vintage hotels, of the fact that in the city are more descendants of *Mayflower* passengers than there are in Plymouth. This

120

The "family trade" gathers at Ocean City

is the way an official Chamber of Commerce statement describes Cape May city:

"No need to pine for the days of yore. . . . Now you can have them today and every day in the oldest seashore resort in America. . . . Cape May stands as a classic out of the past, retaining the full flavor of the gaslight era . . . its Victorian homes, its tree-lined avenues, its wealth of unspoiled loveliness deftly combine with modern advance-

121

ments to achieve a rare and delicate balance of the old and the new that is as inviting as it is unique."

That's official—and that's not the way most resorts talk about themselves, even when their hotels are practically as old (and often much less charming).

Far-reaching changes for Cape and Keys are at hand. Larger crowds are inevitable, bigger and better boardwalk fevers may beset towns which today feel dunes and simplicity and herons and migrating birds are enough. Temptation has transformed other resorts; colonial heritage and memories of bygone glories seldom set cash registers to jangling.

See It as a Beach . . .

Promotion men have found a billion-dollar baby (a billion-and-a-half-dollar baby, some say) where briny sea meets shifting sand on the Jersey Shore. A billion and a half dollars: that's what this 127 miles of beach has been estimated to mean in solid cash each year.

There has to be a reason.

People come, for one thing, because they can find a hotel or motel or cottage in which to rest their amusement-wearied heads. They come because escape from daily care is a never-ending pursuit of mankind. They are lured by newspaper ads and four-color folders—and, to some extent, because Miss America is crowned beside the Atlantic Ocean.

One writer points out that while nature made the sand and sea, it took promotion men to make of these things a commercial beach. Miss Ada Taylor of the Claridge Hotel in Atlantic City puts it another way: "We live on ocean, emotion, and constant promotion!"

Many, too, find year-around surcease by the sea. They are the lucky ones; they know the Jersey Shore in its seasonal moods. Their story is also a part of the charm of the beachland.

Sun and spray reach hotel rocking chairs, too

10. Mine Hosts

Occasionally, when the heat and humidity of July or August turn city apartments into so many Hades-on-Earth, there comes a time when there is scarcely a room of any kind to be had from the Highlands to Cape May.

Gasping humans trot from boardwalk hotel to one-block-back hotel to two-blocks-back boardinghouse to three-blocks-back tourist home. They wave good, crisp folding money, rapidly shift their standards downward from ocean view with bath to attic room with Army cot. Then many go home or, if stubborn, sleep in their cars or under the boardwalk.

One weekend later, chilling rain sweeps the Atlantic coast and rooms— ocean view and attic alike—go begging. Ah, to be a hotel man, gathering ulcers within sight of the beautiful sea!

Presumably there are compensations, not the least of which could be a bank balance, weather and changing public desires permitting. There might be a modicum of cheer also in the knowledge that hotel men played a major role in transforming the New Jersey shore from a barrens into an incredible playground—although that type of cheer warms few lobbies on a cold and wet August Saturday night.

Today the seaside hotel is nowhere near the institution it was a half century ago. Everything in those days revolved around the hotel—sleep, meals, entertainment, romance, social distinction, gossip, fashions— everything the guests believed worthwhile in life.

When guests unpacked their Saratoga trunks back in what hotel men understandably regard as "the good old days," they came for more than dinner. Fifty years ago a stay at a seashore hotel averaged three weeks; today a three-day stay is more the rule.

The automobile has made the difference. Most shore visitors of this era throw bathing suits on the back seat, hop down for their day in the

The Berkeley-Carteret at Asbury Park

waves and hop right back to Philadelphia or Newark at night. That may be fine for the Parkway toll booths, the amusement stands and the hot dog vendors, but it makes hotel managers wonder whether keeping up their multi-million-dollar, multi-storied inns is worthwhile.

Not that the grand hotels overlooking the restless surf are things of the past. Those which have survived changing times, bankruptcy and fire are as impressive as ever. Possibly they are more impressive than ever, considering that major hotel building by the sea has stood still since the late 1920's. Hotels of 30 or more years ago have certain appeals for all that—such things, for example, as space and charm.

On the horizon is a day when the motel, the hotel's informal little brother, will be king (or at least a strong pretender for the crown) of the overnight guest set. Nonetheless, the large hotels will remain—and, in fact, those which meet the competition will be highly significant.

No one knows for sure how many hotels are clustered along the New Jersey Shore. The big question is this: What *is* a hotel—10 rooms, 20 rooms, 100 rooms? The yardstick is highly elastic and often stretches to include some "hotels" which seem on sight to be mighty poor relations of the Waldorf-Astoria, if indeed they are related at all.

By a reasonably strict estimate, there probably aren't more than 75 to 100 major hotels between Sandy Hook and Cape May. Nevertheless, establishments included on promotion lists from town to town would total upward of 1,500 to 2,500 "hotels."

Difficulty in classifying hotels is an old story. Gustav Kobbé, who in 1889 compiled the delightful *New Jersey Coast and Pines*, said he applied a "rigid test" to hotels. He found only 25 hotels worthy of the accolade "first class"—no matter what hotel advertising and other literature said.

"If any reader disagrees with the author in his rating of any hotel," wrote Mr. Kobbé, "he will confer a favor on the author by notifying him thereof." It can be imagined that Mr. Kobbé's mail ran heavy; no one is quite as sensitive as a hotel man, with his sensitivity usually increasing as his hotel's quality declines.

New Jersey's coast hotels in Mr. Kobbé's day were well into the half century of greatest Jersey Shore hotel prominence—those 50 years between about 1880 and 1930.

During that period old hotels gave way to newer models, often after devastating fire leveled old firetraps. That half century brought fireproofing and elevators and private baths and year-around programs.

127

That period also swept Atlantic City into unmatched eminence as a resort city.

Hotel men made Atlantic City. As the resort celebrated its fiftieth anniversary in 1904, the Bonifaces said correctly that "in the amount of money invested, the number of people employed and the volume of business transacted, Atlantic City is pre-eminently a hotel town."

Atlantic City led every resort in the world in the number and splendor of its hotels in 1904—and, for that matter, never had even a near rival until Miami Beach pushed its skyline ever upward and outward after World War II.

Already the first of the long-familiar ocean-view hotels loomed beside the Atlantic City Boardwalk in 1904. That fiftieth-anniversary year the Chalfonte Hotel stretched out to its full ten stories, its management proudly proclaiming their brick structure to be Atlantic City's first fireproof hotel.

Not the first brick hotel, mind you, the first fireproof hotel. Atlantic City's first brick hotel (the New York) arose in 1892, and seven years later, in 1899, the Waldorf-Astoria and the Bleak House became the first Boardwalk brick hotels. Brick hotels would have come eventually, but pause a moment to reflect how an unheralded worker, Herbert McCann, accelerated their arrival.

Herbert, the story goes, left a hose running on the Atlantic City beach in 1883 while he wandered elsewhere for a brief period. The nozzle burrowed deep into the sand and when Herbert returned, he pushed a piece of lumber down beside the nozzle and noted how easily he could drive it downward with the help of the gushing hose.

No idle pastime, that. Herbert McCann's discovery became the forerunner of hydraulic pile-driving. Down into Atlantic City's sands went piles, their way eased by water pressure. Atop those deeply driven piles heavy brick hotels took shape.

The piles, the soaring public demands, the promotion, the improved service—on these Atlantic City's hotels reached new heights. Such still-famed names as the Traymore, Chalfonte-Haddon Hall, the Shelburne, the Dennis, and St. Charles, the Brighton, the Seaside, the Marlborough-Blenheim and others knew considerable glory by 1900.

Elsewhere up and down the New Jersey coast, hotel keepers served a select clientele with a dignity and aplomb inherited in many instances from their fathers and grandfathers before them. The hotel keepers knew their guests and their guests knew them; those days no resort hotel man ran his establishment from an office in New York or San Francisco.

Hotel keepers looked askance at anyone who even dared suggest an alternative to the American Plan (room and *all* meals, for the benefit of those who've come in lately). Guests just naturally wanted meals, not to mention quarters for their maids and valets and coachmen, and stables for their horses and donkeys. There was nothing casual about a visit in those days.

Great hotels attracted wealthy and/or famous people—at Sea Bright, at Long Branch, at Asbury Park, at Spring Lake, at Sea Girt, at Beach Haven, at Atlantic City, at Ocean City, at Cape May. Secretly, many a hotel man wondered how Cape May's old hotel traditions lingered on after all the years.

Secretly, many a hotel man continues to wonder. Cape May's pre-1900 atmosphere still pervades this oldest of resorts—a happenstance which many find tremendously pleasing and which others find annoyingly archaic. Cape May's hotels are old, and that's that.

Hotels out of the past retain in Cape May a veneration seldom found elsewhere, with only Ocean Grove's well-kept establishments offering any rivalry at all. Exhibit A at the cape, beyond question, is Congress Hall, whose history dates back to 1816 (and includes fires which destroyed earlier buildings in 1818 and 1878).

Thomas Hughes built the original Congress Hall in 1816—although it didn't acquire the name until 1828. The present Congress Hall dates from 1879, its 14-inch brick walls and its high pillars giving it a substantial—but old—appearance.

The second Congress Hall had its admirers. One such saw it in 1853 and enthused:

"What else can it be but grand? At night, when this hall is cleared of its tables and chairs, and hundreds of gas jets are brilliantly burning and flickering and the gay and the elite are flushed with the giddy dance, then you behold a hall-scene, beautiful and fair."

Other hotels of splendor and brilliance rose nearby, but none of them matched in grandeur or immensity the Mount Vernon, quite likely the most amazing resort hotel venture undertaken along the New Jersey Shore at any time.

Consider that what its owners call the largest resort hotel in the world today—the Chalfonte-Haddon Hall in Atlantic City—has room for 1,800 guests at absolute peak capacity. Then visualize the Mount

Congress Hall, last rebuilt in 1879, dates from 1816

Vernon, whose walls began to rise in 1852. Plans called for a front section and two tremendous wings, with total accommodations for 2,100 guests, with a bath for every room (in a day when almost everyone, especially doctors, warned bathing might be unhealthy).

Alas, the Mount Vernon never reached completion. The front portion and one wing were finished and the second wing almost completed when an off-season fire in 1857 left only a pile of ashes. Even in its uncompleted state the Mount Vernon won acclaim as the largest hotel in the world at the time.

Fire hung over the old wooden hotels as an always-near threat, but other things—erosion and fickle public enthusiasms, in particular—helped make the life of a hotel entrepreneur no thing of joy.

Pounding seas pulled the land out from under many a hotel—in Cape May, in Ocean City, at Barnegat Light and at Sea Bright, to

The trend is to motels, such as this one in Atlantic City

mention a few spots. Nowhere, however, did hotels suffer in the manner of those ranged along the Long Branch bluff. Several times hotel men at The Branch moved their establishments back or let them wash away— and either way was expensive.

Back in 1880 Long Branch's hotels probably matched or surpassed those of any resort, in New Jersey or anywhere else. Each of the hotels sought to be distinctive. The Continental, calling itself in the 1880's "the Largest Hotel in the United States," commanded 700 feet of ocean frontage; the Stetson, renamed the West End in 1872, attracted the elite; Iauch's Hotel became the magnet for distinguished foreigners, diplomats and fashionable adventurers. Others found enjoyment at Howland's, the Mansion House, the Metropolitan, the Atlantic, the Hollywood or a score of other noted places.

Long Branch's hotels achieved a peculiar architectural distinction. As

131

the correspondent for the *New York Daily Tribune* explained in 1868, the hotels were "not high but very long. . . . In the city a guest is shown 'up' to his quarters; in Long Branch he is shown 'out' to his quarters."

Fashion shifted its attention elsewhere and Long Branch hotel fortunes ebbed. Long Branch's loss meant gain elsewhere—Asbury Park or Spring Lake or Sea Girt.

Asbury Park hotels reached the height of their glory in the years between 1890 and 1930; most observers agree the city does not have the hotel prominence it had in 1910 to 1920—and is not likely to regain it. Back in 1889, to illustrate, Asbury Park had 200 hotels and boarding-houses and many of the hotels remained open all winter. Today few of the Park's establishments are open year-around and few new hotels have been built in the past 40 years.

Only one hotel in Asbury Park, or anywhere along the shore north of Atlantic City, rivals Atlantic City's rooming towers. That is the Berkeley-Carteret, built in the mid-1920's, and now the major year-around hotel on the North Shore. Asbury Park hoped in the 1920's that the Berkeley-Carteret would spark other hotel syndicates into action, but the depression killed that hope.

Most of Asbury Park's hotel world puts up the shutters and silently steals away after Labor Day, or by October 1 at the latest. Large hotels —such as the Monterey, next-door neighbor of the Berkeley-Carteret— remain closed until late spring, despite excellent locations overlooking the boardwalk and the Atlantic Ocean.

That seasonal emphasis affects virtually all New Jersey Shore hotels. Only the Flanders stays open year-around out of Ocean City's numerous hostelries. Hotels at Wildwood, Cape May, Beach Haven and other spots are in the main closed from October to May. Up and down the coast it's somewhat startling—even eerie—in the winter twilight to see the tremendous hotels completely lifeless and completely dependent for revival on a crowd returning in the coming summer.

Spring Lake offers a good illustration. In summer such fine hotels as the Monmouth, the Essex and Sussex, the Warren, the Breaker, the Shoreham and the Allaire are busy and humming with social activity; throughout the winter they are as deserted as the closed Army barracks at Camp Kilmer.

Much of the summertime aura of bygone days lingers about the Spring Lake hotels. Veteran hotel men declare that the average stop in Spring

Handsome hotels front on Atlantic City's Boardwalk

Lake hotels is probably the longest along the New Jersey coast—somewhere in the neighborhood of the old-time three weeks or longer.

Short seasons plague hotel men almost more than anything else. Their big establishments remain empty more than 80 per cent of the time (most hotel keepers would settle for 50 consecutive good days in the summer). Labor is increasingly difficult to recruit on a part-time basis. The average guest no longer takes one hotel above others as a matter of course.

The recourse for hotel men is to build up their seasons wherever they can—through getting people to come earlier and stay later, through winter programs, through stretching out the average stay per guest, through promoting the American Plan or some reasonable facsimile. They must seek guests for the slack mid-week periods which come even in summer; heavy weekends followed by empty rooms Tuesday through Thursday cause headaches.

Atlantic City's hotel keepers, particularly those on or near the 'walk, have won success in two ways—by keeping their rooms heated and open the year-around and by encouraging large conventions to come to their city. Starting when the first hotel (the Brighton) stayed open all winter seeking to recoup losses suffered in the poor summer season of 1876, Atlantic City's hotels have seen the wisdom of a year-around program.

Conventions are the key, of course. A mid-February convention, such as that of the National Association of School Administrators, can bring 15,000 or 20,000 guests to town. Hotels compete for this city-wide convention business—and at times sponsor special meetings and conventions on their own. Conventions are big business to Atlantic City, and hotels and city alike know it very well.

Singling out one hotel for attention could be indiscreet. Nevertheless, justification can be found for so singling out the Chalfonte-Haddon Hall in Atlantic City.

For one thing, as has been noted, the Hall's management says flatly that it is the largest resort hotel in the world, with 1,000 rooms in the combined facilities of the enterprise. Certainly nothing matches the size of Chalfonte-Haddon Hall along the New Jersey Shore. Nothing yet raised in Miami Beach approaches it in numbers of rooms.

Then, too, the Chalfonte-Haddon Hall typifies the family management once a vital part of the Atlantic City scene. Most of the city's original hotels were built by Quakers from Philadelphia or its immediate environs. Today ownership is dispersed; few of the Boardwalk hotels are in the hands of the founding families.

However, the Leeds and the Lippincotts continue to operate the Chalfonte-Haddon Hall. A pair of young Burlington County Quakers, Henry Leeds and J. Haines Lippincott, established this institution on an idea, a prayer and a mother who could cook.

First young Leeds and Lippincott bought Haddon Hall (established 1868) in 1890, and ten years later they added the Chalfonte (founded 1869). Both these famed boardinghouses had been built inland, but when the young men from Burlington County bought them the two frame houses were on either side of North Carolina Avenue near the Boardwalk.

Henry's mother, with knowledge gained by cooking for delicate Sea Girt tastes, came down to run "the back of the house" for the boys. The enterprise prospered. In 1904 the Chalfonte became a ten-story brick building, capable of housing nearly 600; during the 1920's two 11-story brick wings became the new Haddon Hall, with rooms for 1,200 guests.

Today the hyphenated Chalfonte-Haddon Hall is a place where fourth and fifth generations of families return every year. If statistics mean anything, read these from what claims to be the largest resort hotel in the world:

A total of 14,500 meals are served daily, for which 215,000 pieces of tableware are used. Each year 120,000 guests register, and they consume 43,000 pounds of coffee annually, eat a million eggs a year and anywhere from 4,000 to 7,000 pounds of fish each week. More than 700 employees work in the hotel the year around and in summer 1,200 employees make up the staff—often more than one employee for each guest.

Chalfonte-Haddon Hall is only one of Atlantic City's noted Boardwalk hotels, the like of which probably won't be built again on the New Jersey Shore. The future of guest housing seems to be in motels—or, as hotel men say, "motor hotels."

The term "motor hotel" is not without merit. Gone is the day of the poorly built "tourist cabin" with bathroom a short walk away under the stars. Construction is not cheap, and, in most cases, neither are the rates. Many a resort motel now comes complete with parking lot, TV set, swimming pool, lobby and, in some cases, bellboys and tipping (the very things motels supposedly made unnecessary).

Shore motels are often luxurious and often quite large. Wildwood has several motels worth in total millions of dollars. One motel recently built in Atlantic City has 150 rooms. Ten Atlantic City motels built in 1956 cost nearly $2,000,000. Incidentally, many hotel owners in Atlantic City see the motel footprints on the beach; several hotel owners now own or control motels in the city hotels made famous.

The future is catching up with the past in Atlantic City. During the past several years there has been a steady surge of motel building, preceded by a razing of ancient "hotels." As one knowledgeable Atlantic City official put it: "This fall the building is torn down to save taxes, next summer it will be a parking lot and the following spring a motel will start." That's the cycle.

All the while the automobile keeps confounding hotel men. Automobiles bring in more customers; they also take them home in a hurry—or take them to California or Maine or New Orleans. Formerly a family packed its bags and stayed all summer at the shore (or else stayed home to rest up for a 72-hour work week).

Now everybody gets a vacation—and usually drives as far away as possible. But there comes that unbearably hot weekend in summer and shore roads are clogged. Then comes the question: "Why don't they build more hotels or motels or something?" Ah, to be a hotel man. . . .

11. Never a Dull Moment

Aunt Judith Adams knew how to entertain the young folks who rounded Rum Point in the 1840's and set sail for her Absecon Island inn. She left them alone and busied herself getting dinner ready—a wise precaution, considering the goings-on.

Down on the beach, at low tide, the visitors danced to the fiddle. As Dr. T. K. Reed declared in turn-of-the-century reminiscences, before Absecon Island became Atlantic City, "There was none of your mincing and smirking, but genuine fun and frolic—a regular jump-up-and-down, cross-over-Jonathan and figure-in-Jemima terpsichorean fling!"

At high tide they bathed and, in the doctor's words, "The hilarity of the occasion culminated when the young men of the party carried the blushing and screaming maidens to the top of the sandhills, and, tying their feet together, rolled them down to the water's edge."

Reflecting on that lost youth, Dr. Reed wondered: "Where shall we find, in the refinement of the present age, a sufficient compensation for the loss of this rude form of jollity?"—a question as provocative today as when asked in 1900.

Boy still meets girl on the singing sands, but such rude joys as tying together the feet of blushing (that's what the doctor said) maidens and pushing them off sand dunes are frowned on by the teenage columnists. If Dr. Reed thought the seashore amusement world had lost its simplicity by 1900, he should see New Jersey beaches these days.

Millions of people who pause beside the toppling waves must be kept amused. Dedicated to this noble service between June and September is an army of hotel workers, food vendors, night club entertainers, movie moguls, taffy pullers, chair pushers, bingo callers, wheel spinners, party boat captains, jockeys and gamblers (who toil without public praise).

Amusement is a multi-million-dollar industry down where waves

137

A firelit party on Long Beach Island

meet strand. Indeed, seaside amusement may be the biggest New Jersey industry of all. Counting food and lodging, it probably runs to far more than a respectable one billion dollars annually. That's no "rude form of jollity"; some feel it often isn't even jollity.

Lest psychiatrists and theologians hasten to explain our own era's search for pleasure in terms of tranquilizing pills or a world on the chute to perdition, harken to the words of an 1809 Long Branch visitor. He told of "innocent and reasonable" amusements—riding, walking, reading, "a cheerful cigar and a half pint of wine after dinner" or dancing and tea parties ("for the young").

Why have amusements? Said the Long Branch visitor, "They keep off that corroding disease of the mind, 'ennui,' and send the visitors and bathers back to their homes and firesides with improved health and fresh relish for the solid comforts of domestic happiness."

Entertainment today generally revolves around a boardwalk, or, in less democratic atmospheres, around exclusive clubs or casinos. Regardless of whether the individual gets his amusement to the jostling of elbows on boardwalks or to the soft clink of ice in tall glasses in clubs, it usually costs money. Amusement is "refined"—and costly—for those who believe it can only be bought.

Yet hundreds of thousands of people in scores of quiet, unboardwalked New Jersey sea-front towns and back bay villages know simple pleasures which cost little more than opening the eyes to see and the mind to imagine.

It costs nothing, for example, to sit on the sand with a pair of binoculars to watch the ships far at sea (or the bathing suits nearby). It costs nothing to pick up bright shells or to hunt gnarled driftwood. It costs nothing to wander down to the bays to watch the fishing boats come home or to watch sailboats tacking against the setting sun. It costs next to nothing to go crabbing off a dock, to fish off a jetty, to fly a kite off the beach at twilight.

Despite what keepers of the boardwalk might think, the essential amusement element is the sea. This is the sea where people of all ages have found pleasure for centuries merely by exposing themselves to the buffeting billows.

Early records and laws indicate that male bathers enjoyed the ocean without benefit of bathing suit. As late as 1928 one North Shore resort which prides itself on its social standing had to enact an ordinance specifically forbidding bathing in the buff.

A century before that, gentlemen bathers used no suits in the Long Branch surf—if they got there before 6:00 A.M However, ladies received the reassuring word that the bluff kept the beach well hidden from hotel windows, not that any lady would be looking anyway. The first male bathers at Ocean Grove in the 1870's "went off at a distance" and "bathed in the garb of nature." Atlantic City waited until 1878 to require by specific law that a man be "so clothed as to prevent the indecent exposure of his body."

This bathing "in natural garb" died a sure death as the shore became popular—and it never extended to female bathers. When a lady went to sample the surf, she made sure not so much as a square inch of epidermis besides her face or fingers caught the rays of the wicked sun or the leers of wicked males. She wore what one writer has called a "nine-piece suit"—blouse, vest, pantaloons, stockings, kerchief, shoes and a bonnet.

Those early suits took seven square yards of cloth, enough for a fair-sized tent. The *New York Daily Tribune* in 1868 scolded that bathing had become "a social event for no other purpose than to exhibit oneself." As a matter of fact, before the Civil War some of the vain young things who "exhibited" themselves put padding within their vests, although how they expected it to make any difference wrapped in seven yards of flannel is a mystery.

No lady got sunburned, tanned or freckled, the genteel magazines warned. If she did, *Godey's Lady's Book* was right there with a "recipe to remove tan and restore good looks." Very simple: "Wash the face at night with sour buttermilk and in the morning with weak bran tea, with a little cologne and lemon juice put into a cup of milk."

The ladies became more and more daring. In 1897 a scandalized visitor to Ocean City took one look—or several, maybe—and observed: "If some of these women were to come over to Weymouth Township and walk around the way they do here, there would be war!" That same year 200 women had to be "spoken to" at Ocean Grove.

Short sleeves appeared on women's blouses in the 1890's, a bold few wore bloomers at Cape May and Atlantic City in the early 1900's, and in 1907 several shameless Atlantic City hussies rolled their stockings in public. The alert police put a stop to that. Still, epidermis in public view was on its way.

No one needs to be told that bathing suits today are different. They've "shrunk" steadily during the twentieth century—a transformation

140

Playing shuffleboard at Ocean Grove

helped by some of the girls in the early Miss America pageants, who rolled their stockings below the knees, and by pioneers who defied the censors on the Atlantic City beach. It's true—Atlantic City in the early 1920's hired censors who carried rulers to measure suit lengths on both men and women. Skin was all right in the night clubs, but not in the sun.

There is a little footnote to history. When stockings were being discarded everywhere in the middle 1920's, two Cape May ladies clung to the old ways. Then one day on the beach, as the modest pair passed a crowd, someone said audibly: "There go the covered wagons!" That afternoon *all* Cape May limbs caught the rays of the sun—and without fear of tan.

Beach manners have evolved, too. Back in the 1830's no lady appeared on the beach without a male escort; visiting Englishwoman Mrs. Frances Trollope heard to her horror that Long Branch ladies actually asked men to accompany them. Her shocked sensibilities were only moderately appeased when she learned two ladies asked the same man, "as custom does not allow tête-à-tête immersion."

Long Branch contributed something else to seashore culture—the paid escort (the gigolo, in effect). The Branch in the 1890's returned to puritanical ways (at a time when gambling halls ran wide open on the bluff) and a lady needed an escort on the beach. So Long Branch ladies hired them as casually as so many beach umbrellas, by the day, by the week, or, if the young man had real charm, by the season.

The Atlantic Ocean with its undertows and shifty ways lured many a gay vacationer to death, but until amusement began to verge on big business, they died mourned only by their relatives and friends. When hotel keepers, pitchmen and railroad officials began to live off the beach attractions, an ocean death could threaten to plunge their bank accounts into the red.

Thus, after 13 people drowned in Atlantic City in 1865, the hotel men mourned sufficiently to put out ropes. During the 1870's and 1880's lives of bathers rested in the hands of guards sponsored by hotels, railroads, a bit of city money and volunteer subscriptions. Eventually, in 1892, Atlantic City Council organized its widely envied Beach Patrol.

Elsewhere most lifesaving fell into the hands of volunteers who hoped to gain by hauling endangered bathers from the surf. Many fared right well, but occasionally the rescued party clutched his wallet tightly. One such waterlogged miser was hauled from the Cape May surf in 1869 by a Mr. Boynton, a volunteer-hoping-for-a-fee.

Fighting for breath, the man opened his purse and handed Mr. Boynton 50 cents. Mr. Boynton gravely handed back 49 cents in change, remarking that he did not "usually accept more than a life was worth."

Life guards these days adorn practically every beach, perched in bronzed and nose-peeled majesty atop wooden thrones surrounded by loyal, teenage subjects. They do an incredibly fine job, too; rare is the life lost to the sea while the guards are on duty. Atlantic City's Beach Patrol of 135 members, for example, is world-renowned.

Now, off the hot beach and up to the cool boardwalk. That, after all, is where the let's-not-get-depressed boys hold unchallenged sway.

Atlantic City, as has been seen, claims invention of the boardwalk in 1870, but Cape May records show that Cape May had enough beachfront boardwalk in 1868 to merit the name "Flirtation Walk." If Atlantic City didn't invent the 'walk, it did lift planking to its most prominent position in history.

Some 33 miles of the New Jersey Shore now have boardwalks, ranging from the simple, uncluttered strips along the Sea Girt frontage to the money-catchers in Asbury Park, Point Pleasant, Seaside Heights, Atlantic City, Wildwood and a half-dozen other places. Beachfront promenades aren't all pleasure; an occasional town official will declare (off the record) he wishes his town had no boardwalk. A few towns didn't rebuild their plankways after the 1944 hurricane blew them away.

There is not much to be gained by describing boardwalks. Anyone who has trod them knows what they are; anyone who hasn't, can't catch the atmosphere through words. From town to town they differ only in magnitude, each of them trying vainly to emulate in its own small to medium-large way the glitter of Atlantic City's Boardwalk.

Amusements beside that 'walk are fantastic—and have been for 75 years. The amusement piers, for example, date back a half century and more, and through the years they have presented an impressive range of amusements—from Sousa's Band to the Floradora Sextette, from opera singers to diving horses, from freaks to vaudeville stars, from movie premiers to "name" bands.

The "rides" are a usual boardwalk feature everywhere, running the gamut from "kiddie rides" and carousels to "thrill" spins and whirls. Each ride has its own purpose, but possibly there never has been anything like the Haunted Swing, a horror which prospered in Atlantic City in the 1890's.

Patrons of the Haunted Swing entered an ordinary-looking sitting room, complete with kerosene lamps, a filled china closet and a vast amount of heavy furniture. Unsuspecting, they sat in a swing suspended in the middle of the room and the attendant began to push them gently. Movement speeded up and suddenly the patrons seemed to find themselves swinging in a complete 360-degree circle.

Actually the swing moved only a few inches—the room revolved completely! Accounts tell of yelling and screaming, and small wonder. Fortunately the Haunted Swing is but a memory, along with the rack and other instruments of torture.

Atlantic City had its first merry-go-round in 1870, but the city's outstanding contribution to amusement (besides the amusement piers) was the first example of what is now called the "Ferris" wheel. Atlantic City had such a device 20 years before George Washington Gale Ferris erected his wheel at the Columbian Exposition in Chicago in 1893.

For that matter, the modern Ferris wheel is almost identical with a wheel William Somers erected on the Boardwalk in 1891. Somers sought the Columbian concession and later sued Ferris for patent infringement, but the latter died before the suit reached settlement.

Amusement parks grew up largely because the "day trippers" aboard special excursion trains demanded a full day in return for the dollar they spent for the round trip down from New York or Philadelphia. Railroads encouraged merry-go-rounds and beer gardens and Ferris wheels and fortune tellers to supplement their own "excursion houses," complete with dance halls, skating rinks and billiard rooms. If anyone went near the water, that wasn't the railroad's fault.

Day trippers needed something to take home, too. They clutched eagerly at salt-water taffy and picture postcards—and if Atlantic City's publicists may be believed brainy men of the "Queen of Resorts" perfected both.

Salt-water taffy surely is a symbol of Atlantic City, although the "original" can be bought under a variety of trademarks from Sandy Hook to Cape May. This is the way the popular confection came into being, at least according to one version of the story:

Once upon a time in 1883 a young taffy puller named David Bradley found his sweets flooded by the sea, but he sold some anyway to a little girl customer. "That's salt-water taffy, little sister," said the shop-keeper. The little girl's mother—or a bystander, depending on who recounts the story—suggested that the name "salt-water taffy" could be a good sales slogan. Bradley, they say, lettered the name on muslin signs.

Some suspect the story of being apocryphal, but in any case salt-water taffy is big business. It's made in 25 flavors, packed in everything from ordinary boxes to piggy banks and sold by the millions of pounds. If you like to get your teeth into statistics, chew on the fact that Atlantic City alone ships three million pounds annually.

As for picture postcards, Atlantic City claims that Mrs. Carl Voelker saw such cards on a trip to Germany in 1895 and on her return induced her husband to print 10,000 in color—and so introduced postcards to America. If Mrs. Voelker went all the way to Germany to discover

The tracks at Monmouth and Atlantic City have their devotees

postcards, she wasted her fare, because Mayor William Ramsey of Keansburg, as has been seen, printed picture postcards in 1881 and sold them at two for five cents to advertise his resort.

Again, small matter, except for shore postal clerks who, in season, cancel so many millions upon millions of postcards that they must wonder if anyone in the wide world ever writes anything but "Having a wonderful time, wish you were here."

Back in the days when Cape May and Long Branch welcomed Presidents and other great persons regularly, the chief amusement was annoying the notable. Henry Clay arrived at Cape May in 1847, seeking quiet to mourn for his son, recently slain in battle. The ladies pursued

145

him as teenagers now chase popular singers—and those demure females wielded scissors to snip off locks of Mr. Clay's hair as keepsakes.

Mrs. Abraham Lincoln wished for peace in Long Branch in 1861, and said so. Long Branch respected her wishes—with an immense welcoming parade and a series of events such as cricket matches, grand balls and concerts. Vast crowds flocked to Cape May when President Pierce visited in 1855, and when President Arthur came for a single day's visit in 1883, 2,500 well-wishers shook his hand. Small wonder presidents of recent years have avoided resort towns.

In a way, one can't blame the Clay-chasers and the Pierce-pushers. All they had to do in those days was bathe in the surf, flirt, drink a bit of good liquor, walk the beach or "gamble in rooms hotels set aside for them." Sometimes the hotels sponsored formal balls and more frequently guests themselves promoted "hops," a favorite nineteenth-century pastime at every hotel on the coast. The difference between a "hop" and a ball, it was said, was "the difference between a plain dress and one with trimmings."

Things have come a long way since then. Race tracks at Oceanport (near Long Branch) and McKee City (near Atlantic City) help pass the dreary daytime hours when there is nothing out but sunshine. Night clubs while away the awful vacuum between yesterday's last race and tomorrow's first. Golf clubs and tennis courts give the ball-chasers the chance to keep on the run. "Name" bands move the feet of the young, rocking chairs ease the chatter of the old. Band concerts at Asbury Park and Ocean City and Cape May catch a little of the spirit of another day when something didn't have to cost money to be worthwhile.

There are some who contend that the riotous pace of the bars and clubs and movie houses and boardwalks and amusement piers is geared only to the "down-for-the-dayers." There is a sneaking suspicion that many a "down-for-the-monther" is not above seeking divertissement either.

Long stays do give a vacationist a chance to seek the less obvious amusement—to master the intricacies of a sneak box or a Comet on Barnegat Bay, to learn to ride a surfboard through the endless procession of waves, to become a surf caster, to seek fluke in the bays, to have a little power boat tied up nearby, to meet some neighbors for a beach party after dark.

Amusement is a very personal thing, at the New Jersey Shore as well

146

Sailboating means relaxing on broad Toms River

as at home. A person seeking pleasure by the sea can find almost anything his heart desires. A writer for the *United States Gazette* summed
it up rather well in 1832. He makes sense in the Atom Age as well as his
own:

"Those who bathe only may depend on as good a surf as the Atlantic
can make. Those who go to eat will be sure of a good appetite for a
good dinner. Those who are fond of shooting and fishing will find game
in abundance; those who go to read or lounge may read or lounge as
much as they please.

"Old and young will have occasional opportunities to dance a little
in the evening, while those who go to grumble may sit of a hot day
among the adders in the sand or chase the fiddlers in the mud and
grumble to their heart's content."

Anyone for grumbling?

Some of the lensmen who record Miss America's every move

12. Beauty and the Beach

Credit Franklin P. Stoy, mayor of Atlantic City in 1902, with more chivalry than public relations sense. Mayor Stoy stood by while the Floral Parade rolled along the Boardwalk on the first of August of that year, watching the pageant of rolling chairs, in each of which sat a beautiful girl.

"Mayor," said the inevitable bystander, "we ought to choose the prettiest girl."

"Absolutely not," replied the mayor, so firmly gallant that his words are remembered down through the years. "We are going to judge pretty chairs. *All* the girls are pretty. Who would dare to pick out one?"

That reluctance to choose but one has vanished with the passing years. Today, as one writer has put it, the New Jersey Shore "crowns more royalty than Europe." There is a Queen of This and a Queen of That, there are baby queens and college queens and big, grown-up queens. Atlantic City each year dares to choose the prettiest of them all and to call her Miss America.

Occasionally a king is crowned, too—a Marbles King at Asbury Park or a Baby Parade King at Wildwood or Ocean City or elsewhere—but the New Jersey Shore's royalty is essentially female. There is ample reason above and beyond gallantry: The Queen of This or the Queen of That commands almost as much Page One newspaper space as the atom bomb.

If the Queen—of Fishhooks, of Clam Boats, of Seaweed, of Sand—gets on the Front Page, the caption under the picture will mention Asbury Park or Wildwood or Ocean City or Cape May. Someone in Dubuque or Iowa City or Memphis might be tempted to expend a few dollars by New Jersey's rolling waves.

Possibly that sounds crass. Nevertheless, if the Miss America Pageant hadn't lured extra customers to Atlantic City it would stand as much chance of continued existence as snow on the Boardwalk. Beauty and the beach, brought together for purposes of promotion, are vital to the New Jersey Shore.

Promotion can and does take other forms than beauty pageants. Each season a bewildering array of special events is presented by the state's 55 seaside resorts—band concerts, marble tourneys, fashion shows, clam-opening contests, flower festivals, fishing contests, baby parades, and on through a long list.

A single season, according to one commentator on the current scene, brings enough floats to the boardwalks between Atlantic Highlands and Cape May "to supply the Philadelphia Mummers Parade, the New Orleans Mardi Gras and Pasadena's Tournament of Roses for a decade."

Millions of dollars are spent each year to keep the public informed of the merits of the state's coastal resorts. The money comes from many sources—from hotel owners, from boardwalk entrepreneurs, from city budgets, all augmented by a tiny slice from the state budget. The cash goes for many things—for brightly colored and eternally optimistic folders, for advertisements in newspapers and magazines, for publicity staffs, for representatives traveling the country seeking to lure conventions shoreward, and for beauty contests.

Great-grandmother of all promotional schemes involving the decorative young lady is the Miss America Pageant, started in 1921. Although allowed to lapse several times because of financial crises, inept management and lack of interest, the Pageant nevertheless survives as the classic of all pulchritudinal coronations.

Beauty contests everywhere attest Atlantic City's success in getting Miss America (and Atlantic City) in the public prints. Today an estimated 25,000 "queens" are selected in America each year, most of them satisfied with such titles as Vegetable Queen, Miss National Chemical Week, Miss Florida Oranges—and, possibly, some day, the Onion Queen.

Atlantic City didn't invent the use of beauty to advance a cause. The first official beauty queen probably was Miss Myrtle Meriwether of Shinglehouse, Pennsylvania, crowned Miss Rehoboth Beach, Delaware, in 1880. Miss Meriwether became queen by accident; she was in Rehoboth Beach attending a convention of business women and entered the contest without even the formality of first being Miss Shinglehouse, Pennsylvania.

The beauty queen notion didn't catch on quickly, despite the fact that up and down the New Jersey Shore promotion men were beginning to flex the huge muscles they someday would possess. Hotels and railroads advertised widely—without so much as a pretty face or a well-turned ankle gracing their ads.

Asbury Park pioneered the choice of royalty in 1890, when its nationally famed Baby Parade first rolled. Mayor Stoy's later reluctance to choose the prettiest grown-up female had no counterpart in Asbury Park; that resort made its choice in the baby field—and anyone knows that a doting mother whose infant is scorned is far more dangerous than a grown-up female eliminated in a beauty contest.

The Baby Parade caught on rapidly. Within a decade virtually every state sent gaily decorated baby carriages and good-looking babies to the Park. Children and their parents filled hotels for a week or more, which meant the Parade fulfilled the fondest hopes of the sponsors.

Asbury Park added a mature queen in 1901—Queen Titania, a ruling beauty of each year, including movie actresses (notably Mary Pickford in 1915). The city proudly boasted in 1926: "No event in the United States, except the political conventions, gets more linage in the papers."

Festooned baby carriages stopped rolling through Asbury Park between 1932 and 1945; depression and war were to blame. Back bounced the Baby Parade in 1946, bigger and brighter than ever, but changed times did away with the event in 1949. Through the years 5,000,000 people had watched the babies promenade through 45 parades.

The Baby Parade is far from dead, of course. There are those in Asbury Park who hope color TV might revive the city's prime promotion. Several other towns pick the prettiest babies in carriages. Ocean City and Wildwood each year continue their baby parades—both of which, curiously enough, date back to 1909, proving that promotion minds often run in the same channel.

Just so much newspaper mileage can be gotten out of pretty babies of few years. The real gold mine is in pretty babies who've grown up to somewhere between 16 and 25 years of age and who are willing to match their qualities against those of their peers. The wonder is not that there are so many beauty contests, but that there are so few. Queens are sure-fire; flower festival promotions aren't worth a front page paragraph, for all the pleasure they might give thousands of people.

Passing years allegedly have made beauty no longer enough. Today brains and "talent" (much of it authentic) are said to be as important as the ability to round out a bathing suit—but Miss America is lovely first; brains and talent are happy extra dividends.

151

For all its promotional significance, the Miss America Pageant is a handsomely staged show and its backers are sincere enough about the virtues of intelligence to have rounded up nearly $1,500,000 in scholarships over the last ten years. Miss Americas of today *are* bright; bright enough to know that being Miss America is worth at least $50,000 the first year.

It is entirely possible that the first Miss Americas had wise heads on their lovely shoulders, too. No one asked. The Pageant in those days quite frankly stressed tape measurement appeal.

Most historians credit Herb Test of the now-extinct Atlantic City *Gazette-Review* with originating Miss America. It seems that the *Gazette-Review*'s circulation manager in 1921 came home from a meeting in Reading, Pennsylvania, fired up by a circulation scheme. Several papers had decided to choose their town's most popular miss—and as a reward for her helping to boost circulation, to send her to Atlantic City for a week.

Herb Test listened with growing interest. "Since we'll have so many pretty girls here all at once," mused Herb, "why don't we put them all in bathing suits and pick the best?"

They did just that. The "Beauty Maids" from Philadelphia, Harrisburg, Pittsburgh, Camden, Newark, Ocean City, Washington and New York donned bathing suits and joined hundreds of marchers in a Boardwalk parade. Herb Test had worked enthusiasm to a fever pitch by the Tuesday and Wednesday following Labor Day. Atlantic City—the world, for that matter—had never seen the like.

Miss Margaret Gorman, Washington's "most popular," stepped forward to be acclaimed as the "most beautiful bathing girl in America." She dazzled the audience with her full-skirted black suit, dimpled knees peeping daringly above rolled-down stockings, and blonde curls caught in a bandanna. Miss Gorman, all of 16 years old, was Miss America Number One.

Atlantic City gave Miss Gorman something to remember it by— "The Golden Mermaid," a brilliant gold statue to be kept permanently by any beauty who could win it three times. Miss Gorman gratefully posted a $5,000 bond for the honor of keeping the "Mermaid" for one year.

Herb Test's promotion grew to huge proportions within a year. Fifty-seven girls, representing nearly every state, hopefully sought the privilege of posting a $5,000 bond for the 1922 "Golden Mermaid."

From these simple beginnings in 1921 the Pageant has grown

During the parade, Miss Los Angeles tossed oranges to the crowd and Miss Macon kept alive the glory of Georgia by tossing peaches.

One of 1922's 57 varieties of American femininity, Miss Mary Katherine Campbell of Columbus, Ohio, took the promoters seriously about winning the "Mermaid" three times. She posted her bond as winner in 1922 and again in 1923, and seemed about to go on forever— being only 17 when she won the trophy the second time. The promoters met hastily, gave Miss Campbell a replica of the "Mermaid" and told her to go home and compete no more.

Those Roaring Twenties, those days of John Held, Jr., and Bootleg

Gin and raccoon coats, actually witnessed the most modesty the pageant has known. Girls paraded on various ocean piers and could be seen everywhere, but when it came to measuring and judging their figures, the matter became most private. Contestants, judges and chaperones repaired to the high school auditorium, with only the newspaper writers and photographers allowed as spectators—an overflow crowd at that, considering how dear Miss America always has been to the press.

The press had a vested interest in those days. All the contestants were chosen in newspaper contests in various cities and the papers filled their columns with the exploits of their local lovelies. Atlantic City has never had the nation-wide press attention it received as a result of Miss America in the 1921 to 1927 era.

Suddenly everything collapsed. The sponsoring newspapers wondered who was using whom. Herb Test and the sponsors had some disagreement. Many a champion of women's rights felt bathing suit contests degraded women—and many mothers agreed on behalf of their daughters. Finally, and of most moment, the committee found itself losing money every year.

Miss America "died" between 1928 and 1935, except for an effort to revive her in 1933. Then, backed by showmen throughout the country, the pageant gained new life in 1935 and has lived on, growing stronger every year. The new backers decided the "bathing beauty" was "passé." They sought, they said, "charm, poise, personality and talent." The fact that their Miss Americas always looked swell in bathing suits was coincidental, the promoters might have replied in case any happy photographer had wondered.

It remained for Miss Bette Cooper of Hackettstown, New Jersey, to astound Miss America's promoters.

Blonde Bette, 17 years old and with wonderful dimples in her cheeks, entered a contest to choose "Miss Bertrand Island" in 1937—and to her astonishment won. That same naïve amazement stuck with "Miss New Jersey" through a long Saturday night in Atlantic City; she was completely astounded and possibly frightened when she heard Miss Bette Cooper named as Miss America of 1937.

The next morning promoters led photographers to her hotel door, but Bette had fled back to Hackettstown. She refused to budge, to pose for pictures or to make any personal appearances. In June of 1941, after her graduation from Centenary Junior College in Hackettstown,

Bette Cooper won the crown in 1937, "retired" the next day

Bette went on a limited tour with other Miss Americas, but her shyness kept her in the background. Now married, Bette still refuses to have anything to do with the pageant.

Bette's walkout caused a rule change—subsequent Miss Americas have had to be at least 18 years old and have had to agree to give the year of their lives after the coronation to being a Miss America at beck and call of the promoters. In return, Miss Americas in 1938 started building up cash returns for their successes. The days of amateur beauties putting up a $5,000 bond for a cup had long since vanished.

The show officially became "The Miss America Pageant" in 1940 and kept going throughout World War II on a much decreased scale—operating at one time on an annual $16,000 budget. Then, in 1945, direction changed markedly. That year the Scholarship Foundation became official, with $5,000 in the scholarship kitty.

Scholarship awards now reach all the way down to local contests and as a result thousands of young women have attended or are attending colleges and universities in part on scholarships related to the Miss America contest. Today more than $150,000 in scholarships are awarded each year even before the state winners compete at Atlantic City.

Atlantic City awards each year total upward of $25,000 with a $5,000 scholarship going to Miss America and a $3,000 scholarship to the first runner-up. In addition, of course, Miss America indorses enough products and makes enough personal appearances to net her more than $50,000 in the year of her reign.

The Miss America Pageant is strictly and shrewdly run by a full-time staff. Local contests are carefully arranged and the Atlantic City finals are so full of decorum that photographers have on occasion complained the atmosphere seemed more like that of a finishing school than a beauty contest. On a recent occasion pageant directors stuffily ordered photographers not to take pictures showing Miss America's knees during a New York interview.

Nevertheless, when Miss America and her friends appear on the front pages of papers throughout the nation in the week following Labor Day, the odds are high that the pictures will feature a bathing suit. The magic words "Atlantic City" stand a much better chance of catching the eye that way.

Other resort towns along the New Jersey Shore use the good old bathing suit technique, officially and unofficially, to get their names before the public. Most of the queens rise to a moment of brief glory, only to disappear.

Asbury Park gamely tried *Mrs.* America as a promotional gimmick, but Mrs. America and her promoters moved off to Florida. Then Asbury Park chose the National College Queen as a feature of its season. As the publicity boys said, "She should combine a Phi Beta Kappa head with a Marilyn Monroe figure," and she had to prove her literacy by writing a 250-word essay on "What a College Education Means to Me." The winner was assured of scholarships and foreign cruises, but for all its high purpose, the contest didn't prove popular. Asbury Park dropped it in 1957.

New Jersey's second biggest beauty show is the naming of a Miss New Jersey Seafood Princess at Point Pleasant during Big Sea Day in August. Point Pleasant revived the old-time Big Sea Day in 1950 and as a logical climax decided to crown a Miss Seafood Princess. The fete is highly successful, with as many as 300,000 people crowding the city during the day, and it's certain Miss N.J.S.F.P. is as much an attraction as the fact that Indians long ago also celebrated Big Sea Day.

Asbury Park, Point Pleasant, and other towns must admit, nevertheless, that Miss America is every beauty queen's famous "older" sister. Each year, a new Miss America feels the crown nestle atop her cute head, and is linked with the winners of the past—all of them living, and all of them doing quite well as housewives and mothers and career girls. They are, as a matter of fact, living more quietly than might be expected. Many have retired completely from the public eye, eager for privacy for themselves, their husbands and children.

A composite Miss America, statistically embodying the graces of the contest's winners, would be 5 feet, 6½ inches tall, weigh 124 pounds, have measurements of 34½-24½-35, and have reached 19 years of age at the time she won the title. Colleen Kay Hutchins of Salt Lake City in 1952 boosted all the statistics: She was the oldest, at 25; the tallest, at 5 feet 10; the heaviest, at 143 pounds—and the only one to match exactly the fictional 36-24-36 proportions of "ideal" womanhood.

Every year brings its year-around build-up for the week after Labor Day. Thousands upon thousands of girls in farmhouses and city apartments dream of being Miss America, send in their pictures to local committees, lose a pound here or add one there, brush up their voices and piano fingers and dancing legs (talent, that is).

Every time a local queen is chosen along the Miss America trail—in

Iowa or Arkansas or Florida or California—a line is apt to appear in the local paper: "She now will compete in the state contest in the hope that she will be chosen to represent her state at Atlantic City."

Just a line, just a mention. Who knows how many motorists roll into Atlantic City each year on the strength of that? None? Millions? Who knows?

Only one can win

Miss Atlantic City and her gilded key

13. The Year Around

Precisely at 11:00 A.M. on Memorial Day each year, comely Miss Atlantic City trips daintily down to the restless surf, turns a giant, gilded key in an imaginary lock and then returns amid cheers to hand the key to the captain of the Atlantic City Beach Patrol. Officially (for Atlantic City's press bureau, at any rate) the Atlantic Ocean has been "unlocked" for bathing.

The unlocking is a relatively uncomplicated thing these days. Once upon a golden age Atlantic City did it up blue. "King Neptune" and a regal court of beauties performed the gilded key bit with a costumed pageantry that no photographer could resist. Carl Biemiller told the story in *Holiday* magazine of a man suffering from *mal de civilisation* who some years ago wandered out on the Boardwalk during the ceremony.

"What's going on?" asked the bewildered onlooker. "Why, they're unlocking the Atlantic Ocean," said a helpful soul. "That's King Neptune."

The visitor stamped his foot on the Boardwalk. "This thing seems solid enough," he said, as he tacked off into the crowd.

The "unlocking" is a pleasant custom which hurts no one, but it no longer means as much as it did in King Neptune's day. New Jersey's shore is no longer bounded by Memorial Day-Labor Day limitations, any more than there is adherence to the once rigid belief that white shoes were insufferably gauche on May 29 and becomingly chic on May 30.

True enough, the great pleasure-seeking crowds are not commonplace until Memorial Day and after—excepting, of course, the annual Palm Sunday and Easter Sunday throngs. After Memorial Day millions of people merely await the closing of schools to get out from under the cold city pallor and into a nice warm coat of tan.

Nevertheless, two intimately related factors have helped diminish the importance of Memorial Day as an official "unlocking" day. These are the Garden State Parkway and the huge upswing in all-year living which the Parkway has brought about along the shore.

This is what the Parkway does: Let a warm March sun beam through, and automobiles roll shoreward just as surely as daffodils push through the soil. People come to look at their boats, to see if their roofs are leaking, to bring down dishes, to sit by their lagoons and dream. "Bumper to bumper" used to be a phrase reserved for reporters writing of the July Fourth weekend. Now it gets dusted off every bright weekend of spring.

If they could, most shore enthusiasts would return much earlier than Memorial Day. This is particularly true since the Parkway has inspired the building of thousands of vacation homes beside the artificial lagoons in Ocean County. Here are tied up the boats whose hulls lure back devotees in early spring.

More important, the Parkway also has led to an upsurge in year-around shore living that must be reckoned as startling when compared with pre-World War II days. This is particularly true in the North Shore area, from the Highlands to Point Pleasant and in a belt extending 10 to 15 miles back from the ocean.

Some two-score years ago a year-around resident in most North Shore ocean-front towns was a rarity. As one lifetime Ocean Grove resident recalls, "If we kids saw a light in a house near the beach, we figured it must be either a hermit or a burglar." In those days year-around living meant a long train haul to New York or Newark for the breadwinner; few could earn a living all year at or near the beach. Those days are gone forever.

Resort leaders mean something special, however, when they talk about "year-around" business. They mean people spending money in hotels and on the boardwalks and in the amusement palaces. If that trade is to be considered the lifeblood of the New Jersey Shore—and surely it is at least the red corpuscles—then the lady with the gilded key is not without significance, at that.

Most shore resorts stretch and yawn happily just before Memorial Day, signifying an end to the unbroken sleep which began shortly after Labor Day. Not that the charms aren't here after Labor Day. They are. October is a delightful month by the sea, and November can be. April and May along most of the New Jersey Shore are much more pleasant

A Point Pleasant fisherman mends his nets

than they are to the north and west. The catch is that vacations—school and business—offer no recognition of these facts.

Some golden weekends in September give an illusion of wide-awakeness, but by November nearly every resort town is as dormant as a bear hibernating in the mountains. Footsteps echo hollowly at night on dark, deserted boardwalks, and off in the distance on a crisp autumn night a wailing train whistle emphasizes the loneliness.

Possibly nothing is as dismal as a typical small resort spot in winter. Shutters cover windows. Cottages stand empty and shabby. Storm-faded signs flapping in a January gale proclaim the wonders of a program given in the casino a summer ago. Rain beats against the faded poster bearing the face of the "name" band leader who thrilled teenagers last August. Grimy windows hide furniture stacked in restaurant rooms where life abounded in summer. Yachts rest stranded in boat yards. All is still.

A ride from Cape May to Sea Bright in December or January can be disillusioning and depressing; this is a land which needs sunshine and vacationists to be alive. Yet, even in the deepest sleep, awakening begins.

There is much for amusement men to do between seasons. Thousands of boardwalk planks must be replaced. Hotel and motel rooms and grounds must be made livable again. Signs must be repainted, barrooms must be rechromed, ice cream machines must be repaired, kiddie rides must be made safe, beach sands must be sifted clean.

In April hammers sound, saws whine, paintbrushes glide silently over surfaces painted a score of times before. It takes no experienced eye to recognize that a resort town each year needs as much face-lifting as the perennial leading lady getting ready for the next youthful supporting cast.

The old girl who is the New Jersey Shore gets better looking all the time as May progresses. She wears a wig and heavy makeup, but by Memorial Day she has millions of suitors again. People who didn't love her in December love her now in May. Even her ridiculous-in-winter slogans —"20 Degrees Cooler," "Ice Cold"—make sense in the May sun.

Face-lifting on the boardwalk is of interest to the year-around residents, of course, but few of these "new" people have so much as a tent staked out on the beach. These are people who in the main earn their livings in the industrial belt from New Brunswick to Newark; whether the boardwalk thrives or not is only of moderate interest to them.

164

These are people who soundly reinforce a once-uncertain economy subject to the whims of the public and the unpredictability of summer weekend weather. This new economic strength is growing at various speeds up and down the coast. It is firmly rooted in Monmouth County, growing at a rate that sometimes leaves local communities bewildered. The area of growth reaches as far south as Toms River, limited only by the distance a man is willing to drive to work.

Obviously changes will come in the wake of the thousands of new families who have chosen to live in the shore area. Already there are great changes—places like Asbury Park and Long Branch and Red Bank have found their shopping centers growing. Roadside shopping areas have sprung up. Supermarkets have been built—for year-around business.

The vast majority of the newcomers work in relatively nearby industrial areas and they live in Monmouth or Ocean counties because they like to be near their boats, because they feel the air is cleaner and healthier or better for their asthma, because they want room for their children to romp, because they want to get away from the traditional but now rapidly overcrowding suburbs strung in a 30-mile arc around Newark.

A comment made semi-facetiously by Richard Gibbons of Ocean Grove is worth noting. Asked why the North Shore community has expanded so tremendously, he replied, of course, that the Garden State Parkway had to get first credit. Then he added:

"Give second credit to the invention of the asbestos shingle!"

What he meant is that asbestos shingles and other new building materials have been an answer to the problem of combatting the rapid deterioration of wood and paint and metal which occurs when the salt-laden ocean breezes of winter and spring hang over the shore like sodden curtains. Other factors have influenced building—but don't dismiss the Ocean Grove man too lightly.

On down below Toms River, particularly out on the barrier beaches, almost everything is quiet after the sad September song. Areas such as Barnegat Peninsula and Long Beach Island and the Cape May Keys still rest basically on an old-fashioned economy rigidly bound by the closing of school in June and the ringing of school bells in September.

Aylward J. Walnut, a young professional geographer who lives at Barnegat Light, made a close study of business on Long Beach Island in the winter of 1956. He counted 602 business establishments—197 of them open, 405 of them shuttered tightly against the day when summer came again. Mr. Walnut found 51 out of 57 luncheonettes closed, 12 out of 29 grocery stores closed, 34 out of 40 commercial docks closed, 8 out of 10 bakeshops closed, and so on.

Long Beach Island feeds off the vacationist. Only about 4,500 people live the year around on the 19-mile-long island, although this figure is almost triple the winter-level population of 1930. In contrast to the 4,500 "winter" residents, some 90,000 to 110,000 people frequent the strip in summer.

Mr. Walnut found a significant thing, something pertinent to much of the New Jersey Shore—the fact that at least 10 per cent of the island's families spend a minimum of two months in Florida. Those who go south for just a few weeks reach an even larger total.

On down the beach, say in a town such as Sea Isle City in Cape May County, much the same condition exists. William Haffert, Sr., resident of Sea Isle City for more than four decades and formerly its mayor for a long period of time, would like to see Sea Isle City gain more winter residents (it has increased about 500 from the 1950 level of 1,000 permanent dwellers). The thinking down on the Jersey Keys of Cape May, however, is that the soundest growth can come by inducing retired folk to buy or build year-around homes.

Mr. Haffert sees retired people this way: "They bring their money with them, which means they don't need jobs. They won't increase the school population. They won't create any social problem; whatever mischief they're going to raise in life, they've long since raised."

For younger people in the southern New Jersey Shore area, Mr. Haffert admits there are some disadvantages, centered mainly on the difficulty of earning a living. Still, as he puts it, "With a little imagination there are limitless opportunities." He found, for example, in a comparison study of Sea Isle City with Clinton, a similar-sized town in Hunterdon County, that Clinton had about a dozen businesses that no one ever had thought to open in Sea Isle City.

Another thoughtful comment on shore living was made by Jack Lamping of Toms River, who mixes promoting Ocean County with observing the economics of the area. Mr. Lamping believes that three types of people come to the New Jersey Shore for year-around living: the young, who seek a future or a place to rear their children; the retired, who can supplement their incomes with some work in the summer; and, third, those who have had a crisis—health or business failure, by way of illustration.

166

Spring brings work at Seaside Heights—and on all boardwalks

Mr. Lamping is himself a "crisis" fugitive to Ocean County; he came many years ago to get relief from asthma. This third category, incidentally, also includes "many a fugitive from success." These are people who have made a great deal of money elsewhere, then have sought the shore to escape the noise and bother and tension of piling up greenbacks far beyond the point of necessity.

People who live in the lonely stretches of beaches which close down after September must exhibit a degree of independence. As the local saying goes, "Everyone is a tub on his own bottom"—finding much of his own amusement in simple things. There is a minimum of commercial

167

entertainment, and New York and Philadelphia are too far away to run up solely for relief from boredom.

Still, semi-isolation has its advantages. Every person can pitch in to help at church or fire department or library benefits. Few people show great interest in keeping up with the Joneses, in large measure because it's hard to determine who is a Jones worth keeping up with and who isn't. Social distinctions aren't that clear-cut out of season.

There is much to do, provided the doer has a taste for it. There is room for a boy and his dog to frolic on a deserted beach. There is open space to bring peace to a surf fisherman. Off-season is the time to seek shells in the sand. Out in the marshlands are duck blinds calling for hunters. There are migrating birds to watch. There is opportunity to sit quietly in the lee of a dune and watch the ships at sea.

So much for the off-season beach dwellers. It can be a mighty nice life, for those who like it.

For the flockers-together, nevertheless, something livelier is vital, and that can be had in Atlantic City, the only true year-around resort city in the North. Atlantic City owes its unique success to its ability to keep things generating pretty much on a 12-month basis.

Year-around living has brought a heightened weekend business to restaurants in Atlantic City and Asbury Park (and a few other areas). Thousands of couples swarm to Atlantic City on either Saturday or Sunday during fair weekends all winter long, have dinner at a restaurant or hotel, then return to their nearby homes. This is nice business, but it doesn't bolster the basic source of income—hotel reservations.

Once it wasn't difficult to promote winter hotel reservations. Thirty years ago Atlantic City had powerful appeal for New Yorkers through most of the cold months. Fugitives from Broadway found restfulness and warmth in Atlantic City and, to some extent, in Asbury Park. They believed the promotion literature about how warm the Gulf Stream made the New Jersey coast.

Miami Beach has cut deeply into that winter trade. An airplane can whisk a New Yorker to Miami Beach in no more time than it takes him to drive to Atlantic City. And, speaking frankly, Miami Beach *is* warm in the winter; Atlantic City often is not. He who doubts can stride up one of the streets leading away from the beach on a January night when the wind blows briskly in from the northwest.

Conventions are the essential reason why Atlantic City doesn't close up shop after Labor Day, although in the interest of sound judgment, it

Readying the *Little Mary* for another season afloat

must also be pointed out that Atlantic City is a real city of 60,000 all-year residents. Every business day as many as 4,500 automobiles cross the bridges leading to the city, carrying thousands of people to work in the offices and shops on the Boardwalk or on Pacific and Atlantic Avenues, the two streets back from the 'walk. Still, most Atlantic City incomes benefit at least indirectly from the city's amusement and convention superiority.

Pressure from other convention cities is being felt in Atlantic City, but significant numbers of the arrangers of giant conventions feel the New Jersey Shore Queen is superior to places like Miami or New York or Chicago. One prime reason, intriguingly enough, is that in the winter there aren't as many distractions in Atlantic City as in most cities! This is a fine thing, in a city which often boasts of its distractions.

What the arrangers mean is this: Get a delegate out on Absecon Island in January or February, make sure his wife comes with him, then arrange as much of the program as possible right in the hotel where he is staying. He doesn't stray much; he isn't running around madly trying to buy tickets to a Broadway hit or trying to see the floor show at the Latin Quarter. Atlantic City's lively Convention Bureau has stacks and stacks of letters from convention chairmen to back up this theory.

Conventions are big business in Atlantic City. The Convention Bureau works years in advance; already scores of conventions are lined up for the next five years. Exactly what organizations they involve is confidential information; Atlantic City doesn't tell its competitors any more than Gimbels tells Macy's.

Despite the dollar-giving convention business, Atlantic City, too, feels the glow of pleasant anticipation that spring brings to all resort towns. The glow comes first when the Palm Sunday and Easter Sunday throngs jam the boardwalks and spend a bit on souvenirs, deepens when Memorial Day brings reviving business.

Spring at the shore is more than a revival of boardwalk trade or a rise in travel hazards for those who live there all year and roll over the Parkway to work. A magical change takes place.

Whoever travels the ocean avenues any time from October to March is aware of an all-pervading stillness. If he has the heart or the curiosity to peek over the edge of the boardwalk in April, he sees the debris of a half-dozen months littering the strand—huge timbers, crushed orange crates, roots of trees, pieces of furniture—all washed up from no one knows where.

Few of those who think they know the New Jersey Shore well (including the boardwalk concessionaires) ever wander beside the forsaken sands in the months between Labor Day and the few days before Easter Sunday. Few who arrive in town for a convention or a Sunday meal peek over the boardwalk's edge.

More should see the shore in the off months. It's the one sure way to know the magic of spring at the seashore—to know that a frigid, seedy, abandoned, ugly stretch of sand can awaken between May and June to become the siren of allure and warmth which each year calls back so many to seek her charms.

170

See It as the Ocean . . .

Day by day, week by week, the ocean rolls in twice a day—and twice a day it rolls out. Each day, it leaves behind mementoes of its visits: some shifted shells, bits of driftwood, a slightly different shore line. This excites few, except as the sea is itself intrinsically exciting.

Then comes the day when the sea rolls up savagely from out of the depths, whipped to frenzy by a violent wind, pushed on to senseless destruction by the devil in nature. At these times the beach changes radically and an unknown force laughs at man's efforts to keep the shore line in place.

On such dark nights the sea sets her trap for mariners. These days radio and radar and powerful ship engines are nearly always enough to keep the trap from closing, but in years past 500 to 1,000, maybe even as many as 2,000 ships have met ruin off the Jersey Shore.

These desolate nights brought the Coast Guard into being. Such nights still worry the men of *Semper Paratus* reputation, but now the very lure of the sea for boatsmen has created a new problem for Coast Guardsmen: the inexperienced skipper, unfamiliar with the ocean's ways.

Restless, turbulent, romantic, enticing: these are the moods of the ever-changing sea—a sea which can soothe or destroy.

Nature is a tough foe, and she holds most of the weapons

14. The Hungry Sea

Spring smooths the uncertain temperament of the surly winter sea. Waves cease their erosive biting at the beachland sands, as if eager to cooperate fully with those humans preparing to welcome millions of visitors to the Jersey Shore in the vacation months just ahead.

Except for a rare stormy mood in July or August, the Atlantic Ocean in the summer months is as pleasant and as willing to please as a puppy who is genuinely sorry he has just torn up his master's shirts. Rare indeed is the summertime visitor who reflects that this gracious sea holds every bit as much power to destroy as to delight.

This is the paradox of the ocean. The sea which makes the Jersey Shore valuable, is also that very thing which day in and day out fights the seacoast—normally with the tapping deftness of the bantamweight, occasionally with the flailing brutality of a heavyweight. The sea hasn't given that Jersey Shore to mankind forever; it's merely ours on short-term loan.

The battle between sea and Jersey Shore is billed officially as erosion, and possibly nowhere is the problem of erosion more serious than it is along the 127-mile New Jersey beachfront. The state's frontage along the rolling Atlantic is worth something like $5,000,000 per mile in assessed valuations—so when the ocean eats away a few acres it lunches on what amounts to gold rather than sand.

Geologists at times have argued that coast protection is a losing battle, that through passing centuries the forces at work inexorably tend to level landforms. Engineers, on the other hand, argue that while a thousand years may be a short period of time in a geological sense, they must work within the framework of the immediate present. As one engineer has put it:

"Mortgages don't run for a thousand years at the Jersey Shore."

Erosion unquestionably is the number one problem confronting New

Jersey's billion-and-a-half-dollar seashore resort industry. Several beach-front municipalities are in dire circumstances—both economically and physically—because of their battles with the sea. Towns like Long Branch and Cape May find the ocean menacing their very existence as resorts.

Long Branch's erosion problem is dramatic; as recently as 1956, a storm tide threatened to topple a small hotel into the surf. Portions of Ocean Avenue are undermined. It doesn't take an engineer's eye to detect what the sea has done to that pitifully exposed bluff.

Elsewhere the pounding power of the sea is evident—at Sea Bright, where waves break ceaselessly against the massive stone sea wall, at Cape May, where another sea wall holds the sea back from the ocean road, and at Barnegat Light, where a continuing fight goes on to save the 100-year-old lighthouse from destruction.

There are such startling seashore changes as that at Tucker's Island, south of Long Beach Island. Thirty years ago a little village, including a Coast Guard station and a school, existed on that island. Today all human habitation is gone and Tucker's Island is drastically reshaped—for any useful purpose, as good as gone.

Nature is an implacable foe. She holds all the offensive weapons, has on her side every element of surprise, can alternate wild fury with disarming peacefulness. She even has those men fighting her along the Jersey Shore divided as to how erosion can best be overcome or delayed.

Recently the Army Corps of Engineers in cooperation with the New Jersey Department of Conservation and Economic Development completed a massive study of the shore erosion problem between Sandy Hook and Barnegat Inlet. There was widespread agreement with the findings, but many an experienced shore engineer found fault with the study—particularly when its recommendations differed sharply from his own beachfront practices.

Nevertheless that Army survey, plus three others in progress along the shore, estimated to cost about $200,000 (shared equally by the State and the Federal Government), may hold the eventual key to the first coordinated program of New Jersey beachfront erosion prevention and control. The other surveys encompass the Raritan Bay region, the oceanfront between Barnegat Inlet and Cape May and Delaware Bay from Cape May to the Maurice River.

There is one slight problem: money.

The Army report indicated about $25,000,000 would put the Sandy Hook to Seaside Park region in excellent shape—with every resort beach

The southeaster of 1953 crumpled Asbury Park's boardwalk

extending at least 100 feet out from boardwalk or sea wall. Of that total, the Federal Government would put up about $3,000,000—leaving $22,000,000 to local governments and/or the State to raise.

Money and erosion control go hand in hand. Since the turn of the century something like $20,000,000 has been spent in the fight—an appalling amount of it on groins and jetties and sea walls which proved completely ineffective. Between 1940 and 1953 the State put up $8,000,-000 and local municipalities $5,500,000 to combat erosion. A large part of that might as well have been tossed into a September gale. Indeed, the very spot where the most money has been spent—Long Branch—today is probably the worst off.

Early settlers and vacationists observed erosion, as much to while away the summer hours as anything else. Commodore Stephen Decatur, Cape May vacationist, in 1804 measured the distance from Atlantic Hall to the edge of the beach to be 334 feet. Later vacationers noted in 1829 that the waves lapped at the base of Atlantic Hall. The ocean had claimed 334 feet in 25 years!

A comprehensive study released in 1923 gives one of the most intriguing pictures of Jersey Shore erosion ever disclosed. That study, by an engineering advisory board of the State Board of Commerce and Navigation, showed the ocean had robbed New Jersey of 2,496 acres of beachfront in a century.

Take a closer look at that thievery—that was *net* loss. Over-all, 5,521 acres of beachfront property went with the waves in that century, but the whimsical waters gave back 3,025 acres in other places. Some places, such as Atlantic City, Asbury Park, Cape May and Long Branch, saw their beachfronts recede anywhere from 600 to 1,400 feet; others, such as Wildwood, Avalon and Beach Haven, observed their beachfronts build outward from 350 to 600 feet.

Erosion goes on. Recent engineering estimates show an average erosion rate of two and a half feet annually from Sandy Hook to Cape May. Worse, though, 70 per cent of coast locations showed net annual erosion averaging six feet.

Six feet really isn't much. A July bather would be more likely to notice an extra inch around his wife's waist than he would be to notice six feet less of beach. Erosion is subtle; six feet, ten feet, 15 feet, these are scarcely noticed from one summer to another. Sometimes erosion can be spectacular, as for example, during a howling northeast storm— but not many Jersey Shore enthusiasts are around to see such spectaculars, scheduled by nature in off-season months.

Storm damage is an awesome thing, whether viewed in the midst of a roaring gale or merely when viewed in the mound of statistics piled up when the skies have cleared. Take, for example, four major storms in the past 20 years—the hurricanes of September, 1938, and September, 1944, and the storms of November, 1950, and November, 1953.

The Hurricane of 1938 chalked up about a half-million dollars in damage, and the Hurricane of 1944 walloped the Jersey Shore for $7,127,000—more than $4,000,000 in Atlantic City alone. The southeaster of November, 1950, accompanied by torrential rains and powerful winds, totaled $5,877,000 in damages. Finally, the November, 1953, blow, abetted by two full-moon tides, hit the shore with a thunderous smack totaling $7,650,000. That's some $21,000,000 in four major storms. In addition, storm damage piles up, less awesomely, every year.

Such losses make it increasingly difficult for an average shore municipality to shoulder both community reconstruction and beach restoration. Still, such losses as boardwalks and buildings tend to cast into the shadow the really vital loss—the loss of beachfront. Boardwalks can be rebuilt with money; beaches aren't necessarily brought back by expending huge sums.

Rude winds and heavy seas cause the most evident erosion, since waves strike the beach obliquely and scour away the sands well above the normal high-tide mark. Nevertheless, erosion is a 24-hour-a-day undertaking of the surging seas; each grain of sand is moved each day ever so slightly. Joined by countless millions of other grains, moved inch by inch, a grain of sand moves away as surely as the sand riding furiously before a gale.

New Jersey's inability to fend off the ocean stems in large measure from a lack of inter-municipal cooperation. Practically everyone agrees to that; practically everyone has agreed to that for some 50 years or more. Criticism of "piecemeal" attacks on erosion has been appearing in reports ever since a series of winter storms ripped the Jersey Shore in 1913 and 1914.

Those storms had a virtue, because even as they threatened to wash Sea Bright and Monmouth Beach off the map entirely, they pointed up the bitter fact that the battle against erosion should have begun long ago. Those storms brought home what some voices had been speaking into the wind ever since 1870.

Down in Atlantic City, for example, 7,000 persons (mostly out-of-town vacationers) in about 1870 affixed their names to a petition asking Congress to put up the money to halt a serious loss of beachfront. While his neighbors scribbled, Dr. Walter B. Dick, a Navy surgeon of the Civil War, acted.

Dr. Dick owned property in the Brigantine Inlet section and each day he hired boys to row him out into the ocean so that he could study eddies. The doctor built a crude jetty of wooden boxes filled with sand. Neighbors laughed, until Dr. Dick sold lots on land once under water—lots reclaimed by his jetty.

The Federal Government constructed some jetties in 1878, seeking to keep Manasquan Inlet open. The Jersey Central Railroad in the late nineteenth century built a bulkhead on the ocean side of its tracks between Atlantic Highlands and Monmouth Beach and the Army built a sea wall part way up Sandy Hook. It was all very unscientific, very costly and most ineffective.

Concerted action might well have followed those 1913 and 1914 storms, but World War I interfered. Finally, in 1920, the State got into erosion studies in earnest—spurred not only by the wailings from the beach towns, but also by the gentle urging of a Tenafly uplander, J. Spencer Smith.

J. Spencer Smith began to study beach erosion in 1915 when he became a member of the New Jersey Board of Commerce and Navigation. He never stopped until his death in 1953, and in 1926 he organized and became president of the American Shore and Beach Preservation Association. The words of Smith reached from coast to coast; he led the anti-erosion troops into the fight.

Smith said some things the beachfront interests liked, strongly recommending that the State and Federal Governments spend greater sums to halt erosion. Resort towns liked that; J. Spencer Smith would save them some money.

The Tenafly beach preserver also said persistently some things the resort owners didn't like—particularly the unqualified declaration that beaches belonged to all the people, especially if the taxes of all the people were to be spent in the fight on erosion.

Smith liked to recall a "gentleman who called to get the State to protect his property from the sea." This was the problem, as Smith saw it:

"If the State had stepped in and saved his property, would he have been willing for the public to enjoy the ocean breezes on a hot day while making free use of the land to which he held title?"

Various federal, state and municipal studies began in 1920 and have continued ever since, with reports coming almost as often as the year-in and year-out hurricanes. Usually the reports have gently upbraided mankind for tearing down the dunes—nature's protection—for building too close to the ocean, and for undertaking erosion control measures meant to protect one resort without more than casual thought of what a jetty might do to an adjoining town.

Engineers disagreed among themselves and their theories of ocean behavior often contradicted one another. Even to this day there are divergences of opinion among erosion authorities about such matters as

Remains of a completely ineffective seawall at Deal

where the sand comes from in the first place and how it is moved about in the second place. There is a strong school of thought, however, holding that much of northern New Jersey's beach has come from the eroded "headland" of Monmouth County between Long Branch and Bay Head, supplemented by sand picked up elsewhere in the ocean.

Off the New Jersey coast the sand dances in two distinct streams—"littoral drifts," the engineers call them. One flows north, and the other south, with the "nodal" or dividing point well out in the sea, approximately due east of Barnegat Inlet. If no one ever set foot on the New Jersey Shore these streams would cause erosion to go on, of course, cutting away here and adding there, at nature's pleasure. Mankind, by leveling the dunes and by building ill-considered jetties, has hastened the process.

Through the years the ocean has snarled at man's daring to build on land that even casual observation of geological history could have shown

179

would be washed away in three or four decades. The waves have tipped lighthouses into the sea, have washed away mansions and hotels and shacks, have cut the beachfront at Long Branch and Sea Bright back as much as a half mile in 150 years.

How, then, to fight the ever-greedy sea?

Almost 80 years ago jetties stretched out into the Atlantic at widely spaced points—constructed to break up the violently pounding waves and to stop drifting sand. By 1900 it became clearly evident that often jetties made the situation worse instead of better.

Over a long period the building of jetties and groins (essentially the same thing) and sea walls has gone on without signal success. Jetties and groins, to put it simply, are the long-familiar rockpiles (or timber and rock or timber and steel plate structures) extending out into the ocean at scores of points up and down the coast. Sea walls are dikes, built to protect land roads or homes.

Unfortunately jetties often provide the perfect example of robbing Peter to pay Paul. Jetties which preserve Beach A usually ruin neighboring beaches B and C. Sand piles up on one side because the jetty interferes with the littoral drift of sand either northward or southward. On the other side of the jetty, beaches are impoverished.

There are two classic instances, both at jetties built to protect inlets. The first, at Shark River Inlet, shows the beach at Belmar built out to a handsome width on the south side of the jetty. Meanwhile, on the north side, Avon and Bradley Beach have suffered severely because the northward-flowing sand is trapped at Belmar.

The second example is at Cold Spring Harbor Inlet, where a long jetty built in the 1920's to protect the entrance to Cape May Harbor has widened Wildwood's beach to the point where it is the finest in the state—but at the same time has ruined Cape May's shore to the point where there is virtually no beach at all in spots.

Almost everyone interested in preserving New Jersey's beaches knows that "piecemeal" municipality projects may in the long run destroy all but a few resort towns. The answer, carefully spelled out in a dozen or more reports since 1920, is a concerted attack on a regional basis—one region, say, to be within the northerly littoral drift and another region within the southerly flowing current.

There are now 117 groins, six jetties and seven sea walls—with respective aggregate lengths of 43,000, 12,000 and 38,000 feet—along the New Jersey Shore. Army engineers in 1954 expressed the belief that

The worth of this groin depends on which side is *your* beach

more monuments of stone aren't the way to battle erosion. They said that while a few more groins should be built at strategic locations, the essential need is for feeding the beaches with sand dredged up from the bays, from inland or from the ocean itself.

The thinking here is that if the beaches can be built out to a minimum width of 100 feet, then the cruel impact of storm tides can be spent on a shore line well away from homes and roads and boardwalks. This sort of thinking shows only moderate regard for sea walls such as those at Sea Bright and Cape May.

"Sea walls are an admission of defeat," says an official of the New Jersey Bureau of Navigation. "They are a hope that the ocean can be stopped at the wall, but the only way to save the beaches for any length of time is to put a wide strip of sand in front of the sea wall."

Actually, there are many who hold a strong belief that the ocean left to itself would eventually undermine even the massive sea walls now

181

being completed. In a brutal mood the ocean does incredible things; no stone can withstand water forever.

So, say the engineers, build up the beaches by bringing in sand—keeping it in place where necessary with groins, constructed so that the littoral drift could still move relatively freely. Such "nourishment" has been tried at Surf City, Atlantic City, Long Branch, Ocean City and other places, with varying success.

Certainly the sand will move, say the engineers. Certainly it will continue to build up the point of Sandy Hook at a rate of 100 feet or more a year. That simply means more sand must be pumped in, year in and year out. Certainly it will cost money. Engineers aren't interested professionally in the politics or economics or sociology of beaches. They simply seek to know how to build them up.

Yet politics and economics and sociology are as much a part of the erosion problem as the pounding waves and littoral drifts.

Money is the thing from which come all jetties and groins and sea walls and nourishing sand. It is estimated that the over-all army program to protect New Jersey's beaches will call for a sum of $35,000,000 or so. Of this, the Federal Government would pay possibly as much as $10,000,000. That leaves at least $25,000,000 for State and local treasuries to kick around—and that really isn't much money, considering what millions already have been spent on roads to the shore and bridges across bays.

This money shortage has one provocative aspect. Resort areas recently claimed themselves to be an annual aggregate $1,700,000,000 industry. If that is true, the question arises: Why doesn't a goodly bit of that (one per cent would be $17,000,000 annually) go to protect the only real asset the New Jersey Shore has—its beaches?

A State Beach Erosion Commission created in 1949 has been studying the wearing away of the coast. It would like to arouse the entire state to the importance of saving the New Jersey beaches as a state and national playground. Sometimes the commission—composed in 1957 exclusively of men from the four shore counties—wonders why it can't stir enthusiasm for erosion control in the uplands.

The answer lies partially in the make-up of the commission; it would seem reasonable that if counties other than shore counties should be enthused, then they should be represented. The answer, however, lies most strongly (and silently) in the dispute over who owns the beaches and who has the right to say who must keep off and who may go on.

182

This is most evident in the area between Asbury Park and Sandy Hook, the strip of coast where expenditures would be heaviest—nearly $18,000,000, the Army report says, out of the $25,000,000 needed north of Seaside Park. This also happens to be the area least accessible to the public, the area of frequent "Private Property, KEEP OUT" signs.

The question is, very simply: Should public moneys—local, state or federal—be expended to protect private property? There is no easy answer.

Let people argue such a weighty economic and sociological problem; the ocean doesn't care. While man argues (or hides such issues under the table), Old Man Atlantic roars on. He grabs a chunk here, puts it there. He ruins a beach, topples a mansion, threatens a lighthouse, undermines a road.

He never sleeps. He might be checked if enough dollars pile up against him every year, but he'll never be beaten. A year, ten years, a thousand years, ten thousand years—it doesn't matter. He'll get it all back in the end.

Wreck of the ship *Adonis* off Long Branch in 1869

15. Gale and Shipwreck

Call out the melancholy list: the *Sally*, the *Andrew Jackson*, the *Powhatan*, the *Louisa*. Recall the missing: the *John Minturn*, the *Fortuna*, the *Cherokee*, the *Yum Chi*, the *Konig Thryme*. Gone, all gone, wrecked on the New Jersey Shore along with the *Sultana*, the *Lizzie Bliss*, the *Henry Paul*, the *James Fisher*, the *Morro Castle*, the *New Era*, the *Guadaloupe* and a thousand more.

Down through the years these names linger, remembered not because they sailed in dignity but because they perished in agony, when the winds screamed and the spray flew cold in the blackness of coastal storms. They sailed off the wild sea to their fate: stranding on a sand bar, so near to safety yet nearer to death.

From their riggings dropped their crews, from their decks fell their passengers to be swallowed by the sea—then to be spewed forth upon the sands from Sandy Hook to Cape May. The human victims lie now in graves upon the mainland, and the skeletons of lost ships lie buried deep in the sands.

Death on the New Jersey coast from shipwreck is a rarity in the twentieth century, but no one wanders even a short time by that sandy strip without recognizing that seaside disaster has been a significant and harrowing chapter in the state's history. How many ships have met their doom on this coast is not definitely known. The minimum is 500; some estimates range to four and five times that number.

Shipwreck and tragedy were almost as much a part of a seashore visit throughout the nineteenth century as a dip in the Atlantic. Little boys and girls played on the whitened hulls of derelicts; adults painted pictures of them as casually as they now paint Old Barnegat Lighthouse. One storm would hide the timbers of a fine old vessel, only to uncover the remains of another—as, for example, when the noble *Clyde,* wrecked on Sandy Hook on her first voyage, sank beneath the sands, to be uncovered by a howling gale in the late 1880's.

185

Many factors contributed to the piling up of sea-smashed derelicts upon these shores—the heavy traffic bound to and from New York, the shallow shoals of the curving New Jersey shore, the strong inshore currents, the savagery with which storms pound the Atlantic coast, the insufficient navigational aids available to eighteenth- and nineteenth-century sailors. To these add a human frailty: All too often there was evidence that some ship's officers celebrated too well on the last night before docking.

Jacob W. Morris of Long Branch estimated that prior to 1845, at least 15 ships a year came to grief between Sandy Hook and Point Pleasant. A Dr. Reed of Atlantic City reported 64 vessels aground on Absecon Beach between 1847 and 1856. In 1878 the Reverend Mr. Brown of Point Pleasant listed 125 vessels wrecked in the preceding 40 years on 24 miles of beachfront between Point Pleasant and Barnegat. A report to Congress in 1848 told of 158 vessels lost off New Jersey between 1839 and 1848.

These were carefully kept chronicles, and none of the record keepers reached back beyond his own certain knowledge. Wrecks commenced soon after the first colonist began to seek this state. Indeed, about two years after the Dutch established the first colony in Bergen County in 1618, a disaster—worth noting because of Penelope Van Princis—occurred off Sandy Hook.

Penelope and her husband were on a Dutch ship smashed on the Hook in about 1620. The crash severely injured the husband, Penelope stayed to nurse him, and a band of Indians attacked them, slew the husband and left Penelope horribly wounded, with a fractured skull and a deep gash in her abdomen. She lived, married Richard Stout at the age of 22, moved with him to Middletown in Monmouth County, bore seven sons and three daughters, and when she died at 110, left 502 descendants!

Throughout the eighteenth century ship after ship met doom on the treacherous shoals and sand bars of the dreaded New Jersey coast. Seldom were the names of either ships or crew members noted; the deserted beaches enveloped them silently and no one knew who mourned the missing. Only here and there did a record survive: the *Caledonia*, wrecked in Amboy Bay in 1715; the sloop *Ellis,* wrecked near Barnegat in about 1775; the British transport destroyed at Egg Harbor Inlet in 1779.

Wrecks mounted in number as sea traffic increased after the Revolution—and beach dwellers increased in number to speak in awe of terrible nights when great vessels smashed to pieces while the vicious winds sang a mournful dirge. Sometimes a single wreck became famed above all others, and, indeed, symbolized all the others.

Such a symbol was the brig *Perseverance,* out of Le Havre and bound for New York with a cargo valued at $400,000. In December, 1815, she "was spoken" by a passing ship and informed that New York was only 200 miles away. The captain, anxious to make port despite the gales buffeting his brig, spread all canvas and drove the *Perseverance* on—onto the sand at Peck's Beach off Beasley's Point.

All but four of the 17 passengers and crew perished, among the dead being a beautiful young French girl, daintily clad and wearing costly jewels. "She was the concentration of all the graces of the female form," said Cape May historian Dr. Maurice Beasley, who witnessed the tragedy. Silks, satins, china and other rich merchandise littered the beach. So ended the days of the brig *Perseverance,* but poets remembered her for years to come.

Some weeks and months the elements seemed determined to destroy all shipping, and in one long storm period between December, 1826, and January, 1827, 200 vessels are said to have been wrecked or stranded along the New Jersey coast. As many as five were said to have piled up on the Absecon Island beach in a single night.

Obviously the fisher folk and others who lived along the beaches picked up what they saw strewn at the tide marks. Why not? They lived crudely, they knew few luxuries, they wore rough clothing. A shipwreck meant food and timbers and a bit of good living, and who could say to whom belonged the spoils? Many a shack came to harbor fine furniture or beautifully engraved silverware—as out of place as champagne at a fish fry, but pleasant nonetheless.

Down along the shore people chuckled at the tale of a little boy overheard in his prayers: "God bless Mam and Pap and all us poor miserable sinners and send us a wreck afore mornin'." Others told the story of a lookout stationed in the cupola of the Absecon Beach church to watch for shipwrecks during services. No Absecon Beacher was going to let the thieves of Brigantine or Barnegat get to the pickings first.

Stories of plunder grew more and more frequent. There were often-repeated horror stories of scoundrels who lurked on the beaches on stormy nights. People whispered of looted bodies, of many left to die while brutal beachcombers stole from stricken vessels. The whispers

187

reached galelike force after the awful night of February 15, 1846.

That night ten vessels ground into the shoals and sand bars between Sandy Hook and Squan Inlet. The names were on every tongue: the *John Minturn*, the *Mary Ellen*, the *Pioneer*, the *Register*, the *Arkansas*, the *New Jersey*, the *Antares*, the *Lotty*, the *Alabama*, the *Van Zandt*. During the next few days 45 bodies washed ashore, and many more than 45 unquestionably died.

Worst of all was the demise of the majestic full-rigged packet ship *John Minturn*, aground off Bay Head. Nearly all the 51 passengers and crew were drowned or frozen as helpless witnesses stood on shore. Occasionally the blinding snow abated enough for the bystanders to see the stricken ship, but every rescue effort failed.

Ugliness flooded along the coast and through all New Jersey immediately after that sad February night. The State Legislature sent a committee down to the coast to question many witnesses, but the committee found only words of commendation for men who risked their lives to save those aboard the ten wrecks. Piracy, they said, was nowhere to be found.

The looting stories died slowly (and for that matter, continued to be revived through the rest of the century). The tales of plunder and preying had to give way to a greater cause for talk—the birth of the Lifesaving Service on the New Jersey coast, fathered by Dr. William A. Newell of New Egypt.

History shows a turning point in man's fight to save his fellows from the sea: August 13, 1839. That day Dr. Newell stood on the strand at Long Beach Island and watched 13 men of the grounded Austrian brig, the *Count Perasto*, perish as they tried to swim a mere 300 yards to safety. The doctor's quick mind figured that it ought to be possible to shoot a line from a shortened blunderbuss across a stranded ship. That line, in turn, could be used to pull a heavy rope to the stricken vessel.

The Monmouth County physician eventually went to Congress and there in 1848 he pushed through an appropriation of $10,000 for lifesaving stations on the East Coast. The first such station, complete with Dr. Newell's lifeline invention, was built on Sandy Hook—and that tiny building still exists (although recently moved to Twin Lights on the Highlands of Navesink).

Simultaneously, Joseph Francis of Toms River perfected a corrugated metal lifeboat and an unsinkable life car. These, used with Newell's life-

188

line, made the saving of lives a science rather than something governed simply by luck and Providence.

Newell's line and Francis's life car proved themselves beyond question on January 12, 1850, when the Scottish brig *Ayrshire,* with 201 immigrants aboard, bilged and lost her masts off Absecon Beach. Volunteer fishermen towed a life car to the beach and shot a lifeline across the *Ayrshire*'s hull, and for two days they worked—finally rescuing all but one of the 201 imperiled passengers.

Paradoxically, the two victims most ravaged by the dark sea off the New Jersey coast met their fate after the Lifesaving Service began. They were the *Powhatan* and the *New Era,* both wrecked in 1854.

The *Powhatan* grounded off Long Beach Island during a freak April snowstorm in the early morning hours of April 18, 1854. Volunteers struggled to get help to the stricken ship, but all day long the passengers fell from the vessel and drowned in twos and threes. Finally, at 5:00 P.M., a great wave swept over the *Powhatan* and drowned all who remained of the 311 passengers and 29 crewmen.

Stupidity, cowardice and ignorance combined aboard the *New Era* on November 13, 1854, to bring frightful death to more than 300 German immigrants off Deal Beach. The *New Era* grounded 500 yards offshore and panic-stricken officers and crewmen fought one another and the passengers for the ship lifeboats. The captain and three crewmen escaped alone in a boat meant for 50 passengers, followed by the terrified screams of women and children they abandoned.

As darkness fell on November 13, more than 400 men, women and children remained on the *New Era.* Rescuers brought 135 ashore November 14, but before the day ended all the remaining passengers had been swept into the waves. At one time so many drowning passengers floated in the sea that an eyewitness said it looked as if "a great flock of ducks had settled on the water."

While loss of life declined spectacularly, thanks to Dr. Newell's fathering of an efficient lifesaving service and to the crews who manned the stations, wrecks seemed to increase. Indeed, Charles Edgar Nash, in his *The Lure of Long Beach Island,* declares that "more ships were stranded here [Long Beach Island] in the spring of 1864 than at any other known time." He lists seven ships wrecked off the island in one 13-day period that spring.

Then, in its report for 1877, the United States Lifesaving Service called specific attention to the dreaded New Jersey coast: Of 129 dis-

189

asters that year between Maine and Florida, 40—or nearly one third—took place on the New Jersey shoals. Most impressive were *L'Amérique,* stranded January 11, 1877, 150 yards off Sea Bright, and the *Rusland,* smashed opposite President U. S. Grant's cottage at Elberon on March 17, that same year.

L'Amérique's crew remained calm, managed to land nine sailors with a line. A life car was towed out to the ship and all passengers and all but three of the crew were rescued. A wrecking crew went aboard and that crew and the vessel's seamen, a total of 200 men, had to be rescued in turn when another storm threatened the stranded vessel February 23, 1877.

The *Rusland* was hurled ashore at the very spot where the bark *Adonis* had gone down March 3, 1859, loaded with grindstones. The *Rusland* struck the old grindstones and broke up as if she had struck a stone wall or the rock-bound coast of Maine. The entire crew and all 204 passengers were saved from the demolished steamer, however.

The saving of lives became commonplace—400 rescued, 200 safely ashore, 150 saved, 95 landed. The headlines became less bold; helpless vessels with no casualties are important; but dead and missing are far more attention-getting. Not that the toll of wrecks didn't mount. Wrecked in the 1880's and 1890's were such big ships as the *Stephen Harding,* the *Castalia,* the *Light Boat,* the *George Taulane,* the *Zetland,* the *Panchito* and scores of others. Off Bay Head between 1878 and 1889 one ship went down every year, four of them in one identical spot.

The era of broken ships and human victims of the storm had ended, by and large, by 1900. The great steamships stood well off shore in the sea lanes, better weather predicting had arrived, stricter regulations forbade captains to celebrate a landing too soon, lighthouses dotted the coast, and ships used power of their own to combat the power of the winds and waves. Then, as the twentieth century advanced, wireless gave man one more reason to laugh at the elements.

There are a few more melancholy happenings to record. No reporting of New Jersey maritime history would be complete without the *Sindia,* wrecked at Ocean City on December 15, 1901. The *Sindia,* six months out of Kobe, Japan, and scant hours away from New York with her hold filled with Christmas goods, ran high on a sand bar as the ship's officers celebrated a long voyage nearly done. The entire crew was brought ashore, but the *Sindia* and her $1,000,000 cargo couldn't be

The *Morro Castle* beached near Asbury Park's Convention Hall

saved. The *Sindia* didn't break up; she sank gradually through the years and is buried in the Ocean City sands—her rusted rudder post still protruding through the beach.

Long Beach Island, scene of so much tragedy and despair in the nineteenth century, knew some twentieth-century disaster, too, but seldom with loss of life. An Italian bark, the *Fortuna,* out of Trampani, Sicily, was driven hard ashore at Ship Bottom during the 1909-1910 winter. The seas claimed no living thing that night; all on board were rescued, including a newly born baby, a pig and a cat.

A December storm drove the United States troopship *Sumner* aground on Long Beach in 1916, but even as swelling seas broke the ship in two,

191

all 299 passengers (bound for the Canal Zone) came ashore safely. The following September the lumber-laden schooner *J. H. Holmes* struck the wreck of the *Sumner* after being abandoned at sea and broke up a week later.

Seeing a ship pounded to pieces is no pretty thing, but to Long Beachers the saddest sight of all was the *Helen J. Seitz*, five-masted schooner aground in fair weather. Careless soundings led the *Helen J.* aground on February 9, 1907, and efforts to refloat the $130,000 beauty failed. Her captain poured oil over her and set her afire at night, and she went to her death in flaming, if wasteful, glory.

Flaming sacrifice was also the lot of many a cargo ship and tanker off the New Jersey coast in World Wars I and II, although no accurate accounting is available. At least 10 merchant ships or tankers are known to have been torpedoed and sunk within a mile of the New Jersey Shore in World War II. The worst of these, from a casualty standpoint, was the torpedoed tanker *R. P. Resor,* sunk by a German submarine February 28, 1942, with only two of the 49 aboard saved.

Wartime wrecks litter the ocean floor off the New Jersey coast, many of them the homes of fish and the anchorage of party boats which seek them. These torpedo-caused casualties are really another story, not part of the record of ships ravaged by raw natural forces—as is also true of the ill-fated *Morro Castle* and *Mohawk*. No tale of New Jersey's coastal wrecks is complete without those two, however.

True enough, a blustering nor'easter had torn along the coast the September week the *Morro Castle* met her fate, but fire—not storms—destroyed the great liner. The Ward Line ship was proceeding to New York when flames burst out at 4:00 A.M. on September 8, 1934, as the *Morro Castle* steamed past Spring Lake. The least that could be said is that no positive leadership manifiested itself; 134 persons died, many of them trying to swim ashore.

The burning vessel drifted slowly north, came head on toward Convention Hall in Asbury Park, then swung around broadside and beached. There she sat for months, even into the next winter. Bodies from the *Morro Castle* came ashore all the way down to Manasquan, and an emergency morgue had to be set up at Sea Girt. Testimony at the hearing indicated the fire had been incendiary in origin, and it was pointed out that a previous attempt had been made to sabotage the ship.

Four months and 16 days later the *Mohawk*, another ship of the Ward Line, left New York harbor on January 24, 1935, headed for Havana

Only two crewmen escaped this torpedoed tanker in 1942

and Vera Cruz with 55 passengers and 110 officers and crewmen aboard. Temperatures dipped down near zero, but in the warm dining hall passengers were merry. Off Sandy Hook some passengers noted that the engines had stopped, but officers assured them all was well.

Meanwhile the *Talisman*, out of New York an hour behind the *Mohawk*, came into the same lane. The Ward liner swung south by west, directly into the path of the onrushing *Talisman*, and the latter's bow drove through the *Mohawk* amidships. Passengers were hurled to the decks by the impact and crewmen struggled to cut lifeboats loose from icy davits. Two hours later the proud *Mohawk* slid into the sea off Bay Head, taking with her 45 passengers and crewmen.

*Morro Castle, Mohawk, New Era, Rusland, L'Amérique, Sindia . . .
Resor, Seitz, Panchito, Zetland, Adonis . . . Great Western, John Min-
turn, Ayrshire, Powhatan . . . George Taulane, Stephen Hardin, Count
Perasto, Manhattan . . . Cornelius Grinnell, Perseverance, Caledonia,
Ellis. . . .*

Toll the bell, call up the ghosts, summon out the lifesavers and the pirates.

The shoals are there still, the winds howl loud, the rain beats down, the waves burst strong. Some night, in the chill darkness, someone will make a mistake: The sea will show him no mercy.

16. Very Seldom Charlie

Coast Guardsmen along the New Jersey Shore live out their service in A, B, C fashion—or, in service lingo, Alpha, Bravo and Charlie. Alpha is that time when boats are under way on duty, Bravo is stand-by status, ready for quick action, and Charlie is the rare period when boats are laid up for major repairs.

Charlie can mean a few days in dry dock, when the pressures of bucking the cruel sea are relaxed. It can be a good time, maybe a time for small talk and relaxation—even while putting a 600-horsepower motor in shape for patrolling the Atlantic Ocean.

These days, however, as one Coast Guardsman sums it up, "We're very seldom Charlie." That, in its twentieth-century way, is a free and backhanded translation of the very old Coast Guard motto, *Semper Paratus*—Always Ready.

Guarding the coast from outside influences is at the moment of minor concern to the 14 Coast Guard stations between Sandy Hook and Cape May. Their biggest job is to guard the people who frequent the coast— very often to guard them against their own follies.

Today every man who can scrape up a down payment on any- thing from an outboard motor to a yacht is a skipper. Small matter whether he knows the rules of the road from a davit; no one examines him for his knowledge and his transgressions are difficult to punish.

From the time the first boat motors roar in April and May until most private boats are laid up in October or November, the Coast Guard is *Semper Paratus,* and then some. Thousands of fishermen in boats of all sizes stream out into the open sea off the New Jersey coast. Nothing surprises a Coast Guardsman; a 14-foot rowboat with a stalled outboard motor 15 miles at sea is commonplace.

This is a relatively new problem, one assuming tremendous pro- portions in the wake of the phenomenal growth of power boating in

195

A Coast Guard craft emerges from surf at Monmouth Beach

the past decade or so. Far too many of the men who now go down to sea in ships (and rowboats) have neither knowledge of, nor respect for, the treacherous ocean or the shallow inland waterways they travel.

The Coast Guard (by that name) dates only from 1915, the year the Revenue Cutter Service and the Lifesaving Service were combined into one service under Treasury Department control. The Revenue Cutter Service began in 1790, but lifesaving, in an organized way, didn't come into being until 1848.

Volunteers manned the early stations until an 1878 reorganization provided for paid crews from September 1 to May 1. By 1900, 42 stations were strung between Sandy Hook and Cape May, many of them on the wildest portions of the New Jersey Shore. Their success was startling. Between 1871 and 1877, for example, out of 6,327 persons aboard 332 vessels wrecked on New Jersey shores, only 55 lost their lives. In 1890, with 62 shipwrecks, not a soul met death.

The men who went forth from the lifeboat stations had to be dedicated; on a salary "not to exceed $700 per annum" (the 1900 rate) a man didn't get rich. Even the superintendent knew no luxury—he received $1,200 a year for supervising 42 stations along the entire coast!

The number of men in a station crew equaled the number of oars required to pull the station's largest boat, normally six oars. An extra man came on the payroll December 1, to give the crew a man on shore to take care of all shore duties. Sickness or death? Lifesaving crews weren't supposed to get sick or die.

Out in the dreaded winter nights went these forerunners of the Coast Guard, out in sleet and snow and gales and freezing rain. "All I know is the regulations book says you have to go out," declared one old-timer. "It doesn't say anything about coming back." Usually they did come back because this was a rugged breed of man—underpaid, under-equipped, poor in everything but raw courage and eagerness to help victims of the sea they loved.

Gradually the shipwreck threat subsided as sailing vessels gave way to steamboats, as navigational aids increased, and eventually as radio came into full use. The number of vessels pounded to pieces on offshore shoals diminished; actually, at the merger of the Revenue Cutter and Lifesaving services in 1915, shipwrecks had ceased to be a major problem off the New Jersey coast.

The Coast Guard's revenue cutters never received a stiffer workout than that experienced during prohibition. Rum runners found this long coastline, once the natural scourge of legitimate shipping, perfect for getting illegal alcohol to a nation far thirstier than it ever had been before the law said it couldn't drink.

Rum runners flaunted their power—on Raritan Bay, on the 127 miles of New Jersey beachfront, in the inlets and coves, through the thoroughfares and lagoons of southern New Jersey. Their powerful boats roared close to shore, kept in constant discipline by ship-to-shore radio.

Prohibition put the Coast Guard in a thankless position. The "rummies" had everything on their side—money, ruthless leaders, political aid, public opinion. The boats of the rum runners made the Coast Guard's "six-bitters" (75-foot cutters) look like scows. "Rummies" ducked off the sea into inlets; drawbridges opened mysteriously without signal for the lawbreaker, then dropped quickly to hold back the Coast Guardsmen while the liquor went safely inland.

Many a big dollar was made along the New Jersey Shore by the "rummies" and their helpers. Pitched battles off the coast between rum runner and Coast Guard brought sounds of gunfire shoreward on the midnight breezes. Even when bigger and faster cutters gave the Coast Guard partial equality on the ocean, the *Semper Paratus* boys couldn't win. The public thought it needed alcohol; who did the Coast Guard think it was, anyway?

Seemingly the Coast Guard lives under a cloud of ingratitude. Few thanked it for doing its duty during prohibition. Many do not thank it today for its unceasing vigilance, aimed at protecting private boatsmen in an area teeming with potential disaster.

"Potential disaster"—the words are used advisedly. New Jersey's Coast Guardsmen are divided into three groups, with headquarters at Sandy Hook, Atlantic City, and Cape May. Each group is busy, but the Sandy Hook contingent covers what may be the most crowded and the most dangerous shipping waters in the world.

Out in those ocean waters off Sandy Hook are the shipping lanes—Ambrose Channel, carrying ocean liners and freighters to the world's busiest port, and Sandy Hook Channel, carrying tankers and freighters to Perth Amboy and the Kill van Kull. Highly trained veteran pilots guide those mighty ships up the relatively narrow channels.

Coincidentally, off Sandy Hook are some of the best fishing grounds in the country—at places like the Mud Hole, Shrewsbury Rocks, Cholera Bank and the "Acid Slick." To these banks stream thousands of party and private boats from Brooklyn, Long Island and a score of spots

The nation's first life-saving station

along the New Jersey Shore. Unfortunately, unlike the pilots aboard the liners, many who man the boats (not including the skippers of party or charter boats, of course) are trained little beyond the point of knowing how to start an outboard motor.

No one says who can fish, when they can fish, what they must know before heading into the open sea. There are estimated to be between 25,000 and 30,000 power boats of all sizes in the Sandy Hook-Seaside Heights area, and on Saturdays and Sundays thousands of boats vie for position in the inlets and on the high seas. As many as 1,600 boats pass out of Manasquan Inlet on a Sunday morning.

Out of what could be chaos the Coast Guard—and such volunteer aids as the Coast Guard Auxiliary and Power Squadrons—must seek some order. They must shepherd even that occasional "pilot" who resents protection or advice. They must do so discreetly and politely; a harsh word to a rowboat pilot (or yachtsman) drifting in front of an oncoming freighter might start a congressional inquiry.

One way to fight trouble is to prevent it. With that in mind, the Coast Guard's two 83-foot cutters in the Sandy Hook group run constant patrol over and around the fishing banks and through the shipping lanes. The cutters patrol for 48 hours running during the busiest times of year, then slip into port (Manasquan for one, Sandy Hook for the other).

Six hours of Bravo layover is the maximum that can be allowed the 83-footers in summer. That allows for minor repairs and maintenance (sparkplugs, oil change). In rough weather, of course, even the six hours is tentative. As a Sandy Hook officer says: "Heaven help the boat crew that needs six hours to get under way in an emergency!"

This routine patrol by the 83-footers, and to a lesser extent the 30- and 40-footers, never makes the headlines. Such public attention is reserved for the great emergencies—as, for example, that of June 20, 1956, when a Super Constellation bound for Venezuela developed engine trouble and headed back for Idlewild Airport. A Coast Guard air escort from Floyd Bennett Field picked up the crippled plane and escorted it north. Thus far, it was all routine.

Then at 1:15 A.M. the Manasquan station was alerted for possible emergency help, and the crew started to warm up the 83-foot cutter. At 1:35 A.M. flashed the word: "The plane has ditched, 35 miles east of Asbury Park." Within four minutes after being ordered into duty, the cutter headed out through Manasquan Inlet for the disaster scene.

Soon after, the Sandy Hook 83-footer was alerted and for the next 20 or 30 minutes orders came in to dispatch 40-footers from various points. The Manasquan 83-foot cutter arrived on the ditching scene at 4:24 P.M. and other boats arrived within the next hour to take up the apparently hopeless search for the 74 passengers and crew members aboard the missing air liner. Several boats were recalled, but the search went on all day, through the night and through the following day.

Nothing ever was found except some clothing and personal articles, but the Coast Guard didn't stop looking until it became obvious no one had survived. Nevertheless, ordinary work had to go on. Within two days all the excitement was gone—replaced by routine patrol and by a wide range of unspectacular duties. Very seldom are Alpha and Bravo status spectacular.

Speedy rescue vessels at Sandy Hook

Much goes on in and around those neat white "Lifeboat Stations" so familiar to summer shore visitors. Coast Guardsmen's duties include search and rescue (this may get their names in the papers), enforcement of laws (this makes them unpopular), and maintaining aids to navigation—buoys and channel markers, for example—in tiptop shape.

Coast Guardsmen are very seldom Charlie, because they have so much to do. When major jobs at sea are done, they must attend to a multitude of beach duties.

They must keep their boats ready to roar at a moment's notice. They must keep electronic gear in constant readiness. They must regulate the loading of explosives on Navy ships at the Leonardo pier. They must aid in maintaining port security. They must supply personnel and equipment for the lightships and lighthouses along the New Jersey Shore. They must patrol channels. They must make boardings and inspect small craft.

Help comes from the Coast Guard Auxiliary, an outgrowth of World War II, and from Power Squadrons. The Auxiliary and Power Squadrons, both composed of qualified New Jersey Shore boatsmen, conduct classes for motor boat enthusiasts. (One recent class at Manasquan High School drew 250 persons.) The Auxiliary also conducts courtesy examinations of boats to check equipment and issues a decal of approval (something like an automobile inspection sticker).

Two periods of time particularly plague the Coast Guard—April and May, when boatsmen are getting the bugs out of their craft, and August and September, when fishing is best offshore. Still, Coast Guard action is a year-around matter. In an average year for the Sandy Hook group alone, as many as 2,300 boats are boarded for inspection and as many as 1,200 calls for assistance are answered.

This activity threatens to engulf the thinly spread ranks of the Coast Guard, now operating much of the time with station complements at 75 per cent or lower of authorized personnel. Coast Guard recruits are not as readily available as they once were, but it is interesting to note that at Cape May, New Jersey plays a significant role in preparing "boots" for action.

Cape May's receiving center is the only Coast Guard recruit training camp now in operation east of the Mississippi. Here 12 weeks of training get as many as 1,200 men ready at once in a rigorous program designed to give the "boots" both theory and practical sea experience. The base, originally a World War I Naval Training Station, has been a Coast Guard boot camp since 1948.

Out of Cape May go the "boots"-turned-Coast Guardsmen. They go to patrol in the frigid Arctic waters, to far-off weather patrol, to maintain buoys and beacons in many harbors and, if war comes, to man the landing boats on distant shores. In philosophy and spirit the crews aboard the sleek 83-footers are one with the volunteers of days gone by.

No matter what else they learn at Cape May, the boots know well the meaning of *Semper Paratus*. They are Always Ready because they mean to be Coast Guardsmen, who will rest only when the sea no longer seeks to victimize those who flirt with it. They seldom sit still; their lives are strenuous, ranging from Alpha to Bravo and (very seldom) Charlie.

See It as Few Do . . .

The sand and the waves and the sunlight are the tinsel and sequins on the Jersey Shore, but there is more to the shore than glamour.

There is the Inland Waterway, coursing down through bays and sounds and inlets and sedgy islands of the Shore's back yards. Yachtsmen—and adventurers in rowboats—know the Waterway, and they are lucky.

Biggest of the "back yards" is Barnegat Bay, an area where legend and fact are blended, an area where past and present merge on the pathway to the future.

If the Waterway and Barnegat Bay are several shades away from beachfront glamour, even farther removed are the men who go down to sea to fish—both those who must fish for a living and those who fish because they consider it a sport to arise before dawn and ride seaward on a rocking party boat.

Down on the ocean-front sand itself is excitement unconnected with the heralded amusements of boardwalk and nightclub. This is the search for treasure as God made it—the treasure of gnarled and knobby and strangely shaped seashells, the treasure of shore birds on the wing. The sophisticated might scorn it; the knowing find calm and satisfaction in getting everything from the beach that is there to find.

Glamour? Who needs glamour?

The Inland Waterway cuts through Ventnor's neat back yards

17. Inland Waterway

Traveling the Inland Waterway from Manasquan Inlet to Cape May forces a man to recognize that there is far more to the New Jersey Shore than its heralded beachfront glamour. At times this can be a bit disillusioning—something like discovering that your prom date is wearing loafers rather than silver slippers.

The Waterway, after all, touches the back yards—the fishing piers, the marshy islands, the rough fishing shacks out on the sedges. It is a place for those who like a boat under their feet or a sail over their heads. It is a place teeming with potential excitement—more excitement, for many, than is offered by the party-dressed boardwalk.

New Jersey's 116 miles of Inland Waterway is but a small part of the ocean bypass leading all the way south to Florida (or, in season, all the way north to New Jersey). The section between Manasquan Inlet and Cape May with its twistings and turnings and its shallowness is by no means the best stretch of the Waterway—but, like most byways, it offers fascinations not found where speed is possible. And to the yachtsman, it offers protection from the wildness of the ocean.

The Inland Waterway has a formal name—the Intracoastal Waterway—but rare is the person who gets that formal. Many a veteran traveler calls the New Jersey section "The Ditch," or worse; a boating expert called it "a muddy nightmare" in a 1956 article in *Sports Illustrated* magazine. He dwelt on the shallowness of the Waterway—often less than five feet.

Veteran travelers can be wrong—particularly those who view life merely as getting from one place to another as quickly as possible. For thousands of persons in no hurry the Inland Waterway is a delight.

Certainly "The Ditch" must be known to be appreciated. There are several ways to know it vicariously—with books such as Fessenden Blanchard's cruising guides or the delightfully informal *We Took to*

Cruising by Talbot and Jessica Hamlin. Armchair trips are also possible through imaginative use of the cruising guides put out by the gasoline companies or the official charts issued by the United States Coast and Geodetic Survey.

Dream travel always leaves much to be desired. Nary a book or a chart will show how the gulls sweep in to grab a bit of food tossed in the air. Nor can an armchair view encompass snowy egrets standing in the marshes or the drama of a thunder and lightning storm flashing in the west. Neither can vicarious travel convey the comradery to be found on the Waterway.

The best way, then, is to course the Waterway by boat—yours, a friend's or, if you're a lucky newspaperman, aboard the *Navigator*. The *'Gator* is a trim 46-foot cabin cruiser owned by the State Department of Conservation and Economic Development and used to patrol that part of the Inland Waterway within New Jersey.

Riding the *Navigator* is a joy under any circumstances; she's a good ship—complete with galley, four bunks and some of the comforts of home (in case any very important people such as legislators want to inspect the Waterway). The *'Gator* is big and roomy, and her twin engines make her move along briskly.

Still, it takes a skipper to make a boat come alive. Aboard the State's boat, that skipper is Captain Raymond Huber.

Quiet, but friendly, in the distinctive manner of most veterans of the New Jersey Shore, Ray Huber has lived on or near the Waterway all his life. He has worked on the Inland Waterway since 1927, when he "shipped on" a State job at the age of 19. He has held every type of job on the Ditch; perhaps no one knows this inland sea road better or loves it more than Captain Ray Huber.

Everybody on the Waterway knows the captain—the bridge tenders, the yachtsmen, the clammers, the skippers who gather on the porches of the yacht clubs. Most hail him simply, "Hi, U-Boat." Captain Huber explains with a grin:

"That's a hangover from when I was a kid on the Atlantic City docks. We were all excited over the German submarines off the coast, so I never minded when the boys changed 'Huber' to 'U-Boat.'"

New Jersey's section of the Inland Waterway begins where boats duck into Manasquan Inlet off the Atlantic Ocean. Fessenden Blanchard, recognized as the guide to the waterways, calls Manasquan Inlet "first class, easy to enter or leave except during an off-shore blow." Through this inlet each year pass thousands of boats whose skippers are pleased to be safe from the treacherous sea.

When Captain Huber heads the *Navigator* between Manasquan's stone jetties, riders get the same sense of being introduced to the Inland Waterway that thousands of small boatsmen experience every year. Past the jetties, through the draw of the upraised railroad bridge, under the Brielle highway span and southward through the Manasquan Canal to Bay Head goes the *'Gator*.

Captain Huber keeps the powerful engines of his craft throttled down through the canal, and, indeed, doesn't open up until the boat slips past the draw at Mantoloking. The surging wake of the ship at full speed makes it evident why skilled pilots throttle down in narrow or heavily populated areas; waves rippling off to shore from such a wake would be enough to smash a boat tied up at dockside.

Below Mantoloking the full glory of Barnegat Bay stretches before the viewer. A stimulating spot, this bay can be treacherous for the unwary. Charts show why. Often shoals give less than a foot of water on either side of the channel. A first trip is no time for speed.

A first trip is a time to study the channel markers. Boatsmen should know them well (although there is ample evidence that many of the new breed of skippers are less interested in safety than horsepower). Channel markers serve exactly the same purpose as highway signs; on the Waterway boats keep to the right, as on highways. The markers—combined with common courtesy—can make the Inland Waterway as safe as a back yard.

Captain Huber shares the worries about the Inland Waterway (and all New Jersey's tidal waters) that are common among thoughtful boatsmen and the state officials charged with keeping the waters safe. "There are just too many boats," says this Waterway veteran. "Thirty years ago there were few boats. Now everybody is his own captain. Why, I think you could walk across this bay—boat to boat—on a Sunday."

The boating fever continues to rise, heightened by the growing popularity of man-made lagoons leading off Barnegat Bay. Between 1950 and 1955, 30 additional miles of waterfront were created along such lagoons in coast counties and by 1962 an estimated additional 60 miles are projected. Figuring 100 waterfront lots per mile, and a boat to every lot, that will be 9,000 additional boats which didn't exist in 1950—just in those lagoons alone!

Right now those lagoons and developments along rivers leading to the bay have caused terrific marking and dredging problems for the State. Every channel must be designated with triangles (to starboard) and squares (to port) to guide the sailors home.

Fortunately New Jersey no longer is responsible for dredging and marking the main stem of the Waterway. The federal government took over that responsibility in 1953; now the Coast Guard does the marking and the Army Engineers the dredging. Both of these had been State responsibilities since the major part of the Waterway was opened to traffic in 1915.

Relinquishing control of the Intracoastal Waterway has permitted the State to spend more time on the tributary channels—and that is a big job, a job too long delayed. In addition to dredging, the channels must be marked. Flashing beacons must be put at entrances, and more than 200 barrel buoys in the channels and 3,800 channel stakes (each bearing a triangle or square marker) must be maintained.

There are many tributaries worth exploring off Barnegat Bay— Metedeconk River, Toms River, Forked River, Oyster Creek and so on. One especially appealing is Forked River, where both a State Marina (berthing spot) and the headquarters of the channel marking and maintenance crew are located.

New Jersey's first marina was completed at Forked River in 1934 and now has 108 berths available. On the east end of the marina is the headquarters for the crews charged with maintaining New Jersey's part of the Inland Waterway. Often the *Navigator* is tied up here, particularly when the State's unique work boat—the *Transit III*—is out in the channels.

This third craft in a line of State work boats would win no beauty contest, but she does an important job. Seventy feet long with a 20-foot beam, the latest *Transit* has been on the Waterway since 1951. Her shallow draft (four feet) permits her to move almost anywhere and her bulky shape has been designed to carry everything her eight-man crew needs to mark and maintain the channels.

Forked River is diverting, but nothing on the Inland Waterway quite matches the atmosphere on and about Barnegat Bay. Boats move by constantly, almost without variance showing the greatest courtesy both for one another and for tiny rowboats anchored beside the channel. Town after town lies low on the horizon to seaward; westward, green woods edge down to the bay, the treetops broken only by villages huddled beneath church steeples.

Transit III is the workboat of Inland Waterway crews

Barnegat Light dominates a broad area of the bay. The red and white shaft is as much a beacon for Inland Waterway tourists as it has been for ocean-going vessels for a century. As the light falls behind to the northeast, the *Navigator* slips under the new high-level bridge under construction at Manahawkin, moves beyond the end of Long Beach Island and into the choppy waters of Little Egg Inlet.

This inlet can be rough, since it is not really an inlet at all, but rather a broad, open stretch between Long Beach Island and the nearly deserted islands of Great Bay. The Atlantic Ocean sweeps through the inlet in power, forcing the Waterway Channel to hug the blunt peninsula on which Little Egg Coast Guard station stands.

Crossing Little Egg Inlet reveals a new facet of the Waterway, something to be encountered all the way south to Cape May. Now on all

209

sides are seen the vast numbers of low-lying sedge islands through which the Inland Waterway twists and turns like a constantly coiling and uncoiling snake.

Spread over these flatlands 10 miles northwest of Atlantic City is the Brigantine National Wildlife Refuge—16,000 acres of fresh-water ponds and tidal marshes set aside to protect the natural life threatened by development everywhere on the New Jersey Shore. The wildness of the refuge is in startling contrast with the towers of Atlantic City, shadowy in the distance.

Atlantic City is a good first-night tie-up for anyone who has been poking in and around the Waterway, bent on exploration rather than speed. The Atlantic City seen by the water traveler is sharply different from Boardwalk views familiarly associated with the famed city of amusement.

Many boatsmen tie up at the Atlantic City marina (which will have berths for approximately 350 boats when finished). Other yachtsmen tie up at private docks along lagoons leading into the back "yard" of Atlantic City. Here there is no tinsel or gaudiness; here truly is a queen in comfortable old clothes. The waterfront looks more like a New England fishing village than the supposedly sophisticated city of gaiety.

Yachtsmen who know their navigation find their way to the Tuna Club, which claims the largest boat club membership in the world. The clubhouse has handsome appointments, but skippers love best its broad porch overlooking the lagoon. There they relive their days on the decks.

At the Tuna Club—or at any of the 20 to 25 yacht clubs along the shore where yachtsmen tie up—tales of giant catches are swapped. These fish never get away, and most of them are larger than any in the sea. One skipper in describing a huge haul may begin: "You remember that white whale? That Moby Dick? Well. . . ."

Next morning, at an hour whose earliness depends on how much larger than "that white whale" the fish eventually become on the Tuna Club porch, skippers slip out of the Atlantic City harbor and idle downstream again. They try to reach the railroad bridge between 20 minutes and 30 minutes after any hour, because those are the only minutes when the bridge will be open.

The State boat captain tells a beginner that 23 of the 29 bridges between Bay Head and Cape May are tended—and the beginner can

210

judge for himself that bridge tenders are not chosen for fleetness of foot. Still, the job gets done. Out on the Waterway few chafe about such things as slowly opening draws—nor should they. If the beginner happens to have been one of the thousands of motorists caught by an open drawbridge while a single yacht went through on an August Sunday, he is not unduly sympathetic.

Just south of Atlantic City is Ventnor, whose back "yard" must be judged the most appealing on the New Jersey Shore. Good-looking houses overlook the Waterway (called Inside Thorofare at this point) and trees rise behind the bulkheads. Many New Jersey Shore areas claim to be the real "Venice of America." Ventnor comes closest in appearance, at least.

On and on the *Navigator* moves, down past Ocean City, past Strathmere and Sea Isle City and Townsend's Inlet, across Great Sound and through Great Channel and Dung Thorofare to Grassy Sound and Richardson Sound.

Everything is personal down in this Cape May back-yard meadowland. Names of islands and thoroughfares and sounds are those of long-gone discoveries or storytellers. Interestingly enough, down here bays are called "sounds" all the way from Ocean City to Cape May (excepting only Ludlam Bay). This is different country—birds of all kinds, including the beautiful egret, fly or stalk over the flats where wild rice billows in the soft breeze.

The twists and turns through Cape May's islands make it clear why yachtsmen call this waterway a "road." The wake of the boat is clear far to the rear as it curves gracefully around and between the sedges. At one particularly twisting point Captain Huber looks back at the wake and remarks:

"We call this 'Snake Alley.' You'll find it on the charts as 'Crook Horn.' "

Wildwood's Otten Harbor is a must for an exploring visitor, although a cruising yachtsman usually passes it by. Northbound, he has just left Cape May; southbound, he is too close to Cape May to stop. If curious, however, he'll at least have a look at Otten's Harbor—and if he's lucky enough to arrive when a kicking ocean wind keeps boats to harbor, he'll see Otten's alive with the big commercial fishing fleet berthed there.

The *Navigator* slips in and out of Otten's Harbor, glides through Jarvis Sound and soon is inside Cape May's splendid big harbor, un-

Captain Ray Huber, veteran pilot of the *Navigator*

questionably one of the best small boat anchorages on the Atlantic coast.

Boats of all sizes swarm through the harbor, many of the larger craft being based at the Coast Guard training station at the head of the harbor. Fishing vessels tie up here or stop for fuel and supplies; often three or four of the big menhaden fishing boats stop by for a brief respite from the sea.

Most boatsmen tie up at Scotty's Warren (more formally the Cape May Boat Marina). There is a quick and easy friendliness, a pleasant inspection of gear and a spirited interchange of chatter. These are people at home with one another, joined together by their love of the water and their familiarity with the Inland Waterway.

Cape May is a vital stopover on the Waterway, one of the most important between New York and Florida. Close by is the Cape May Canal, completed in 1942 to link the harbor and Delaware Bay. Four miles through that canal and 55 miles up the Delaware is the Chesapeake and Delaware Canal, inland route to Chesapeake Bay.

Eventually anyone bitten by the boating bug to the extent that he contracts an incurable disease travels up the Delaware to the C. and D. Canal and on to the South. This trip on the *Navigator* is an exposure instead of a real bite, an effort to experience in some way the symptoms of the boating fever. So, instead of the restless moving south, the *Navigator* reverses herself and takes the visitor home to Bay Head.

Much later the visitor finds in the library a book by Talbot and Jessica Hamlin. He feels a kinship with them when they reminisce about some thoughts they had as they lay over at Scotty's Warren during a four-day blow:

"Sometimes we think all boat dwellers, ourselves included, of course, are just a little mad—mad by the standards of the world. It is a charming madness, and that is one of the common bonds of those afloat; it is why they understand each other."

Perhaps, they conclude, "It is the land people who are mad and we on our boats are truly sane." It's possible, you know.

Crabbing in Barnegat Bay

18. Barnegat Bay

Barnegat Bay is at that point in time where its future as a well-populated—perhaps typically overcrowded—New Jersey Shore resort is clear. Yet, even as new housing developments and lagoons and boat basins come to the bay, much of the charm and romance of this great body of water remains for those who seek something other than slick modernity.

Five to ten years ago the bay might have been looked upon as one of the last frontiers along the coast. Today, gaudy sign after gaudy sign proclaims that the bulldozer and the easy payment plan have brought summer dwellings to land that muskrats not long ago called home. Barnegat Bay has ceased to be a frontier: It merely gives that impression at times because the past is so near at hand.

The merging of past and future has been, more or less, "as ca'm as a clam at low tide," to borrow a Barnegat expression. There are those real estate men who claim that they discovered Barnegat Bay (they hint such in their roadside signs extolling the merits of their developments). Tell them that the bay is merely returning to long-past vitality and you'll be rewarded with the look usually reserved for outlanders.

Barnegat Bay's sudden upsurge in popularity is explained in many ways. Many attribute it almost entirely to the Garden State Parkway. That's too easy an explanation, even though the Parkway is an important factor. Much more to the point is the tremendous rise in boating interest since World War II—an interest combined with enough easy money to put a boat within reach of thousands who once merely daydreamed about a little craft of their own.

Anchorages on the ocean side long ago became crowded and expensive. The answer, developers figured, was to get new anchorages, develop the land side, to cut up the marshes, dig out lagoons, throw up little houses, appeal to the boating enthusiasts. The plan worked; as

215

Where the Metedeconk River and Barnegat Bay become one

one real estate man near Forked River puts it: "They buy a lot and put up a house just so they can tie up their boat."

The number of boats along Barnegat Bay has to be seen to be believed. There are literally thousands of new boats—rowboats, sailboats, small craft with inboard or outboard motors, and on up to big cruisers. It's a common sight to see a cruiser (or maybe two cruisers) tied up in a lagoon in front of a house not much larger—and certainly cheaper—than the boat.

This fundamental love of the water and the sport available on the 70-odd square miles of water is the element which persists on Barnegat Bay. It is the element which Gustave Kobbé recognized in 1889 when he noted in his charming little book, *Jersey Coast and Pines:*

"Barnegat Bay is all sport. In summer, hundreds of little vessels scud over its waters to the fishing grounds near the inlet; and on the early mornings in winter, the figures of gunners may be seen dimly outlined against the horizon as they row their sneak boxes out of the creeks toward some sedgy island or point."

Add some water skiers, a huge number of power boats, fleets of slick sailboats, some late-model bathing suits (and some late models to wear them), and what Mr. Kobbé said in 1889 is in large measure valid for today. The boats still scud, the fishermen still go out, the hunters in fall and winter still wander out in the sedge islands in the hope of bagging some brant or broadbills or black duck.

The surprising thing is not that developers have finally turned their eyes and power machines to Barnegat Bay, but rather that it took them so long to catch up to its evident charms.

Barnegat Bay has been in the written literature of the land since 1609, when the keeper of the log aboard Henry Hudson's *Half Moon* wrote: ". . . we came to a great lake of water, as we could judge it to be, being drowned land which made its rise like islands, which was in length 10 leagues. The mouth of the lake had many shoals, and the sea breaks upon them as it is cast out of the mouth of it. And from that lake or bay the land lies north by east and we had a great stream out of the bay."

The man at the log showed himself to be a bit of a real estate man at heart, too, when he added: "This is a very good land to fall in with and a pleasant land to see." That's what the home sellers of the present day are trying to get over in somewhat lengthier prose.

Barnegat Bay has some elastic boundaries. Some say it stretches all the way from Manasquan Canal at the north to Beach Haven Inlet on the south. Others see Barnegat as ending down near Gunning River where it meets Manahawkin Bay. Most, however, agree that the water between the canal at the north and the Manahawkin-Ship Bottom causeway on the south is the most logical area of the bay.

The bay is indeed very close to being a quiet salt lake. Down its eastern side are the long bars of ocean-front sand—Barnegat Peninsula, Island Beach and Long Beach Island—which ward off the potential violence of the Atlantic. Only Barnegat Inlet prevents the sand bar from being continuous all the way from Bay Head down to Beach Haven Inlet.

Barnegat Inlet is the key to the bay behind the sand islands. Incredible amounts of water pour through the inlet every time the tide changes. One writer estimated that 2,000,000,000 cubic feet of water swirl in and out of the inlet every day—an amount three times, he said, the volume of water flowing from the Hudson River watershed in the same period of time.

Left to its own devices, nature probably would eliminate Barnegat Inlet entirely and would cut a new inlet through Long Beach Island farther south. That's the classic way of inlets, always shifting. The fact that Barnegat Inlet has lasted at least 350 years is both something of a phenomenon and a tribute to man's determined, if not always effectual, efforts to control the tides.

There are those who theorize that some wild night soon nature will have its way, cutting through a new inlet in a matter of hours, then returning methodically to silt in Barnegat Inlet. This might well have happened years ago except for more than $2,000,000 spent since 1925 for jetties and dikes to keep within boundaries the sea surging through the inlet at the foot of Barnegat Light. Whether a new inlet happens or not, the bay is oriented in large measure toward Barnegat Inlet.

Ever since mariners have sailed off the New Jersey Shore they have both loved and feared the bay inside the inlet, their love or fear usually in direct ratio to the amount of water their vessels drew. Very early, charts warned of the flats inside the bay; today yachtsmen are warned to stick to the well-marked channels or risk stranding on shoals and sand bars a foot or less below the surface.

Nevertheless, boatsmen now hold Barnegat Bay in high regard. They know that the inland waterway channels will handle most of their

218

Island Heights, called "Pearl of. Resorts" by John Wanamaker

palatial yachts, and they know that boats designed specifically for Barnegat Bay, such as the sneak box and the garvey, will negotiate safely all except the shallowest flats. And even if a sneak box or garvey nudges up on a shoal, it can easily be refloated.

The bay has changed only moderately through the years. Very early maps showed it to be about four miles at its widest point, between Barnegat Inlet and Waretown, the same as today. Since recorded time it has been filled with low-lying sedge islands ("sedge" from the fact that many of the islands have grown from sedge grass which only partially rotted and through the years caught debris to build up islands).

Early settlers plotted the tricky bay, first in their minds and then on

219

crude charts. Today charts, bearing the same hard-won knowledge of those pioneers, are available at the nearest marine gas station, warning boats drawing more than four feet to stay in the carefully defined channels. The Inland Waterway through the bay, started in 1908 and fully dredged eight years later, cuts through the bay from Manasquan Canal southward.

Barnegat Bay is, of course, salt water, but it is characterized all along the land side by fresh-water cedar creeks trickling into it from the upland pine forests. These are the streams often visible to motorists along the Garden State Parkway—slow-moving, cedar-colored (and cedar-smelling) streams. They move to meet the bay at Metedeconk Creek, Toms River, Forked River, Cedar Creek, Oyster Creek, to name a few spots. Salt water mingles freely with fresh far up the creeks. Toms River (the town), for example, is at the point where tide water comes all the way up the river from the bay.

Tidewater towns like Toms River and Waretown and Barnegat assumed colonial importance, sending fleets of vessels into the Atlantic Ocean laden with lumber and farm products from inland. Sea captains and their families frequented the bay villages—real, ocean-going sea captains who bucked the waves (some of Barnegat's "captains" today hold a courtesy title, somewhat like the colonels of Kentucky).

The land side of Barnegat Bay in those days held the utmost importance. Conversely, few went to Island Beach or Long Beach except possibly to hunt. During the Revolution, Barnegat Bay's sailors sallied out to harry British shipping, skipping blithely back through an inlet in their shallow-bottomed boats and making their way home through well-known "thoroughfares" or "slews" (sluiceways). Woe to the British captain who risked the shoals and flats without a local pilot.

The passing years brought a decrease in prestige to the land side. The loss of Cranberry Inlet in 1812 intensified the isolation and by Civil War time, the sea captains began either to move elsewhere or to turn to relatively tame inland water shipping.

Railroads doomed the sloops and schooners in Toms River and the other bay ports, but subtly railroads wrought the change which in the long run will mean most to the bay—they brought in seekers of recreation. Hunters and fishermen came down to grow vacation beards and to swap stories in the old inns and hotels and to enjoy the excellent bay fishing and waterfowl shooting.

Others, particularly Philadelphians, came for genteel enjoyment of

220

the beach. They depended on inland boatsmen to ferry them across the broad reaches of the bay to the island sands on the edge of the Atlantic. A few came to vacation on the bay side—notably at Island Heights on Toms River, where in 1878 Methodist camp meetings started and where in 1903 John Wanamaker of store fame built a summer resort for his employees. Mr. Wanamaker called it the "Pearl of Resorts."

Naturally, just as simply as two men in sailboats on a broad expanse of water means a contest, yacht racing came to Barnegat Bay. It started most informally, with one sea captain racing another in their catboats. Soon businessmen from Philadelphia owned catboats, too, and since businessmen-turned-sportsmen have ever needed organization, the Toms River Yacht Club was organized in about 1870. Its purpose: to promote official races to prove the fleetness of the boats rather than depending on the speed of a racer's anecdotes.

Island Heights had a yacht club in the late 1880's, and by 1900 clubs had been formed at Seaside Park and Bay Head. Today there are a dozen or more clubs along the bay.

Club racing gave fame to Barnegat Bay boats. Some of the fastest catboats in the world sailed the bay, augmented later by noted racing sloops known as "tuckups" and that unique Barnegat Bay boat, the sneak box. The latter, developed before the Civil War, reached its peak of perfection in the hands of C. Howard Perrine of Barnegat. Mr. Perrine died in June of 1956, just as another season was getting under way.

Today yacht racing on Barnegat Bay is of supreme importance. Sneak boxes are generally reserved for younger boys and girls, but all types of sailing boats skim over the bay all summer in formal or informal races. The bay is said to have the second largest fleet of yachting boats in the country.

While sailing is picturesque and cabin cruisers heading out to deep-sea fishing are glamorous, less spectacular uses of small craft make up the bulk of bay boating interests. The little boats, powered by small engines, get fishermen out in the bay to where the weakfish and blowfish and flounders and fluke are biting. Often they serve as well to cruise through narrow and shallow thoroughfares on trips to show visitors the bay.

Barnegat Bay has other lures besides boating and fishing. For one thing, it is easier to swim in the bay than in the rolling ocean. Lagoon-side or bayside docks permit diving into the bay waters, a sport unknown on the ocean. Water skiing is also popular on the generally calm bay.

The bay offers opportunities for anyone to fish off the banks, unlike the ocean, where only an expert can cast into the waves. Youngsters particularly enjoy the good crabbing, and some amateurs join professionals in seeking the splendid Barnegat Bay clams resting out on the flats.

Summer visitors who like local "flavor" have the opportunity to get it in those areas still stubbornly resisting real estate developers. Towns like Barnegat and Waretown have a charm based largely on antiquity. In these areas many weatherbeaten buildings offer the photographer opportunity to test his skills.

Off the beaten path in Waretown and Barnegat are clam depots, where the clammers sell their cherrystones and little necks—sometimes as many as four million clams are purchased by a single buyer in one year. Clammers are like everyone else: Questioned about their work they talk readily—a fact which few summer visitors ever fail to find "quaint."

In startling contrast to the newness, and therefore unproved quality, of the present-day developments are some of the old churches found along the bay. Surrounded by cemeteries, wherein headstones carry Barnegat Bay names generations old, these time-worn places of worship are reminders of almost-forgotten days. One good example is the Friends Meeting House established in Barnegat in 1767. The Quaker church rests under high trees beside the main road leading in from the bay.

Near Lanoka Harbor, in the midst of an area where builders talk freely of 1,500 or 3,000 new homes in any of several developments, is the Good Luck Church at Murray Grove. This colonial church, built in 1760, is where the Reverend John Murray in 1770 conducted the first Universalist Church service in America.

Simplicity always has been all about for those who seek it at Barnegat Bay. Take, for example, still-existent place names. Nice and simple and descriptive place names: Clam Island, Oyster Creek, Sloop Point, Applegate Cove, Toms River—all of them reminiscent of people and things and happenings.

There are family names which appear again and again—in graveyards, on store fronts, in modern, thriving business, even in the names of towns and villages. These are typical family names of Barnegat Bay: Woodmansee and Applegate and Salter and Eno; Perrine and Cranmer and Osborn and Soper. Time isn't likely to change quickly this aspect of the bay area.

Time will not quickly eradicate its natural beauty, either, although the onrushing tide of building seems determined to try.

222

A house, a boat, a bayside lagoon, can add up to happiness

In the marshlands—such as the great stretches near Waretown and Barnegat—tall reeds grow, their stalkiness relieved in August by the native marsh mallow and the larger rose marsh mallow, sedge-land flowers whose wide, fragile blossoms of pink and white speckle the land. Muskrats tunnel through the sedges in the winter. In autumn, the crescent-breasted lark returns and much of the time the snipe, the sandpipers, the warblers and the blackbirds frequent the meadows. Sometimes the solemn blue heron stalks the water lapping the shores.

The upper part of the bay, the arc from Mantoloking around westward to Bay Head and down through Metedeconk toward Toms River, has been rather well settled for 20 to 30 years. Still, even in that upper part of the bay, wide areas of marshland or woodland continue to defy human interlopers. The lower part of the bay, down toward Waretown and Barnegat, is just now in transition from the very simple past to the more complicated present.

Sophistication and mahogany planking and aluminum masts and gorgeous yachts have been moving into the bay for some time, but the balance as of now probably remains just a bit on the side of nature and the native. How long that can last is anybody's guess.

Indeed, there is a saying that "Once the natives used to sit on the fence and watch the strangers; now the strangers sit on the fence and watch the natives."

19. Fishing for Fun

Lights twinkle on in four homes in Essex and Morris Counties as Shorty, Doc, Al and Red climb out of bed on Sunday at 4:00 A.M. or so, with an alertness they can't possibly match on weekdays when they arise at 7:00 A.M. for work. This is different; this is the day Shorty, Doc, Al and Red have set aside to pit their wits against the wary fish in the Atlantic Ocean.

Elsewhere the same morning—in New York, in Philadelphia, in Newton, in Vineland and hundreds of other spots—other men (and a few women) also get ready for deep-sea fishing with the fumbling heavy-handedness accompanying the ritual of getting-out-without-disturbing-the-family. Already dawn pinkens the east, and the time has come to hurry.

Down to the shore the early risers stream. Some spread out and head for the party boats and the charter boats berthed at nearly 40 basins and docks between Raritan and Delaware Bays. Many hustle to rent some of the five or six thousand rowboats tied up at a hundred liveries along the coast. Others go to seek good spots on a score of fishing piers, to get elbow room on a shore river bank or a rock jetty, to cast in the surf before the bathing suit crowd arrives hours later.

Together they form a mighty army engaging in what very well may be New Jersey's biggest participation sport—salt-water fishing. There is no positive way of knowing exactly how many fishermen seek the blues and weaks and porgies and stripers and cod and other fine-finned friends, but reliable experts figure as many as 1,000,000 persons fish along the New Jersey Shore during the year.

The hardy ones fish all year, of course; men who wouldn't walk to the corner store for a newspaper on a Tuesday night in January lest they catch cold, find health values (or some value, at least) in riding a boat out to seek cod the next frigid Saturday or Sunday morning. However,

A surf fisherman finds riches beyond the value of his catch

these year-arounders are but the rear guard engaged in holding action; the main army doesn't appear until June, July and August, when summer residents are about.

These are the vacation months, and fishermen haunt the docks and piers and jetties. Coincidentally, the fish are pleasantly cooperative; June, July and August just happen to be the best fishing months. No one in his right mind can declare that the fish aren't doing their scaly best to be cordial.

Shorty and Doc and Al and Red enjoy most these summer months (although they also are among the wintertime cod seekers). They are old-timers, old-timers enough and affluent enough to hire a charter boat for their very own occasionally. Usually, however, they board one of the party or "head" (so much a head) boats to join 50 to 100 others for a day of sport and/or seasickness.

As old-timers, Shorty and the gang invariably go to the same dock, board the same boat, speak the same greeting to the same captain, rig their same gear in the same way, share the same happy ease they've shared so many times before.

"Shorty," says Doc every Sunday, "you get over on the other side with the rookies, unless you want to stay over here with us professionals and bait my hook." Shorty does the same slow burn he's been doing since 1935, and snorts: "Ah, you guys is just along to open the beer."

Meanwhile, out on the docks as sailing time approaches (anywhere from 6:30 to 8:00 A.M. in summer months), activity proceeds with orderly tumult. Music blares from loud-speakers, refreshment stands dispense breakfasts meant for cast-iron stomachs, and tackle shops do a lively business. Mates from party boats try politely to steer newcomers to a particular boat. Each arriving party totes enough food and drink to last a week. Everywhere there is conversation.

Old-timers (whose old-timeness may have started last week) lament the rookies. Says one: "You hook a fish. Them amateurs stand around with their feet in their mouths, get you all tangled up. I lost 300 yards of line that way last year. No more. I just yell, 'Coming through!' and I come through." That evidently means something to his listeners. They nod sympathetically, at any rate.

Finally sailing time is at hand, sailing time in summer being when the head boats have enough "heads" and in off season being when all are aboard who're coming aboard. Off go the party boats in more or less regular procession, since a captain doesn't dare delay his fishermen much beyond the time the first boat slips away.

Out chug the boats, loaded with hope and eagerness. Shorty and Doc and Al and Red maybe have a beer or, in the kindly way of men who recognize kindred souls, help a wide-eyed little boy straighten out his gear. Through the inlets and out from the bays swarm the party boats, out to the deep holes and the sunken wrecks where porgies, sea bass, tautog, ling and whiting abound.

Party boats embrace a wide range of craft, anything from 26-foot cabin cruisers to 110-foot converted sub chasers, their similarity lying in the willingness to take fishermen aboard at so much apiece ($4 to $5, including bait). The average neophyte is introduced to deep-sea fishing this way, particularly if he just ups some morning and decides to go fishing.

Often, however, the neophyte gets his initiation as one of five or six fellows from the office or the lodge or the Sunday Afternoon Napping and Poker Club who decide to charter a boat for their very own for a day. This represents a somewhat more glamorous fishing experience, featuring trolling up to 12 miles or more at sea. It has the added advantage of limited numbers around to tangle the lines or to drink up the beer.

Charter boats are large cabin cruisers, from 26 to 45 feet, and can be readily differentiated from other boats by their tremendous outriggers— used as fish finders or as a means of adding trolling lines. The boat, skipper, tackle and lures are for hire by the day at a fee ranging from $50 to $75.

Unlike the head boat captains, charter boat skippers aren't apt to be active along the New Jersey Shore until April, when the striped bass migrate northward along the coast. Then, in October or November, when the striped bass return to their winter homes, the charter boat skippers pull in their outriggers and either go into drydock or head for Florida.

Naturally there is a difference between the fish hauled in by the "heads" and those boated by the "charters." The former get such fish as porgy, sea bass, fluke, ling, cod, blackfish, mackerel and weakfish. The "charters" seek bluefish, striped bass, mackerel and fluke, perhaps some tuna or albacore—with emphasis on the blues, those fighting fish which also are good to eat. Still, when the "big ones" aren't being chummy, charter boats have been known to settle for a catch of pan fish.

228

While deep-sea fishing is the most glamorous, most costly, and probably most successful form of angling along the New Jersey coast, it is far from being the only one. Thousands of fishermen set foot on party boats or charter boats only on rare occasions, if ever. These are the fishermen who prefer rowboats or U-drives, who cast from the surf into the pounding waves or who fish from the banks and jetties and piers.

Rowboats (once propelled only by muscle power, now usually outboard motor driven) are thick in the bays and rivers—in Raritan Bay, Barnegat Bay, the bays and sounds in Atlantic and Cape May Counties, and on such rivers as the Navesink, Shrewsbury, Shark, Manasquan, Toms and Mullica.

It isn't difficult to find a rowboat livery. A recent survey showed nearly 100 rowboat leasers, many of them with 75 or more hulls for hire (one in Sea Bright having 249 rowboats). The rowboat fisherman is usually skilled and knowledgeable. He knows the fishing spots (or claims he does), and he anchors over them or drifts over them, casting all day long or trolling for hours on end, hoping for a strike from a weak, a striper, a blue or a bottom-loving fluke.

Possibly Shorty and Doc and friends and all the thousands who fish each day from boats wouldn't acknowledge it, but the most natural shore fishing of all is that done from the banks and docks on the rivers and bays. True, the skilled and the semiskilled gather for this fishing, but this is also the place where the little boy or girl with a drop line gets a start.

From the banks and docks the youngsters graduate to the jetties and fishing piers and party boats or perhaps join the thousands of surf fishermen who persist in enjoying what many believe has become a dying sport as beaches grow more and more commercial. Surf fishing opportunities today are nowhere near what they were 20 years ago.

Surf fishermen are apt to be lone wolves, although occasionally they gather in twos or threes. Generally, though, the surf fisherman stands by himself, seemingly oblivious of the deserted beach spread on either side of him in off season or in off hours during the height of the swimming season.

It's not uncommon to see the surf fisherman trudging in solitary bliss along the streets of seaside towns, headed for the sea as darkness starts to fall in summertime. He carries an impressive amount of equipment, including chair and lamp, and he sits or stands on the beach for three

One minute the Brielle fishing fleet is in . . .

or four hours. There are those who suspect he gets as much joy out of contemplating the sea and in flexing his muscles to cast out beyond the breakers as he does in catching fish.

Indeed, if fish were the main object, then those who fish from the banks and jetties and those who surf cast could do better on a party boat. A state survey showed in 1953 that 6,600 men fishing from bay banks caught an average of only 0.69 fish per man hour. Also, 2,800 men fishing in the surf caught an average of 0.37 fish per man hour. The same survey showed, incidentally, that the average value of fish per man caught on 20,000 fishing trips was 72 cents' worth at Fulton Fish Market prices! The commercial trawlers are not likely to become obsolete.

230

. . . thirty minutes later it is off for the deep

Certainly the value of sport fishing shouldn't be measured in poundages or dollars, nor should it be measured in terms of the money it attracts each year to New Jersey coastal towns, but the fact remains that sport fishing is a major industry by the sea. There is a tremendous investment in docks, boats and equipment—and just the money expended by day's end on film to record the catch must insure a third-quarter dividend for the photographic suppliers.

Figures which are generally agreed to be most conservative put the number of man days spent fishing between May and December along the shore at 3,000,000. Say each man day is worth $10 (again, a highly conservative estimate). That's a $30,000,000 industry, which gives economic stability to such communities as Belmar, Brielle, Atlantic

231

Highlands, Barnegat Light, Beach Haven, Forked River, Ocean City, Wildwood, Cape May and a score of other towns, including Atlantic City.

If appraising fishing in terms of money is unsporting, then consider it in terms of fish caught. There is one group of salt-water anglers which grumbles that commercial fishermen are getting all the fish. Roy Younger and James Zamos, who conducted an intensive study for the State between 1952 and 1954, came to the significant conclusion that —excluding menhaden—sportsmen caught almost as much fish as men who earn their livings by fishing.

Younger and Zamos said that non-commercial anglers in 1953 caught 13,302,000 pounds of edible fish, compared with 16,735,000 pounds caught by the business fishermen. Considering the differences in equipment and methods the slightness of the disparity is striking.

The sports and commercial interests have been clashing for almost a century and probably will go right on clashing as long as the sea lures both. Undoubtedly there are commercial fishermen who have not the slightest interest in conservation, but they share their disinterest with the sort of fishing hogs who, as Henry Schaeffer of *The Newark News* has written, "catch enough fish to feed 400 families or to fertilize a 40-acre field."

Sports fishing in New Jersey waters goes back to very early days. Early histories are filled with tales of sportsmen from Philadelphia who frequented the barren stretches of southern New Jersey's coast seeking fish. Nevertheless, not until the 1870's and 1880's brought their influx of new families lured by the railroads did sports fishing become both a vital industry and a major recreation.

Nearly all the nineteenth-century fishing was in the bays and rivers, although an occasional commercial fisherman would take anglers outside on the ocean if his pound nets weren't bulging. Catboat captains at Toms River offered their boats for charter at $5 per day, and other skippers at ports all the way down to Cape May sailed occasionally with charter fishing parties aboard.

One writer of the 1880's described the Shrewsbury Rocks as excellent fishing grounds—and they are that to this very day. He told of Sea Bright fishermen who would take sportsmen out for fees ranging from $5 to $20, "the higher charge being made when the fishing is very good, when, indeed, it is very hard to get a fisherman to take you out at any price."

232

Better bargains could be struck at Asbury Park, where sailboats rested at anchor offshore, ready to take passengers fishing at $1 a head. One famous Asbury captain was Harry Maddox, whose big sailing vessels, the *Emma B.* and the *Carib*, made two trips daily from the Asbury Park beachfront to the deep-sea holes.

Surf fishing had its devotees in those days, too. An article in *Harper's Weekly* for July 3, 1880, tells of bluefish two and three feet long being hauled in by surf fishermen at Asbury Park. Such bluefish would be amazing today, but there are those who recollect that once big blues were so plentiful on the New Jersey Shore that farmers came down to the shore and carted them off by the wagonload for fertilizer.

Three factors—ever-improving transportation, perfecting of marine motors and leisure time for working men—have combined in the twentieth century to bring New Jersey Shore sports fishing to the high economic and recreational position it now enjoys.

First of all, the railroads between 1890 and 1920 ran highly successful "Fishermen's Specials" out of Philadelphia to Atlantic City, Wildwood and Cape May. The trains pulled out of Philadelphia before dawn, thundered across New Jersey in darkness and rolled up to the piers at dawn. Accounts of the day tell of coaches "bristling" with fish poles protruding from windows.

The automobile, whose evolution coincided with the perfecting of inboard and outboard motors and larger cruising yachts, killed the train specials, but built up a still larger potential clientele on wheels. Then, after Shark River and Manasquan Inlets on the north shore and Cold Spring Inlet at Cape May were completed in the 1920's and early 1930's, new boat basins sprang up. Brielle, nearly deserted in World War I days, became by 1935 a vital sports fishing center and is today the largest sports fishing area on the East Coast (some say the largest in the world).

Finally, the twentieth century has brought leisure time to nearly everyone. Once upon a time, even as late as 1930, only the wealthy could really afford deep-sea fishing. The ever-increasing pay of the working man, on the rise in the late 1930's, has risen still faster since World War II. All recreation, including sports fishing, is within the easy reach of most people.

One excellent example of the broadening of sports fishing interests has been tuna fishing. Thirty years ago a man had to be wealthy enough to afford a yacht of his own before he took out after the great game fish. During the 1930's it became common for groups of five or six

233

to charter their own boats and head out for the tuna banks. Many a relatively unskilled fisherman brought in tuna weighing upward of 300 pounds.

Tuna fishing is in abeyance at the moment, but its return is possible any time. After splendid catches in the middle 1930's, the giant fish seemingly disappeared—to the extent that in 1949, 300 anglers in the annual United States Atlantic Tuna Tournament out of Brielle boated exactly five tuna. The tournament moved out of New Jersey in 1950—ironically, just as big tuna returned with a rush for a brief time in July and August of that year. That year, indeed, Ray Fromm of Lavallette fought and conquered a 787-pounder on a boat out of Brielle for the state tuna record. Big "tunny" have been scarce since 1950.

Other fish have come and gone in cycles. The bluefish has done the same appearing and disappearing act through the years. At the moment blues are running well again. As one Point Pleasant captain put it when bluefish returned a few years ago, "We were so glad to see them back we didn't even ask where they'd been!"

Salt-water angling in the past decade has picked up many a fresh-water addict who has tired of standing with other enthusiasts four or five deep along upland trout streams. Again quoting Henry Schaeffer, "Many have learned they can have more exciting action in one day chumming for bluefish than they can hope to have in a month of fishing on any of the state's overcrowded bass lakes or trout streams."

Mr. Schaeffer is an advocate of light tackle for deep-sea fishing, particularly for blues or albacore. "If the object is sport," he has written, "the fly, spin and plug casting equipment very definitely belongs on the boat."

Fishermen are not likely to agree on tackle, on bait or on exactly what kind of weather is best for fishing. That's what makes them fisher-men, in a way. The possibility of discussion and debate is what brings them down to the docks an hour or more before any boat could possibly sail. They don't expect to be convinced or to convince anyone else, for all the vehemence of their arguments at times. They just like the comfort of being with those who share their fun.

This sort of thing is likely to confuse the newcomer, of course, but he would do well to put himself in the hands of the skipper or the mates on his first trip (after that he's picked up enough lingo to pose as a real old veteran). There is one point to remember: The captain is as eager to catch fish as any "head." Three or four trips without fish would put the skipper landside.

Party boat: fish and lunch, snagged lines and talk

Captains pick up reputations as fish-finding people. Some anglers swear their favorite skippers are better than electronic fish finders. There is a fierce loyalty on the part of many fishermen to certain skippers, and, in all truth, some do have an uncanny knack of locating fish and coaxing them to jump at the hooks of the customers.

In the long run, the fisherman must choose his own boat—because he likes her looks, because a friend in the office suggested her, because she has his wife's name, because she has the name of a horse who once won the Kentucky Derby. Or, he might just walk down to one of the scores of docks and say, "Eeny, meeny, miney, mo. . . ."

After all, Shorty and Doc and Al and Red picked their boat and their skipper 20 years ago by the "Eeny, meeny" method. It was a good choice, good enough to get them out of bed nearly every Sunday at a time when most people are turning over for another pleasant four-hour sleep.

235

A pound boat "off the beach" at Long Beach Island

20. Fishing for Dollars

Captain Tonnes Anderson of Point Pleasant eased his 61-foot *Jenny* through the swelling Atlantic on April 22, 1956, carefully picking his spots to get the best use from the net dragging the ocean floor abaft of the stout fishing boat. Routine, sure, but exciting, too, in a mild sort of a way—for that net always offered the possibility of riches snatched from the sea 100 miles off the New Jersey coast.

Suddenly the *Jenny* came to a staggering halt, pitching Captain Anderson against his wheel and flattening his crew against the deck. The winch cable to the dragnet stretched taut; to the crew's horror the trawler began to back up. The *Jenny* found herself battling in her net something far greater than even a giant tuna.

"A whale!" screamed a crewman as the *Jenny* wavered crazily on a rolling crest and threatened to capsize at any moment. Captain Anderson struggled with the wheel, fighting to keep the pitching boat on course, aware this battle with the unknown could mean disaster for him, his crew and the boat he loved so much.

The steel cable tautened still more, then snapped with the crack of a rifle shot. Relieved of her tormentor, the *Jenny* shuddered violently again, then slipped down through a wave trough, her broken drag cable slapping against the hull. No more fishing for the netless *Jenny* this trip. Back to Carlson's Dock in Point Pleasant she hastened.

Four days later the atom-powered submarine *Nautilus* surfaced at Groton, Connecticut, wearing on her top gear the dragnet snatched from the *Jenny* and Captain Anderson. "When Tonnes hooks something," laughed a Point Pleasant mate, "he hooks 'em big!"

It ended well, of course. The government paid the captain $1,300 for his gear. Television crews and newspapermen swarmed over Carlson's Dock, suddenly a place of importance. Above all, the *Nautilus* gave Tonnes Anderson a tale to top all tales of fabulous catches. As long as New Jersey Shore fishermen gather anywhere to recount their legends, someone will always say:

"Remember the time Tonnes Anderson caught that giant, that *Nautilus* or whatever you call it?"

Legends and yarns there are aplenty when commercial fishermen gather—tales of whales and swordfish and giant tuna wrapped in trailing nets, tales of pound nets filled with a thousand boxes of butterfish, tales of tension and danger and disaster. Down on New Jersey's commercial fishing docks a special breed of men lives and works, close to the elemental excitement of the sea.

These are men who work hard—incredibly hard at times, particularly when fishing is at its height in June and July. Often they are up at 4:00 A.M., work until midnight and then rise again at 4:00 A.M. to start all over. These are men who know heartbreak, who seek uncertain rewards, who never know when their meal tickets will disappear completely—as, for example, the mackerel have disappeared in the past six or seven years.

Probably few of the men who gamble their time and money in the hopes of earning a living with their nets and their muscles are even casually aware of the economic significance of commercial fishing in New Jersey. Most fishermen are rugged individualists; if their nets have "drawn water" today, that is for them the significant thing, not the fact that fishing is a $10,000,000 to $12,000,000-a-year industry in New Jersey.

Nevertheless, the fishermen and those thousands of visitors who seek the salty and picturesque fishing docks should know that only three states—California, Washington and Massachusetts—clearly outrank New Jersey in value of fish caught. Virginia is neck and neck (or is it net and net?) with this state, so New Jersey is sometimes fourth, sometimes fifth, nationally and hasn't been lower than sixth for decades.

True, this lofty standing is largely because of the massive hauls of menhaden brought in to the three menhaden processing plants within New Jersey, but a fish is a fish. Menhaden counts, tremendously—in 1956, 461,000,000 pounds of these oily fish were landed in New Jersey ports at a value of $6,975,000.

There were tons of other fish—6,000,000 pounds of fluke, 5,500,000 pounds of porgy, 4,000,000 pounds of sea bass, 2,000,000 pounds of whiting, all of which are edible fish. In total, New Jersey fishermen last year brought in some 30,000,000 pounds of fluke and porgy and bass and whiting and 40-odd other types of fish.

United States fishing statistics show that some 5,000 men are engaged in commercial fishing within New Jersey, practically all of them, of course, down along the shore. They use nearly 2,000 boats (about 400 of them major-sized) to chase the elusive fish.

Commercial fishing is much more than numbers of dollars, numbers of men, numbers of fish. Anyone who strolls down to the docks recognizes that. The average visitor quite likely wouldn't know a croaker from a cod or a sea robin from a sea bass, but that in no way impairs the enjoyment of the docks. On those wharves there is all the romance that so many hope to find near the sea, because fishing is about as close as a man can get these days to earning his livelihood as his forefathers did through countless centuries.

Fishing docks have a never-ending fascination. About them and on them lie neat rope coils. Nets dry in the sun. Broad-bottomed boats back from the sea snug in tightly to the docks, their masts and chains and hawsers begging to be photographed. Sea gulls, the fisherman's good luck symbol, scream overhead. There is no pretense, no effort to make the weather-beaten docks sparkling and modern. You like the docks as they are—or go away; you won't be missed.

Excitement rises when the boats come home, trailed by raucous gulls. Even the old-timers, beached by time, edge up to the front. "How many?" they ask tersely. "A thousand," calls a laconic crewman from the deck of the boat being eased up to the dock. Everyone falls to sorting the fish—laughing, joking, glad to be home.

Most fishermen along the New Jersey coast are Scandinavian, for Swedes and Norwegians have dominated commercial fishing on the New Jersey shore for 75 years—except at Sea Isle City, where a group of Italian fishermen pit themselves and their boats against the fish.

Naturally commercial fishing has a long history. Whalers first settled the coast, and in 1683 East Jersey Governor Gawen Lawry was instructed in London that he must "take particular inspection into the convenience of fishing . . . lest the fishermen be drawn elsewhere for want of encouragement."

There was no want of encouragement. Indeed, by 1878, when New Jersey passed its first law to regulate seine fishing in bays, commercial fishing had become a $3,000,000-a-year business—so profitable an enterprise that bitterness and dissension swept over the fisheries.

Warfare broke out. In 1885 fishermen at Holly Beach (now Wildwood) fired cannon balls at menhaden boats close offshore. Up near Galilee and Nauvoo (Sea Bright) the "hook and liners" rowed out to the pound nets at night, covered them with gasoline and burned them to the water's edge. Men fought as if every fish hauled ashore would be the last.

Never again is commercial fishing apt to be as colorful as in the days between about 1870 and 1910, when the beaches at Sea Bright swarmed with hundreds of fishing boats drawn up from the surf and beached on the sand.

Fishermen had come to what is now Sea Bright as early as 1820, lured by the famous fishing ground around Shrewsbury Rocks and the easily sloping beach which makes the launching of boats less dangerous than at other portions of the coast.

The fishermen built shanties and erected icehouses and by 1880, fishermen flocked to Nauvoo and Galilee (as the settlements came to be called) from as far away as Cape May. During the summer many Swedish sailors left their ships for a summer's fishing at Nauvoo—and from this beginning dates much of the Scandinavian influence along the docks today.

Old-timers, like the veteran Axel Carlson of Point Pleasant, remember well those Sea Bright two-man skiffs—16 to 18 feet long, topped by a small sail. There were as many as 300 boats before World War I, and since the average "fare" per boat reached as much as 150 pounds a day, the average net "fare" soared to as much as 45,000 pounds daily —an astounding total when it is remembered that most of this was done with simple hook and line.

"Hook and liners" have not vanished by any means. Scores of them still go out in skiffs, seldom more than 30 feet long. They fish the grounds frequented by sports anglers, fishing either at night or early in the morning before the party boats appear to disturb them. These are the true independents. They fish two or three to a boat, using hand lines and gill nets. Often they have incredible catches. When bluefish or mackerel are running heavily, there may be as many as 1,000 fish to show for a night's work.

Impressive though that may be, considering the relatively crude methods employed, the "fares" of those skiffs fade into insignificance when weighed against the menhaden (pronounced men-HAY-den).

240

Thousands more menhaden head for the mother ship's hold

This is far and away the most important commercial fish, nationally as well as in New Jersey. Nevertheless, it is possibly the least known of all commercial fish.

The menhaden is little known principally because it is too oily for average human consumption. It has picked up some uncomplimentary names: mossbunker, pogy, bony fish, bugfish, fatback, old wife and hardhead.

"Menhaden" comes from a noble Indian word, meaning "that which enriches the earth," and it's likely that a menhaden was the fish dropped into each Indian corn hill in pre-colonial days. For years the primary reason for harvesting menhaden was to grind them up as fertilizer, but in recent times the lowly menhaden's oil has come to be tremendously valuable—not only for fertilizer, but for use in making soap, linoleum, oilskin clothing, paints, varnish and plastics. It's used even in tempering steel, but the processing of menhaden is mainly to produce dairy and poultry feed.

Menhaden (or bunker) boats are a familiar shore sight during much of the year, since they often come in close to shore and their bulky lines are familiar, especially because of the crow's-nests in the masts. From these nests, schools of the silvery-sided menhaden are spotted—although airplanes today supplement the search from the crow's-nest.

Once a school is sighted, a "striker" or a "catcher" from the mother ship rows out over the school in a dory. Behind him trail two "purse" boats, which encircle the school and quietly play out a net to surround the fish. Then the "purse line" is quickly drawn on the bottom, thus preventing the fish from "sounding" and escaping under the net.

At this point the menhaden are in a broad net bag, or purse. Crews burst into rhythmic song, singing sea chanteys handed down through the years and designed to ease the work of drawing in the purse and transferring fish to the mother boat. Once the thousands of fish had to be shoveled into the mother boat; now they are hauled in by suction.

Menhaden fishing is big business, and getting bigger all the time. In 1952, 231,000,000 pounds of menhaden reached New Jersey landings; by 1956 that total had doubled to 460,000,000 pounds! The menhaden is a delightfully cooperative little fish, reproducing at a rate to keep up with the demand. There seems no end to his good-natured growth—and since the menhaden eats only vegetable matter, he doesn't ruin other fishing. Further, since the menhaden doesn't run with other fish, few edible fish, if any, are netted when the purse string is drawn.

Menhaden are brought into three chief points in the state: Belford on Raritan Bay, Crab Island near Tuckerton, and Wildwood, where huge processing plants are located. The Belford operation, complete with an airstrip for spotting planes, also helps keep alive one of New Jersey's distinctive fishing techniques—pound fishing.

Pound fishing thrives in Raritan Bay because menhaden are trapped there for the Belford plant. Once pound fishing centered almost completely in the Atlantic Ocean; in 1914, the first year statistics were kept, there were 112 pounds in the Atlantic, only 35 in Raritan Bay. Today, thanks to hurricanes, high labor costs and poor runs of fish, there are a mere 17 traps (pounds) in the Atlantic and 93 in the bay. In these bay nets are trapped as many as 40,000,000 pounds of menhaden in a year (ocean pounds are set to catch edible fish).

Nearly everyone who has been at the New Jersey Shore is familiar with pound nets, or at least with the poles which support them a couple of hundred yards off shore. The nets themselves, 50 feet square and as much as 60 feet deep, are hidden beneath the surface, fastened to the poles.

Long nets stretch out underwater from one end of the pound like funnels. Fish swim into these, fight their way forward toward what seems freedom, then abruptly find themselves trapped in the pound. Once each day, from March to September or October, the pounds are visited and emptied. Sometimes the haul is tremendous (Axel Carlson caught 1,000 boxes of butterfish in one trap in 1947; it took three days to get the catch in to dock). At one time huge tuna—up to 1,000 pounds—were found in the nets. Sometimes the haul is worthless sea robin, or worse, a "water haul."

Hurricanes ripping up the coast in 1944 and again in 1950 provided the final blows, but pound fishing had been declining before that. Nevertheless, 20 years ago one of the really spectacular sights was the launching of the pound boats from the beaches at a score of spots. Today all but two fisheries on the entire coast berth their wide-beamed 30- to 35-foot "mackerel" boats in bays or lagoons.

Basically, what appears to be wrong with pound fishing these days is that fish must come to the pounds—and that's archaic, in an era when draggers and seiners can go far out to sea and locate schools of fish with electronic fish finders.

The draggers and seiners do just that, sweeping out for a day, two days or several days. Draggers or trawlers haul their nets behind, seeking

243

to entrap fish in the open-throated net held open by "otters" (doors) on the sides or by beams on the bottom. Seiners surround their quarry and pull tight the purse—catching menhaden, porgy and (a few years ago) mackerel.

Draggers and seiners have been active in the open seas for about a half century, but their reach has been lengthened by the fish finders. Small wonder, then, that while New Jersey fishermen still bring in some 30,000,000 to 40,000,000 pounds of edible fish each year—about the same as 50 years ago—most of it is brought in by the boats which go to the fish.

It hasn't been easy, of course, for the draggers and seiners. There are two depressing factors—fluctuating costs of fish (a man can be pushed to the wall in a hurry) and the absolute unpredictability of fish.

Whoever questions that fish are unpredictable can ponder the mackerel situation. For decades the great fishing fleets of Boston and Gloucester each year in the early spring swept their seines over the Atlantic off the New Jersey coast. For many years the Gloucester fleet sought refuge and fresh drinking water inside Sandy Hook. Later the New England vessels put into Cape May harbor year in and year out. Mackerel was a tremendous business—worth $2,000,000 to $3,000,000 every year in New Jersey.

Oddly enough, the greatest catch in history just preceded the abrupt demise of the business. Mackerel fishermen in 1949 reported 17,000,000 pounds of mackerel caught by seine boats off the New Jersey Shore. The following year the huge fleet came back—and caught 250,000 pounds, give or take a few thousand pounds. The year after that a scant 25,000 pounds of mackerel were netted. In two years, mackerel dropped from 17,000,000 pounds to 25,000 pounds!

The mackerel haven't returned. Most fishermen think they will come back, perhaps as suddenly as they disappeared. It has happened before with other fish. During World War I, for example, the menhaden—the prolific menhaden—seemed completely gone from these same waters. Who knows, one of these fine spring nights a lookout may spot the "fire in the water"—the flashing sides of the mackerel.

Commercial fishing has many aspects, enough to fill a good-sized book. There are little fellows as well as big—the hook-and-liners mentioned previously, the gill netters and the rugged individuals who every spring set their sea bass pots out by sunken wrecks. Every April the docks in Wildwood and several other spots are covered with the black tarred pots—similar to lobster pots—ready to be strung out near sea bass grounds.

Another aspect of commercial fishing is the rapid increase of dredging for surf clams (an odd name, since "surf" clams burrow on the sea bottom). This has become big business since the clam chowder and clam freezing interests found ways to clean the sandy mollusk.

Clamming has enticed many an erstwhile dragger or seiner to buy several thousand dollars' worth of gear to seek surf clams far at sea— often a full day's trip from shore. The result has been a huge rise in clam hauls—from about 250,000 pounds in 1942 to 11,000,000 pounds in 1956 (valued at $1,212,000). Some say surf clams "saved" the Wildwood fishermen.

Few landlubbers ever take a trip to sea on a commercial fishing vessel, but they can—and do—experience the vicarious thrill of home-coming.

Home-coming time means much at fisheries in Belford and Monmouth Beach and Point Pleasant and Ship Bottom and Atlantic City and Wildwood and Cape May. It seems, however, to touch most intimately Sea Isle City, where fishermen live close by the lagoons from which they sail before dawn and to which they return at night.

Fishing has been a way of life at Sea Isle City for three generations. Poor hauls can mean a disaster on the back docks, which lack the resort splendor surrounding most other fishing areas. Elsewhere, too, many sit by with poorly hidden tension while they look for the return of the fishing boats. As they "mug up" constantly from the coffeepot with its thick, black liquid, they reminisce, they guess at what the oncoming boat may bring.

Then the boat comes in—loaded. The price is good. There is joy on the docks. If the boat has been at sea six or seven days the men get paid and "pack out" to home or possibly a nearby bar. (There's a saying, "If you want to talk to fishermen you have to know how to be able to take a drink.")

In the happiness an old, retired captain leans his chair back in the sun and watches the younger men working, their sweating muscles rippling. He lights a pipe and says in his Scandinavian way:

"Dey tink dey voork. You tink dey voork. Dese boys never voork like old man. . . ."

The "boys" look up and grin. "Ah, get outta here, Pop," says one. "We work as hard as you guys ever did." And, to a bystander, it *does* seem like work, at that.

Watching the gulls is endlessly fascinating

21. Treasure on the Beach

Everywhere along the New Jersey Shore there is treasure—if the mind and heart are receptive. There probably is actual hard-cash treasure: enough old gold and silver coins are found each year to keep alive the dream that someday a wild northeast storm will lay bare the buried chests of the buccaneers—at the very moment when *you* are standing there.

That will-o'-the-wisp is worth contemplating, provided it doesn't divert the eyes and ears from treasures much closer at hand—treasures to be had by casting one's eyes along the edge of the strand where seashells are jumbled in wild profusion, treasures to be had by listening for the cry of the laughing gull or by stalking the egret with binoculars and camera.

What child would exchange for a doubloon that first fascinating moment when she holds to her ear a huge conch shell and hears—or thinks she hears—the roar of the surf within? Who needs a thousand pieces of eight when he finds on a Wildwood beach a perfectly preserved sand dollar?

Nor can money buy more than that still, silent moment of wonder when the herons come home at sunset to roost at Stone Harbor. Rich and poor alike can laugh at the sandpiper teetering and dancing on the very rim of a wave, as if afraid to get his feet wet. To a bird lover—or even a casual flirter with nature—this is treasure on the wing, to be stored in memory rather than in a bank vault.

Expensive equipment and extensive scientific background aren't necessary to become a shell collector or shore bird enthusiast. Indeed, more than a little learning can be a dangerous thing from the standpoint of innocent merriment—the conchologist might never settle for less than a perfect shell and the ornithologist can become so obsessed with species that he finds it impossible to understand why a person who never

Point Pleasant's commercial wharf is a photographer's joy

bothers to know a laughing gull from a herring gull can still enjoy both.

These paragraphs must not be considered more than an introduction to the joys of shell hunting and bird watching by the sea. Those snared eventually by their treasure hunts into a desire for wider knowledge can find a shelf full of books on the subjects at any public library.

Consider shell hunting first. It's as natural as a child seeking a big clam shell to use as a scoop. It's as cheap as breathing or walking. It requires no more skill to enjoy than the ability to differentiate between colors or to tell one form from another.

Shell hunters—regardless of age—move slowly, although invariably they are amazed at how far they have wandered. They zigzag down the beach, veering off to both sides of the reasonably well-defined line of shells strewn at high-tide mark. They move alone, even if they started out with a group. Each sets his own pace, establishes his own standards, assigns his own values. What the first casts aside, the second snatches up. One man's oyster shell is another man's pearl.

Rachel Carson fixes the mood in *The Edge of the Sea*—that "strange and beautiful place." On no two days, as Miss Carson points out (and as anyone can observe), is the shoreline precisely the same. That is why the shell hunter goes out day after day, to comb the "infinitely mysterious" strand.

Unfortunately New Jersey's beaches offer none of the exotic colors and shapes of shells found in Florida and other tropical climes. Without the exotic, there still is much to seek.

Possibly the New Jersey shell most sought by the amateur is the conch (pronounced "konk" by those who know). It's a large, spiral shell, anywhere from four to nine inches in length, with a delicately curved orange or rose-pink opening. This is the shell which a child can hold to his ear in mid-February and hear again the sea, even as it sleets outside his home in Newark or as a blizzard rages past his farmhouse in Kansas.

Conches are of two varieties—channeled and knobbed. The names are descriptive: the channeled has a groove or channel along its outer spiral, the knobbed has little knobs or horns on the spiral. Both are subject to ruinous battering from the waves; thus chances of finding whole specimens are best on the bay sides of the barrier beaches or on islands out in the bays. Bay-side, however, the conches are usually covered with a hairy matting which tends to hide their attractiveness.

The conch's beginnings are of interest, since the neophyte beachcomber is unlikely to link the big shells with the necklacelike strings of conch (or whelk) egg cases found often on the beach. The cases, each about the size of a quarter, are like parchment in texture and color. There are nearly a hundred cases on a string, nearly 40 eggs in a case. From these are hatched the young conches, the size of a grain of rice, but perfectly formed.

The conch shells are the most spectacular of the single spiral shells, but the range of these univalve shells is reasonably broad on New Jersey beaches. This family of "sea snails" varies downward in size to the periwinkles, oyster drills and little dog whelks. Periwinkles, long ago prized by Indians as wampum (treasure is a changing thing), are found in the salt marshes between half tide and high-water mark. Often they are found clinging to reeds.

Oyster drills serve a predatory purpose in nature. The drill is brown or green in color and uses its long filelike "tongue" to cut through a shell to kill and eat the oyster within. The drill is common and prettily shaped, and shell collectors need be only moderately concerned with its killer role.

Another predator prized for its appearance rather than its habits is the moon shell, enemy of the clam. Two kinds are found on New Jersey shores—the more numerous "shark eye" or southern (lobed) moon shell and the northern moon shell. The slightly advanced shell collector knows the difference: The northern shell spirals around an opening in the bottom; the "shark eye" has that opening covered by a callus. Small matter to the initiate, who finds any moon shell a bright addition to his collection.

Most of the shells along the New Jersey beaches are those of the bivalve or mussel family—the clams and oysters and scallops. Commonest of all is the big surf clam shell, about six inches across and so easy to find that most of them are left to bleach white. Often after a fall or winter storm the beaches are covered with surf clams.

Surf clams are a child's favorites because of their numbers, because of their size, because they make handy sand scoops, because their size and shape prompt painting as ash trays for grandfather at Christmas time. The supply appears inexhaustible; for every one taken away, two seem to take its place.

Other clam shells include that of the quahog or hard clam, about five inches in diameter and readily identified by the purple color inside its shell. Indians prized this shell also as wampum, back in the days when

Shell hunters know wealth is more than pirate's gold

applied conchology could make a man more money than it makes him today. Related, too, are the small, stout, little ribbed shells of the bloody clam and the three-inch shells of the ponderous ark.

The most curious of the clams is the razor clam, about six inches long, handsomely colored and most fragile. It is difficult to find whole along the beach front because the pounding of the waves soon destroys the thin shell. The razor when alive inhabits deep, sandy bottoms and disappears rapidly at the approach of danger—faster, it is said, than a man can dig. The "sailor's razor," therefore, is not easy to find—but it's worth the search. More common is the so-called "stout razor," a shorter, stubbier, hardier first cousin.

Every amateur's collection has an oyster shell, probably many, because these six- to ten-inch long shells are seldom alike and they come in a sufficient variety of colors to make it seem natural to pick up many of the crusty shells.

Obvious on every New Jersey beach is the scallop, the fan-shaped shell whose form has become familiar because of the advertising of a gasoline company. The scallop is a fine shell, delicate in appearance, yet sturdy enough to remain whole on the beach. The scallop comes in a number of colors; no beginner's collection is complete without several scallop shells.

The range of collecting possibilities extends through some 75 varieties of shellfish in New Jersey waters. Beaches are littered with the little, smooth-surfaced blue (or black) mussel, varying in length from an inch to three inches. Nearby can be found the ribbed mussel, whose mother-of-pearl luster in the center of the brown-edged outer shell makes it easy to identify.

Nearest to treasure in appearance are the thin little jingle shells. These crisp little shells, which can be crushed between the fingertips, have waxy lusters of silver and gold and a variety of other colors through black. Sometimes they are confused with the "dead sailor's toenails," but that hard, yellowish, waxy "toenail" is not a shell at all. Rather, it is the "door" which the moon shell uses to close its opening when disturbed.

Any New Jersey beachcomber considers it a day well spent when he finds a sand dollar (or sea cookie). This is the delicate, flat, whitish shell of a kind of starfish, a little round shell whose surface bears the mark of a star and five identical perforations.

Equally, there is a thrill in finding a sea horse, a perfect starfish, an uncrushed king crab. These are the animals of the sea, the relics of days long eons ago—the days when life began in the ocean. The king crab, for example, is related to the extinct trilobites and is virtually the same in appearance as its ancestors of 250,000,000 years ago.

A shell seeker wanders down the beach, gently nudging aside a shell with her toe. She stops to examine a specimen, picks it up, studies it in relation to everything else she has. She keeps it, throws away something originally prized. Her male partner, several paces behind and lost in the realm of univalves and bivalves, picks up the shell she has discarded as the very thing he needs.

Meanwhile, up the beach, a man with binoculars seeks treasure, too, as he sits in his beach chair. His binoculars pick up an osprey, the great bird of the telephone pole set. The osprey whistles piercingly, then plummets unerringly out of the blue sky into the sea to snatch a fish from the water. Then up from the waves it rises and levels off, to feed the young in its bulky nest atop a utility pole.

The man with the binoculars may be a dedicated, admitted, sworn bird watcher. In that case, he won't mark the osprey down on his chart of "birds seen." He will have seen so many ospreys that his interest now far transcends mere identification. If he is a dedicated bird watcher, he's at the right place; few areas in the country offer so much opportunity as the New Jersey Shore to see so many birds.

Perhaps the man is merely interested in nature and natural settings. He's still in the right place, and he'll do himself a big favor if he eases himself out of his beach chair to visit Brigantine National Wild Life Refuge, 11 miles northwest of Atlantic City and easily reached by automobile off Route 9. This 16,000-acre refuge is a veritable bird's paradise—and where there is paradise for birds, there, too, is a paradise for those who only stand and watch.

Development of the Brigantine refuge since the first land was purchased in 1939 has centered on dike construction to create fresh-water marshes. About 900 acres of the normally salt marsh area have been diked, and the dikes serve a double purpose—in addition to defining the fresh-water marshes, they permit an autoist to drive much farther out into the salt marshes than ever before possible.

Brigantine is fascinating the year around. In winter more than 140,000 brant (a type of duck) use the refuge as a winter home. The conjunction of salt- and fresh-water marshes make it astoundingly rich in birds in spring, summer and fall. Out in those marshes 17 avocets were seen nesting last summer, a surprising thing when it is considered that the avocet has not bred in New Jersey since 1859.

The avocet is possibly of greater interest to the long-time bird fancier than it is to the beginner. Nevertheless, the beginner foresighted enough to bring along binoculars can see a brilliant array of birds. Hundreds of egrets crowd the flats and many other large birds are there in August.

Frank McLaughlin, executive director of the New Jersey Audubon Society, runs trips out to the refuge. On one trip he took along a Texan of the caricatured "what've-you-got-that-Texas-doesn't-have-bigger-and-better" type. Mr. McLaughlin promised him a minimum of 50,000 birds and the Texan laughed heartily, ignoring the information that 219 different species of birds have been catalogued at the refuge. Out at Brigantine the Texan swept his glasses around in an arc and slowly took in an estimated 80,000 to 100,000 birds of all sizes and types.

"I'll be danged," said the Texan in awe, "I wouldn'ta believed it. Not outta Texas, I wouldn'ta."

Brigantine refuge is worth seeing, even if the visitor thinks he cares for birds only on Thanksgiving Day. Nevertheless, there are dozens of other places where quantities of birds may be seen, with the opportunities increasing as the nature enthusiast proceeds southward along the shore. Crowded conditions along the north shore have reduced breeding areas and consequently reduced adult bird life.

The southern tip of Long Beach Island is an excellent area to watch shore bird migrations, beginning in late July and picking up pace through August and September. That sandy region, now a protected refuge, is alive with black skimmers and common and least terns. This is also a breeding ground; in late June and July the young shore birds can be seen—often hiding in the shade of a big clam shell to ward off the cruel rays of the sun.

Island Beach is a prime place to watch shore birds, of course, but it has the double disadvantage of being not readily accessible and requiring a permit to visit. Much easier to see are the broad stretches of still unspoiled lands in Cape May County.

Surely a visit to the heronry at Stone Harbor is rewarding to anyone. No heronry in the country is as easy to observe, because this municipally owned preserve is right on Ocean Drive. Here can be seen American egrets, snowy egrets, little blue herons, black-crowned night herons. The thick forest shelters thousands of the birds in summer breeding season, and during that time the adult birds are in and out of the tree-tops all day long carrying refreshments to the young.

Thirty-five years ago Stone Harbor's heronry would have been considered impossible. Wanton slaughter of egrets and herons of all kinds continued through the latter part of the nineteenth century, as no lady worth her keep considered herself well dressed unless a half-dozen birds had been sacrificed to make her hat. Records tell of professional egret hunters "knee deep" in birds in Cape May County in the 1880's.

Even as recently as 1930 the total count of snowy egrets in all New Jersey was a mere nine. Today, because of protection, the snowy egret is common in the southern New Jersey Shore marshland. For all his commonness, he is a bird of rare beauty—beautiful enough for a hat, true, but so much more striking alive, as he rears his gracefully curved neck over the marshland reeds.

Cape May County is one large year-around bird haven. Its location—Cape May Point is on the same latitude as Washington, D. C.—mingles southern and northern birds. Its unusual merging of upland pastures and woodland with marshes and barrier beaches means a large spread of shore, marsh and upland birds. Finally, the Cape is important to birds (and those who watch) because it is a prime migratory center.

Each October bird watchers from all over the East converge on Cape May to witness birds in migration. A northwest wind will make the cape thick with birds; as many as 180 different species have been sighted on a single weekend! Birds at times are everywhere: thronged in the trees, clustered on the boardwalks, thick on the rigging of ships close to shore, and, when exhausted, even resting on the shoulders of watchers. There is a recorded instance of a breathless hummingbird resting for 15 minutes on the scarlet shirt of a newspaper photographer.

Cape May Point's sanctuary, fittingly enough, is named for the late Wittmer Stone, the revered and learned bird watcher whose definitive *Bird Studies of Old Cape May* is must reading for anyone who decides the time has come to know a common (or even a "least") tern from a robin. Mr. Stone's two books are long and detailed, an unfortunate thing in a way; because his passion for detail often obscures his charming ability to write about nature.

There is no real way to get to know the names of shore birds except through a bit of reading in or through any of the good books on birds (most of them nowhere near as long as Mr. Stone's work). Neverthe-

Where no man has trod, there nature reigns supreme

less, not knowing names doesn't necessarily limit the enjoyment to be gained from watching birds.

It isn't necessary to know, for example, if the gull tacking into the face of a stiff breeze is a laughing or herring gull. His zigzagging and graceful perseverance can still be worth seeing. It isn't vital to know a sandpiper from a plover to enjoy the dance of the little birds at wave's edge. The sheer handsomeness of an egret glimpsed "close up" through binoculars isn't necessarily enhanced by knowing whether he's an American or a snowy.

Still, why be lazy? Find out—and really get far more pleasure out of an inexpensive hobby than the expenditure of a little reading time would indicate. It *is* worthwhile to know a tern from a plover! Such a book as Roger Barton's *How to Watch Birds* can get an amateur off on the right eye and ear.

There is treasure to be found, then, and the greater the digging, the greater the treasure—whether the hoped-for treasure be gold and silver, seashells or birds. The whole thing is cumulative. The gold digger can become a shell seeker; the avid shell hunter is likely to become at least a casual bird watcher and vice versa. Fresh air and the excitement of finding something new are the common denominators.

And so—off across the dunes . . .

The Jersey Shore in Print

Understandably, a great deal has been written about the Jersey Shore, but much of it has been fleeting—words in newspapers, scrapbooks or diaries. The following list represents a culling of the books used in preparation of this work, with the aim of giving the interested person a basic guide to further reading. In addition, most libraries along the Shore have copies of local newspaper anniversary editions, newspaper clipping files, and so forth, which are easily used (although seldom conveniently arranged for the average reader).

A Book of Cape May, N. J. Cape May, The Albert Hand Co., 1937. (Chronological history of Cape May from its beginnings until 1937. Well-written and readable.)

Alexander, Robert C., *Ho! For Cape Island!* Cape May, N. J., privately printed, 1956. (A delightful account of the Cape from 1796 to 1856.)

Barber, John, and Howe, Ward Henry, *Historical Collections of the State of New Jersey.* New York, S. Tuttle, 1844. (An easily obtained book giving a contemporary view of New Jersey more than a century ago.)

Butler, Frank, *Book of the Boardwalk.* Atlantic City, The 1954 Association, 1953. (An encyclopedia of information about Atlantic City, conveniently arranged to present a great deal of fascinating material in capsule form.)

English, A. L., *History of Atlantic City.* Philadelphia, Dickson and Gilling, 1884. (An account of the city as it grew to resort greatness, enhanced by attractive illustrations.)

Hall, John F., *Daily Union History of Atlantic City and County, N. J.*, Atlantic City, N. J., Daily Union Press Co., 1900. (A comprehensive, if wordy, story of Atlantic City as it neared its fiftieth anniversary.)

Heston, Alfred, *Heston's Handbooks, or Queen of the Coast*. New York, privately printed, 1887-1908. (Unabashed adoration of Atlantic City, by one of its greatest publicists.)

Kobbé, Gustav, *The New Jersey Coast and Pines*. Short Hills, N. J., Gustav Kobbé, 1889. (A "must" for anyone interested in the Jersey Shore, or, for that matter, for anyone interested in good anecdotal writing.)

Leonard, Thomas Henry, *From Indian Trail to Electric Rail*. Atlantic Highlands, The Atlantic Highlands Journal, 1923. (The best study of the Highlands of Navesink and Sandy Hook, although the over-long book suffers from the author's inability to separate trivial detail from major fact.)

Mandeville, Ernest W., *The Story of Middletown*. Middletown, N. J., Published by Christ Church, 1927. (Much of this well-arranged book deals with the Highlands and its legends, including those of the pirates.)

Nash, Charles E., *The Lure of Long Beach*. The Long Beach Board of Trade, 1936, 1947. (A delightful word picture of Long Beach Island, especially as it was in days gone by.)

Nelson, William, *New Jersey Coast in Three Centuries*. New York, The Lewis Publishing Co., 1902. 3 vols. (Carefully written study of the entire Shore of more than a half century ago. A good beginning point for a general study.)

Pullinger, Walter F., Jr., *The Island: A Photographic Impression*. Beach Haven, N. J., Published by The Schooner Lucy Evelyn, 1956. (The finest collection of Jersey Shore pictures ever published. While the pictures deal only with Long Beach Island, their appeal is to anyone who loves the seashore—any seashore, anywhere.)

Sachse, Julius F., *The Wreck of the New Era*. Lancaster, Pa., privately printed, 1907. (A detailed, but somewhat opinionated, account of New Jersey's most appalling shipwreck.)

Stone, Witmer, *Bird Studies of Old Cape May*. Philadelphia, Academy of Natural Sciences, 1937. (A monumental two-volume study of birds in Cape May and, in effect, for most of the Shore. An intriguing, detailed, painstaking work.)

Weygandt, Cornelius, *Down New Jersey*. New York, Appleton-Century Co., 1940. (Intimate glimpses of people and places in Southern New Jersey, with many a long look at the Jersey Shore. Brightly written.)

Wilson, Harold F., *The Jersey Shore: A Social and Economic History*. New York, Lewis Historical Publishing Co., 1953. 3 vols. (The best modern general-purpose study of the Shore, although the mass of detail incorporated makes it a difficult work for the average reader to use easily.)

Woolman, H. C., and Price, T. T., *Historical and Biographical Atlas of the New Jersey Coast*. Philadelphia, Woolman, 1878. (Valuable for the nicely balanced text and a pleasant surprise for anyone who likes handsomely finished pencil sketches of a vanished era along the Shore.)

Index

Publisher's Note

Since 1953, *The Newark News*, through Publisher Richard B. Scudder and Editor Lloyd M. Felmly, and the Rutgers University Press have cooperated in the publication of three books by John T. Cunningham on various aspects of life in New Jersey, both past and present. *The New Jersey Shore*, fourth title in this joint enterprise, is evidence of the continuing interest of the *News* and the Press in making available to the people of the state books which not only entertain and instruct, but which, it is hoped, contribute to their readers a justifiable pride in being citizens of New Jersey.

The New Jersey Shore, like the three previous books (*This Is New Jersey, Made in New Jersey*, and *Garden State*), appeared first in the *News* as part of its well-known series on the New Jersey story. Rutgers University Press is happy to present in permanent form a continuing portion of a newspaper program highly regarded by educators, statesmen, librarians, and general readers throughout the state.